Praise for 7

"Who Lost the Lost Orders? is the greatest single mystery of the Civil War. But chasing its answer has frequently distracted attention from the larger mystery of what George B. McClellan did with the discovery of the Lost Orders. For almost a century-and-a-half, opinion has followed McClellan's legion of critics in blaming him for 'dawdling,' even with the greatest intelligence coup of the war in his hands. Gene Thorp and Alexander Rossino beg, very pointedly, to differ. In *The Tale Untwisted*, they offer an alternative view, with McClellan in heated pursuit of the Confederate army, managing a badly demoralized and hastily improvised Army of the Potomac and deploring a lackluster surrender of Harpers Ferry that ought never to have occurred."

— Allen C. Guezlo, author of *Robert E. Lee: A Life* and *Gettysburg: The Last Invasion*

"Thorp and Rossino make a very persuasive case for McClellan having received the Lost Orders in mid-afternoon and sending his dispatch to Lincoln at midnight on September 13, 1862. If I were writing my Antietam book today, I would follow their account."

— James M. McPherson, author of *Crossroads of Freedom: Antietam* and the Pulitzer Prize-winning *Battle Cry of Freedom*

"This well-documented and logical explanation of the controversial Lee's 'Lost Orders' debate finally puts the actions of General George McClellan in a proper context. Before a single Union soldier took a step in response to any order based on finding S.O. 191, Lee remarked that he found the Union army 'advancing more rapidly than convenient.' Now we know why."

— Thomas G. Clemens, ed., *The Maryland Campaign of September 1862*, Vols. 1-3

"A clear, extremely well-researched study exploring when Lee's famous 'Lost Orders,' S.O. 191 came into McClellan's possession, and how he responded to them. Anyone with an interest in the 1862 Maryland Campaign will find it a fascinating and illuminating read."

— D. Scott Hartwig, author of *To Antietam Creek: The Maryland Campaign of September 1862*

THE TALE UNTWISTED

*General George B. McClellan, the Maryland Campaign,
and the Discovery of Lee's Lost Orders*

Gene M. Thorp & Alexander B. Rossino

SB

Savas Beatie
California

Names: Thorp, Gene, author. | Rossino, Alexander B., 1966- author.

Title: The tale untwisted : General George B. McClellan, the Maryland Campaign, and the discovery of Lee's lost orders / Gene M. Thorp, & Alexander B. Rossino.

Other titles: General George B. McClellan, the Maryland Campaign, and the discovery of Lee's lost orders

Description: El Dorado Hills, CA : Savas Beatie, [2021] | Includes bibliographical references and index. | Summary: "In this detailed new study, authors Gene Thorp and Alexander Rossino document exhaustively how 'Little Mac' rapidly reorganized his army, advanced on Frederick with more speed than previously thought, and then moved with uncharacteristic energy to counter the Confederate threat and take advantage of Lee's divided forces. The Tale Untwisted is a beautifully woven tapestry of primary research that proposes to put a final word on the debate over the fate and impact of the Lost Orders on the history of the 1862 Maryland Campaign"— Provided by publisher.
Identifiers: LCCN 2022007363 | ISBN 9781611216226 (paperback) | ISBN 9781954547445 (ebook)
Subjects: LCSH: Maryland Campaign, 1862. | McClellan, George B. (George Brinton), 1826-1885. | Lee, Robert E. (Robert Edward), 1807-1870. | Military orders—Confederate States of America. | Confederate States of America. Army of Northern Virginia. Special Orders No. 191.
Classification: LCC E474.61 .T46 2022 | DDC 973.7/336—dc23/eng/20220216
LC record available at https://lccn.loc.gov/2022007363

First Edition, First Printing

Savas Beatie
989 Governor Drive, Suite 102
El Dorado Hills, CA 95762
Phone: 916-941-6896 / sales@savasbeatie.com

Savas Beatie titles are available at special discounts for bulk purchases in the United States. Contact us for more details.

Proudly published, printed, and warehoused in the United States of America.

For my grandfather Robert Edwards, whom I never met in life, but whose books and legacy inspired my interest in this tragic period of American history.
— Gene Thorp

For my grandfather Clifford Mersereau, who introduced me to the history of the American Civil War.
— Alexander Rossino

GEN'L. GEO. B. McCLELLAN.

Entered according to Act of Congress in the year 1861, by M.
B BRADY, in the Clerks' office of the District Court of the District of Columbia.

Table of Contents

Table of Contents (continued)

An exclusive excerpt from Alex Rossino's *Six Days in September,*
a novel of Lee's Army in Maryland, 1862, follows the index

About the Authors

Endpiece

List of Maps

Photos have been placed throughout the book for the convenience of the reader.

Acknowledgments

Gene and Alex came to the subject of George McClellan and the Lost Orders from different directions. Gene's views on George B. McClellan evolved tremendously over time. His awakening to the other side of the McClellan story came during many camp fire talks with living historians whom he fell in with as a volunteer at the Antietam National Battlefield Park. Among this group of experts, William Sagle was especially prominent in convincing Gene to reevaluate his opinion of the general. Jeff Driscoll of the same group then introduced him to the tremendous volume of Civil War primary source materials available. Gene is deeply indebted to both for challenging him to be a better historian.

For Alex's part, he discovered Gene's deep knowledge of McClellan while researching *The Guns of September: A Novel of McClellan's Army in Maryland, September 1862*. After comparing notes, he realized before long that we had more than enough material to produce a detailed study of McClellan and the Lost Orders. The product of our combined efforts is the book in your hands.

Many other individuals contributed to bringing us where we are now. We are grateful to Maurice D'Aoust for his discovery and publication of Lincoln's midnight time-stamped version of the so-called "trophies" telegram. We appreciate the valuable insight and strong support and encouragement Moe has provided since Gene's 2012 online debate with Stephen Sears in *The Washington Post*.

Our sincere thanks as well to Tom Clemens, editor of the Ezra A. Carman papers and co-founder of the Save Historic Antietam Foundation. We are grateful for Tom's friendship, advice, deep knowledge, and support of Gene's research dating back to 2001. Tom generously provided us with many primary sources that form a critical part of the arguments in this book.

We would also like to acknowledge the contributions of Scott Hartwig, who generously made available primary documents he discovered while working on his own books about the Maryland Campaign, and his willingness to review and provide comments on our initial manuscript.

We are grateful to Michelle A. Krowl of the Manuscript Division, Library of Congress, and Trevor Plante and Paul Harrison of the National Archives, who enthusiastically guided us to source materials and provided supervised access to original telegrams and letters when the microfilm versions were not legible enough to interpret.

Our thanks as well to all the individuals who spent the time and resources necessary to made their collections of primary material publicly available online. This includes people like Carolyn Ivanoff, who shared a transcribed the diary of Sgt. C.D.M. Broomhall, 124th Pennsylvania Infantry, and Charles B. Dew, who provided additional information about the Samuel E. Pittman Papers.

Most of all, we are indebted to our families for their consistent support while we pursued the truth about McClellan's actions. Gene's parents, Marilyn and Merle, and brothers John and Bob, tolerated his incessant history questions growing up. Wife Diana and children Kate and Jack, provided their love, patience, understanding, and support during long days of writing, and as they traveled with Gene to myriad obscure historical sites associated with this book.

Alex, meanwhile, must acknowledge the endless patience of his wife, who tolerated many weekends lost to the writing of this book. We are both truly blessed to have such unwavering support.

Last, but not least, we would like to thank our publisher, Theodore P. Savas for his belief in us and for the good folks at Savas Beatie, including but not limited to, Sarah Closson, Sarah Keeney, Lisa Murphy, Donna Endacott, Veronica Kane, and Lee Merideth, for their continued support. Without them this book could not have been produced and distributed. Our copyreader, Dr. Wayne Wolf, also provided a sharp eye and excellent editing suggestions, for which we are grateful.

Preface

The book you are now holding is a greatly expanded version of an essay published as part of Savas Beatie's Civil War Spotlight series in 2019. That earlier essay, available in digital format only, focused tightly on the events of September 13, 1862, when troops with the Army of the Potomac's Twelfth Corps discovered a mislaid copy of Robert E. Lee's Special Orders No. 191 lying in a field near Frederick, Maryland. Passing up the chain of command, the "Lost Orders," as they have come to be known, eventually reached General George B. McClellan, who used the information contained in them to lead his army to its fateful clash with Lee's Army of Northern Virginia at South Mountain, and shortly afterward, at Antietam Creek.

Publishing online presented challenges for those of the reading audience who wanted a hard copy of the essay for their Civil War book collections. We also received numerous requests for more information concerning General McClellan's direction of the Maryland Campaign from the beginning of September until the eve of the South Mountain fight on September 14. This expanded version of our study provides the new information requested and a great deal more, including sections on the historiography of the Lost Orders debate and an exploration of Civil War-era telegraphy meant to clarify where the incorrect "12 M" timestamp on McClellan's "trophies" telegram to President Lincoln on September 13 might have originated.

It is our hope that this study answers many of the questions we have received from readers of the earlier digital essay. We anticipate as well that this study will clear up flawed interpretations of the evidence that historians and others have used over the years to unjustly criticize McClellan's performance in Maryland. Had the general not risen to the task and provided the shattered Federal army in the east

Hd Qrs Army of Northern Va
Sept 9th 1862

Special Orders }
No 191 }

III   The army will resume
its march to-morrow taking the Hagerstown road Gen Jacksons command
will form the advance and after
passing Middleton with such portion
as he may select take the route toward
Sharpsburg cross the Potomac at the
most convenient point & by Friday
morning take possession of the
Baltimore & Ohio R.R. capture such
of the Enemy as may be at Martinsburg
and intercept such as may attempt
to Escape from Harpers Ferry

IV   Gen Longstreets command will
pursue the main road as far as Boons
-boro when it will halt, with reserve supply
and baggage trains of the army

V   Gen McLaws with his own
division and that of Gen R.H. Anderson
will follow Gen Longstreet. on reaching

Geo H. Stew   Alex ...

22878201320436

201609216 / 0100005fhxel / 65087 / 01-07 / 87

with capable leadership, the United States as it existed might have permanently ceased to be. Defeating Lee north of the Potomac in September 1862 saved the Union at its moment of greatest peril and George B. McClellan deserves praise, not condemnation, for having accomplished it.

Gene M. Thorp & Alexander B. Rossino
Glenwood & Boonsboro, Maryland
September 2021

"I have thus far abstained from any public reply to the various criticisms and misrepresentations of which I have been the subject, and shall probably preserve the same attitude during the remainder of my life. Certainly, up to within a brief period, party feeling has run so high that the pathway for the truth has been well-nigh closed, and too many have preferred to accept blindly whatever was most agreeable to their prejudices, rather than to examine facts. . . . I have, therefore, been able to maintain a calm front under abuse, and—while far from claiming immunity from error—have remained satisfied with the conviction that, after my death at least, my countrymen will recognize the fact that I loyally served my country in its darkest hour."

— Major General George Brinton McClellan,
Nov. 8, 1881
(four years before his death).

Chapter 1

How We Got Here:
The History of Writing about
George McClellan and Lee's Special Orders No. 191

Every so often one of the American Civil War's most enduring controversies erupts into public awareness, stirring renewed debate among historians and enthusiasts alike. One of those controversies is whether Major General George Brinton McClellan, commander of the Army of the Potomac, dawdled after receiving a mislaid copy of Robert E. Lee's Special Orders No. 191 on September 13, 1862.

The lost orders were discovered in a field southeast of Frederick, Maryland, three days after Confederate troops marched out on September 10, providing McClellan with Lee's operational plan for the capture of Harpers Ferry. The "Lost Orders," as they have come to be known, clarified to McClellan the meaning of various pieces of information that had been coming in for several days from Governor Andrew Curtin of Pennsylvania, General Alfred Pleasonton's cavalry, President Abraham Lincoln, and the War Department in Washington. These disparate sources painted a jumbled and often conflicting picture of Rebel movements, with some stating that Confederate columns had been spotted in Hagerstown, while others said Rebel troops were crossing the Potomac River back into Virginia at Williamsport.

With Lee's orders in his hands all of these scattered bits now made sense to McClellan. He understood that Lee had split his army into multiple columns, that taking Harpers Ferry was Lee's immediate objective, and that the opportunity had presented itself to destroy the separated parts of the Army of Northern Virginia in detail. This information enabled "Little Mac," as many of the men in his army fondly called him, to devise a plan for attacking Confederate forces at the gaps in South Mountain.

Federal troops with the Sixth, Ninth, and First Corps did exactly this on September 14, successfully driving Lafayette McLaws's, James Longstreet's, and Daniel Harvey Hill's portions of the Rebel army back toward Virginia, effectively wrecking Lee's plans. Yet despite the passage of more than a century and a half debate about the steps McClellan took—or failed to take—continues to swirl. Exactly when this controversy began and why it has persisted for so long are fascinating tales in themselves because it is the things written about the Lost Orders over the years that first fanned the flames of controversy into life and which keeps them burning to this day.[1]

Thanks to leaks from the Army of the Potomac (or possibly the War Department) information about the discovery of Special Orders No. 191 first appeared in major newspapers within days after McClellan had received them. The *Washington Star* reported on September 15, 1862, that, "A member of Colonel Colgrove's regiment found a paper purporting to be Rebel Order No. 119."[2] Although someone clearly leaked this information, there does not appear to have been any explicit political intrigue connected with it. Indeed, politics did not figure into the picture until 1863 after George McClellan himself attempted to defend his actions during the Maryland Campaign by passing a copy of the orders to his friend William Cowper Prime.[3]

Prime, the editor-in-chief of the New York *Journal of Commerce*, a newspaper critical of the Lincoln administration's handling of the war, published the orders on January 1, 1863. McClellan then testified in March of that year before the congressional Joint Committee on the Conduct of the War that he had been handed Lee's orders at Frederick. This news became public in April with the release of the committee's official report, but while criticism of McClellan by the committee certainly provided the backdrop for these events, no controversy

---

1 This chapter examines writing on the Lost Orders from the predominant Northern and European perspectives. It is not a comprehensive review of all the literature dealing with the subject. Literature produced by Southern authors in the latter half of the 19th century has not been included as it tends to focus on the issue of who lost Special Orders No. 191 and not on what George McClellan did with the information he learned from reading them.

2 Stephen W. Sears, "The Twisted Tale of the Lost Order," in *North and South*, Vol. 5, No. 7 (Oct. 2002), 61 and Scott M. Sherlock, "The Lost Order and the Press," in *Civil War Regiments: A Journal of the American Civil War*, Vol. 6, No. 2 (1998).

3 Sears, "The Twisted Tale," 60.

erupted concerning his handling of Special Orders No. 191.[4] Just the opposite occurred, as the committee, being more interested in the conduct of the Peninsular Campaign and allegations that McClellan had not done enough to support John Pope before the Battle of Second Bull Run, made barely any inquiries about the conduct of the Maryland Campaign. To all intents and purposes, the discovery of the Lost Orders proved to be a non-issue.

This might have remained the state of affairs had two important events not occurred: the announcement in October 1863 that McClellan intended to run for president on the Democratic ticket in 1864 and the publication in February 1864 of a 480-page report written by McClellan defending his time as the Army of the Potomac's commanding officer. Intended to justify the decisions he had made and rebut accusations that had surfaced during the Radical Republican-controlled Joint Committee hearings, McClellan recounted succinctly in his report that, "On the 13th [of September 1862], an order fell into my hands issued by General Lee, which fully disclosed his plans."[5]

This bland statement of fact might have gone unnoticed had McClellan not followed it up with the assertion that he "immediately gave orders for a rapid and vigorous forward movement" to save the endangered Federal garrison at Harpers Ferry. This claim contradicted on-the-record comments made by General-in-Chief of the army Henry W. Halleck before a military commission investigating the circumstances surrounding Harpers Ferry's fall in September 1862.[6] Testifying that, "after having received orders to repel the enemy invading the State of Maryland, [McClellan] marched only six miles per day, on an average, when pursuing this invading enemy." Halleck implied that the general had been guilty of foot-dragging when the relief of Harpers Ferry required swift action. To this Halleck added, "in his opinion he (McClellan) could, and should have relieved and

---

4 U.S. House of Representatives, *Report of the Joint Committee on the Conduct of the War in Three Parts* (Washington, DC, 1863), 439. Referred to hereafter as *JCCW*. Bruce Tap, *Over Lincoln's Shoulder: The Committee On the Conduct of the War* (Lawrence, KS, 1998), 137 concluded in his study that following McClellan's dismissal from command by President Lincoln in November, "When Congress met in December 1862, the committee launched a five-month effort to ensure that McClellan and his notion of limited war remained politically and militarily vanquished." This illustrates just how powerful the general's enemies were in Washington.

5 George B. McClellan, *Report on the Organization and Campaigns of the Army of the Potomac* (New York, NY, 1864), 353.

6 For the complete record of the military's investigation see *The War of the Rebellion: A Compilation of the Official Records of the Union and Confederate Armies*, 128 Vols. (Washington, DC, 1880-1901), Series 1, Vol. 19, Part 1, 549-803. Cited hereafter as *OR*.

protected Harper's Ferry," a statement with which the commission said it fully concurred.[7]

In other words, the accusation of tardiness that subsequently became a hallmark of Little Mac criticism started with Henry W. Halleck in an effort to shift blame from himself for the disaster that befell Col. Dixon S. Miles and his men at Harpers Ferry. Halleck proved so successful at contriving this bit of subterfuge against McClellan that even President Lincoln shared the belief, telling Senator Orville Hickman Browning in November 1862 that McClellan "could and ought to have prevented the loss of Harper's Ferry, but was six days marching 40 miles, and it was surrendered."[8]

The release of McClellan's report lit a bonfire of public criticism, prompting William Swinton, a wartime correspondent for the *New York Times*, to pursue a literary scorched earth campaign against the now Democratic party presidential candidate. Swinton railed mercilessly against McClellan's command decisions in a series of articles published by the *Times* from February through April 1864. These screeds, published as a collection by the Radical Republican Union Congressional League under the provocative title *McClellan's Military Career Reviewed and Exposed: The Military Policy of the Administration Set Forth and Vindicated*, made it clear from the outset that Swinton did not intend his critique to be an honest comment on military policy. Rather, he contrived from the very beginning to influence the outcome of the presidential race, arguing in the first sentence of his first column that General McClellan, "Having won whatever reputation he enjoys in the field of *war* . . . is now running on this reputation as the Presidential candidate of a party whose creed is *peace* . . . [he] will only be certain of being President of our country when it is certain we have no country at all."[9]

Turning to the general's lengthy report, Swinton lambasted it as "an elaborate political manifesto" produced by a man "struck by the fever of the White House ... while his soldiers were being struck down by thousands with the fevers of the Chickahominy." McClellan sought to "vindicate his conduct and arraign the Administration" in his "so-called 'Report'," argued Swinton, demanding a critical analysis of the document out of concern for "the welfare of the country not less

7 OR 19:1, 786, 800, and McClellan, *Report*, 355.

8 Theodore C. Pease, ed., *The Diary of Orville Hickman Browning, Volume I, 1850-1864* (Springfield, IL, 1925), 590.

9 William Swinton, *McClellan's Military Career Reviewed and Exposed: The Military Policy of the Administration Set Forth and Vindicated* (Washington, DC, 1864), 3.

than the truth of history." Swinton self-righteously dedicated himself to this task, promising

> to pierce to the historical truth underlying the veneer which General McClellan has spread over event[s], to endeavor to seize by the guiding-clue of unpublished dispatches how much here set down as original motive is really *afterthought*, and to examine the foundation of the charges which he heaps upon the Administration. If I do not succeed in proving by documentary evidence that *every one of General McClellan's failures was the result of his own conduct and character* [emphasis added]—if I do not prove his career as a whole to have been a failure unmatched in military history, and if I do not fasten upon him conduct which in any other country in the world would have caused him to be court-martialed and dismissed the service,—I shall ask the reader to accept his plea in abatement of judgment and accord him the patent of distinguished generalship.[10]

Following this declaration of intent, Swinton proceeded to develop the disparaging portrayal of McClellan's "flaws" and "failed decisions" that remains with us to this day. He dissected McClellan's claims from the Peninsula Campaign about the overwhelming strength of the enemy while minimizing the number of his own men, accusing the general of producing "a series of winnings and whimperings for troops, the most extraordinary ever put on record." Swinton questioned McClellan's complaints about the weather hindering his operations and statements that the men of his army were neither disciplined enough nor sufficiently well-trained to take the field. He outlined McClellan's refusal to promptly execute orders, accused him of foot-dragging, described his reluctance to bring on engagements, and argued that after the reverse experienced outside of Richmond McClellan, "brought back an army demoralized, worn down by useless toil, [and] reduced by sickness, almost unmatched in the annals of war."[11] To all of this Swinton added the undermining of John Pope, closing with the statement that while he had hitherto questioned McClellan's capacity as a commander, the failure to support Pope called into question even the general's loyalty to the nation.

Turning finally to the Maryland Campaign, Swinton pontificated that it was not his purpose to review it in detail, his true aim being

> not so much to dissect the historical facts themselves as to *dissect General McClellan's character and conduct* [emphasis added]. . . . We are presented with the same characteristics of

10 Ibid., 4. The emphasis on "afterthought" is Swinton's.

11 Ibid., 8 and 24.

genius and generalship which we have already discovered—the same unreadiness to move promptly and act vigorously; the same clamoring for "more troops" before advancing; the same reference to the great superiority of numbers on part of the enemy. It is, after all, a dismal story, and has probably already tested the human stomach to its utmost limits.[12]

When Swinton came to the discovery of Special Orders No. 191, he called Lee's operation against Harpers Ferry "bold," arguing

the rebel general should have been made to pay dearly for venturing upon it. And yet, if we consider that the combinations of a commander are necessarily largely influenced by his knowledge of the character of his opponent, we must admit that *Lee, aware of the tardy genius of McClellan* [emphasis added], was authorized in taking a step which, against a vigorous opponent, ought to have secured his destruction. At any rate, the event fully justified his action. McClellan, intrusted with the duty of meeting and crushing the invading army, moved out by slow and easy stages—at an *average of six miles a day* [emphasis added] and accommodated Lee with all the time he needed. Of course, he was able to accomplish his designed object—the capture of Harper's Ferry, its garrisons and stores.[13]

Here we find Swinton airing the first public reproach of McClellan's handling of the Lost Orders. Readers familiar with the Maryland Campaign will recognize the many elements of the story that have become hallmarks as it has been passed down. Swinton claimed that Lee made his plans based on an assessment of McClellan's timidity, including a word-for-word recitation of the accusation hurled by Halleck that McClellan's advance averaged only six miles per day. Never mind that in the campaign's early phase McClellan marched the exhausted remnants of John Pope's army north thirty to forty miles to cover Washington and Baltimore, or that as it approached Frederick the Ninth Corps' columns actually marched at twice the daily rate asserted by Halleck.[14] Swinton never asked about any of that. The journalist-turned-military expert found it easier to cherry-pick Halleck's statement and use it against McClellan than to verify the details. After all, and this is important to remember, *Swinton did not intend to seek the truth.* His *New York Times* columns

---

12 Ibid., 29.

13 Ibid., 29-30.

14 Steven R. Stotelmyer, *Too Useful to Sacrifice: Reconsidering George B. McClellan's Generalship in the Maryland Campaign from South Mountain to Antietam* (El Dorado, CA, 2019), 10-14 argues Halleck's statement about McClellan's slow advance was a patent fabrication.

represented little more than an openly declared effort to assassinate the character of Abraham Lincoln's political opponent in the upcoming election.

Worse yet, Swinton claimed that "the moment Lee crossed the Potomac, the forces at Harper's Ferry were placed in a false position and should have been promptly withdrawn. But we find no recommendation to this effect by General McClellan during the period in which it was possible to carry it out." In other words, he made the entire sorry debacle at Harpers Ferry George McClellan's responsibility despite the fact that as commander of the Army of the Potomac McClellan did not receive the required authority *from Halleck* to issue orders to Col. Miles until September 12, only three days before Miles surrendered.

Never mind either that at the end of its proceedings the Harpers Ferry Military Commission investigating the debacle concluded "that Colonel Miles' incapacity, amounting to almost imbecility, led to the shameful surrender of this important post . . . Harper's Ferry, as well as Maryland Heights, was prematurely surrendered."[15] Halleck's effort to cover up his own blunders thus proved to be spectacularly successful thanks to his use of McClellan as a scapegoat and William Swinton's enthusiasm as a Radical Republican attack dog.[16]

Unfortunately for Little Mac, the politically-motivated broadsides fired by Swinton would not be the last heard from him concerning the Lost Orders. Styling himself a scholar after the war, Swinton published a history of the Army of the Potomac in 1866. In this work, the fledgling military historian revealed his own duplicity by changing the thrust of his critique. Reading somewhere along the line that Lee had said McClellan advanced his army more rapidly than was convenient during the campaign, thereby disrupting his plans, the Federal commander suddenly

acted with energy but not with the impetuosity called for. If he had thrown forward his army with the vigor used by Jackson in his advance on Harper's Ferry, the passes of South

---

15 *OR* 19:1, 799-800.

16 Swinton developed a very poor reputation among senior Federal commanders during the war. He unwisely distributed derogatory comments about President Lincoln uttered by Joseph Hooker in Spring 1863 and narrowly escaped being shot as a "libeller of the press" by Ambrose Burnside in 1864. He also ran afoul of George Gordon Meade and betrayed the trust of U. S. Grant, who had him expelled from the army. See Louis M. Starr, *Bohemian Brigade: Civil War Newsmen In Action* (New York, NY, 1954), 194 and 279. Also see Ulysses S. Grant, *Personal Memoirs of U. S. Grant*, Vol. 2 (New York, NY, 1886), 68-71. Swinton first met Grant after visiting the general's headquarters with Congressman Elihu Washburne, demonstrating how deep his connections with the radical faction of the Republican party ran.

Mountain would have been carried before the evening of the 13th, at which time they were very feebly guarded, and then debouching into Pleasant Valley, the Union commander might next morning have fallen upon the rear of McLaws at Maryland Heights, and relieved Harper's Ferry, which did not surrender till the morning of the 15th. But he did not arrive at South Mountain until the morning of the 14th; and by that time the Confederates, forewarned of his approach, had recalled a considerable force to dispute the passage.[17]

Now, therefore, McClellan moved fast in response to reading Lee's orders, but just not fast enough, and as a result the Confederate army was able to defend the South Mountain passes in time to capture Harpers Ferry. The failure on McClellan's part suddenly became the fact that he did not attack the South Mountain gaps quickly enough, a variation of the slow marching accusation that Swinton had made so much of in 1864, but which now held little water in light of Lee's published comment. Despite these subtle changes in his condemnation, and knowing Lee's opinion of McClellan's industry during the campaign, Swinton never offered a retraction of the slander he had penned in 1864 to influence the outcome of the presidential election. Those deliberate and malicious misrepresentations lived on unchallenged.

Following Swinton another writer, the talented renaissance man, John W. Draper, picked up the twisted tale of Special Orders No. 191. A scientist, photographer, and physician, Draper included the subject in a multi-volume *History of the American Civil War* that he published in 1868. In this work he claimed, without offering a detailed elaboration, that after obtaining the orders McClellan "had it in his power, on the 14th, to have overwhelmed the division of the Confederate General McLaws and relieve Harpers Ferry." This time, though, the failure was not McClellan dawdling, it was that instead of attacking McLaws's command the general "followed the main body of the Confederates toward South Mountain, for they lingered in their march to give time for the reduction of Harper's Ferry."[18] Making such a statement amounted to damning with faint praise because while Draper praised McClellan for acting decisively, he also criticized him for moving in the "wrong" direction. Curious in regard to Draper's history at this point is his apparent ignorance of Swinton's history from two years earlier. Neither

17 William Swinton, *Campaigns of the Army of the Potomac: A Critical History of Operations in Virginia, Maryland, and Pennsylvania from the Commencement to the Close of the War, 1861-1865* (New York, NY, 1866), 201-202.

18 John W. Draper, *History of the American Civil War*, Vol. II (New York, NY, 1868), 452.

mentioning nor citing Swinton, Draper appears to have arrived at his own conclusion concerning Little Mac's handling of the Lost Orders, and while he did not applaud the general's effort, he at least acknowledged action on McClellan's part based on an independent reading of the sources.

Swinton's and Draper's interpretations of the event remained the most prominent until the appearance in 1876 of a history of the war written by Louis-Philippe d'Orleans, otherwise known as the Comte de Paris. A Frenchman who had served on McClellan's staff during the war, d'Orleans also turned out to be a skilled and even-handed historian. He blamed Col. Miles for "shutting himself up at Harper's Ferry" instead of retiring out of harm's way and wrote of the Lost Orders that while they provided "a splendid opportunity [for McClellan] . . . the danger at the same time was imminent; for it was evident that Miles, of whom the Federals had heard nothing more, was allowing himself to be hemmed in on the right bank of the Potomac. It was necessary, therefore, on the one hand to prevent the capture of Harper's Ferry, and on the other to attack the Confederate army before it should be able to reunite."[19]

Little Mac rose to this challenge, according to d'Orleans, as "Federal troops immediately took up their line of march toward Middletown . . . [while] Franklin, bearing to south-westward with the left, was to carry the pass of Crampton's Gap, proceed rapidly down Pleasant Valley on the track of McLaws, attack the latter vigorously with all his forces, rescue the garrison of Harper's Ferry, and finally, without losing a moment, taking this garrison with him, overtake the rest of the army through Rohrersville."[20]

The French Count then took time in his analysis to address Little Mac's critics, particularly those who claimed the general had advanced too slowly. Writing that these voices "might perhaps blame [McClellan] for having lost a few hours in the execution of this plan, to which the incapacity of the defenders of Harper's Ferry was to give a decided importance," d'Orleans argued,

> instead of condemning so trifling a delay, we feel convinced that impartial history will render justice to the really extraordinary results he obtained through his activity, the precision of his orders and the prestige of his name in leading to the pursuit of a victorious enemy the routed bands he had rallied ten days before in sight of the capital. He could not

---

19 Louis Philippe d'Orleans, *History of the Civil War in America*, 4 Vols. Trans. Louis F. Tasistro (Philadelphia, PA, 1876), 2:318.

20 Ibid., 2:318-319.

make them march with the regularity of tried veterans, nor could his lieutenants, notwithstanding their zeal, always conform strictly to the orders he gave them. It followed that Sumner, on the evening of the 13th, had not left Frederick, that only a single corps of the right wing, Reno's, had reached Middletown, while the greater portion of the left wing was still on the banks of the Monocacy. The execution of the great movement, in fact, was only commenced on the morning of the 14th.[21]

These movements resulted in the capture of the South Mountain gaps and a reverse for Lee's army; outcomes, the Frenchman concluded, representing an

important success for McClellan [that] restored confidence to his soldiers and opened to him at the same time the entrance to the valley of the Antietam, where he hoped to strike his adversary before Jackson should have returned from Harper's Ferry. If he had been able to begin the battle sooner, he would have inflicted upon Hill, who was isolated, a much more serious reverse, and by obtaining control of the South Mountain passes before night, he would have definitely prevented the junction of his adversaries. But the Federal general could not foresee the failures which were to result in the premature surrender of Harper's Ferry, and he had reason, . . . to felicitate himself upon the result achieved and the unquestionable victory he had just obtained.[22]

Although in writing these words d'Orleans could be accused of making excuses, the Count freely admitted that McClellan could have started his advance earlier. At the same time, he also gently placed blame for the Harpers Ferry disaster squarely on the shoulders of Dixon Miles for surrendering prematurely. This represented a significant departure from portrayals of the events thus far because it exonerated McClellan for the fall of Harpers Ferry. The Count used a noticeably different tone in his writing as well. For the first time, a former Union military man and veteran of the war had taken up his pen to publicly analyze events surrounding the discovery of Special Orders No. 191 and the surrender of Harpers Ferry. As such, d'Orleans's perspective provided a professionally-based balance absent from the amateurish efforts of Draper, and especially Swinton, whose poisonous influence continued to rear its head in the decades to come.

Six years passed before another veteran of the war took up the subject of George McClellan, Harpers Ferry, and the Lost Orders. This next man, Francis Winthrop Palfrey, served with distinction during the war. Wounded and then

21 Ibid., 2:320.

22 Ibid., 2:323-324.

captured at Antietam, Lieutenant Colonel Palfrey rose to the rank of colonel after his exchange, eventually attaining the rank of brevet brigadier general for meritorious service in 1865. Palfrey's volume, *The Antietam and Fredericksburg* appeared in 1882, calling the discovery of Lee's orders "a piece of rare good fortune [that] . . . placed the Army of Northern Virginia at the mercy of McClellan, provided only that he came up with it and struck while its separation continued." Palfrey, though, quickly returned to the theme of Little Mac's sluggishness, echoing William Swinton's overstated version of Halleck's accusations.

Writing, "It cannot be said that he [McClellan] did not act with considerable energy, but he did not act with sufficient," Palfrey lazily repeated the claim that Little Mac had missed the chance "to interpose his masses between the wings of Lee's separated army."[23] With fair weather on September 13 and the "roads in good condition," Palfrey continued

> There was no reason why Franklin's corps should not have moved that night, instead of at daybreak the next morning. As McClellan respected the night's sleep of Franklin and his men, so did he that of the rest of his army. No portion of it was ordered to move that night, with the possible exception of [Darius] Couch, who was ordered to join Franklin 'as rapidly as possible,' and no portion of it other than Franklin's was ordered to move so early as daybreak the next morning. . . . [McClellan] was not equal to the occasion. He threw away his chance, and a precious opportunity for making a great name passed away.[24]

Palfrey's depiction of these events offered nothing new to the history. Rather, it was his glowing war reputation that made the difference because as a respected veteran officer Palfrey gave credibility to Swinton's Halleck-derived accusations. If a former officer of Palfrey's standing thought Little Mac guilty of acting too slowly then it must be what happened. Even in the 1890s, Ezra A. Carman, the grandfather of Antietam studies, could not help but agree with Palfrey in his then unpublished manuscript. Stating that, "As far as it went [McClellan's 6:20 p.m. order to William Franklin] was good," Carman agreed with Palfrey "it did not go far enough." Indeed,

> It did not set Franklin and the entire army in instant motion, and there were no valid reasons why this should not have been done. . . . McClellan did not rise to the occasion; he

23 Francis Winthrop Palfrey, *The Antietam and Fredericksburg* (New York, NY, 1882), 22 and 29.

24 Ibid., 29-30.

did not take advantage of the long afternoon; he did not order [a] night march and thereby missed the opportunity of his life. At noon he dispatched President Lincoln that his 'army was in motion as rapidly as possible' . . . [But] as a matter of fact nearly the entire army, at that hour, was at a dead halt, and McClellan did not rise to the occasion to lead it forward.[25]

Lincoln biographers John G. Nicolay and John Hay relied on the influential Palfrey, too, commenting in volume six of their monumental work on the late president that, "General Palfrey's criticisms of McClellan in this campaign are entitled to careful study. They are, as he says, 'The expressions of conclusions arrived at with deliberation by one who began as a passionate enthusiast for him, who has made his campaigns the subject of much study and thought'." What conclusions concerning McClellan and the Lost Orders did these Lincoln partisans reach? Nothing less than complete condemnation of the general. Repeating the usual bromide that when he saw the copy of Lee's dispatch, "McClellan received information which was enough to put a soul of enterprise into the veriest laggard that ever breathed. There never was a general so fruitlessly favored by fortune," Nicolay and Hay proceeded to repeat Halleck's six miles a day marching claim augmented by the usual judgment that "it was not in his (i.e., McClellan's) nature to act promptly enough."[26]

Concerning the 6:20 p.m. attack orders to Franklin, they fell back on William Swinton, arguing that McClellan, "wrote at his leisure a long and judicious instruction directing him to march . . . the next day. The weather was perfect; the roads were in good order." These judgments might be excusable had Nicolay and Hay simply used the standard histories of the time to write a dispassionate history of the events, but the evidence shows that this was far from their intent. As Michael Burlingame has pointed out concerning the two men, "Publicly, Nicolay and Hay did not acknowledge their partisanship . . . in the introduction to their biography,

---

25 Ezra A. Carman, *The Maryland Campaign of September 1862, Vol. 1: South Mountain.* Thomas G. Clemens, ed. (El Dorado, CA, 2010), 291. Carman wrote his manuscript after corresponding with as many participants in the Maryland Campaign as he could identify. His influence on the history of writing about the Lost Orders is therefore subtler than the other authors considered here. We have chosen to include his work here because of Carman's role in developing the history of the campaign, even though his manuscript remained unpublished until the twentieth century.

26 John G. Nicolay and John Hay, *Abraham Lincoln: A History*, 10 Vols. (New York, NY, 1890), 6:135-136.

they emphatically asserted their impartiality."[27] Nothing could have been further from the truth. Hay flatly admitted in an August 1885 letter to Nicolay that he had, "toiled and labored through ten chapters over him (McC). I think I have left the impression of his mutinous imbecility, and I have done it in a perfectly courteous manner. . . . It is of the utmost moment that we should *seem* fair to him, while we are destroying him."[28]

The story as first described by William Swinton thus remained intact until the publication of Jacob Dolson Cox's war memoir in 1900.[29] Formerly the commander of the Army of the Potomac's Ninth Corps after the mortal wounding of Jesse Reno at Fox's Gap on September 14, Cox appeared to offer inside information on the army's workings, including his interaction with George McClellan. Cox, however, did not strive for dispassion, repeating old tropes in his telling of the tale:

> McClellan telegraphed to the President that he would catch the rebels 'in their own trap if my men are equal to the emergency.' There was certainly no time to lose. *The information was in his hands before noon, for he refers to it in a dispatch to Mr. Lincoln at twelve* [emphasis added]. If his men had been ordered to be at the top of South Mountain before dark, they could have been there; but less than one full corps passed Catoctin Mountain that day or night, and when the leisurely movement of the 14th began, he himself, instead of being with the

---

27 Michael Burlingame, "Nicolay and Hay: Court Historians," in *Journal of the Abraham Lincoln Association*, Vol. 19, No. 1 (Winter 1998), 3. Available online at https://quod.lib. umich.edu/j/jala/2629860.0019.103/—nicolay-and-hay-court-historians?rgn=main;view=ful ltext#note_13.

28 John Hay to John G. Nicolay, Aug. 10, 1885, Hay Papers, Brown University. Cited in Burlingame, "Nicolay and Hay," 3. The emphasis on "seem" is in the original.

29 Even the eminent military historian John Codman Ropes did not depart from the version of events propounded by Swinton and Palfrey, writing, "McClellan, it is plain, did not propose to hurry his movements, even when Fortune herself beckoned him on to victory. Instead, therefore, of ordering his army to march at nightfall of the 13th, which would have brought the troops to the Gaps in the South Mountain range by daybreak, McClellan postponed their advance till the morning of the 14th. There was no reason in the world why he should not have called on his troops for a night-march in this emergency. Since leaving Washington they had been marching very slowly; the weather was fine; [and] the roads were excellent ... had McClellan acted with energy and promptness the moment he came into possession of Lee's plans, the Federal troops would have forestalled their adversaries." See John Codman Ropes, *The Story of the Civil War: A Concise Account of the War in the United States of America between 1861 and 1865* (New York, NY, 1895), 342-344.

advance, was in Frederick till after 2 P.M., at which hour he sent a dispatch to Washington, and then rode to the front ten or twelve miles away.[30]

Cox's interpretation of the events did add two new elements to the condemnation already heaped upon McClellan for not ordering a general advance on the night of September 13—the first published mention of a noontime telegram sent by the general to President Lincoln and McClellan's own alleged failure to ride to the front when the fighting began on September 14. The communication referred to by Cox is of course the now famous telegram from McClellan to Lincoln timestamped "12 M" for "meridian" or noon. McClellan informed the president in this message that he had the "whole rebel force" in front of him and had put "the army . . . in motion as rapidly as possible" after it. Adding in a clear reference to Lee's orders that he possessed "all the plans of the rebels," McClellan promised to "catch them in their own trap if my men are equal to the emergency."[31]

To Cox, "The failure to be 'equal to the emergency' was not in his men," it was in McClellan himself. Squandering twenty-four hours, the general lost the garrison at Harpers Ferry and all of its stores to the Rebels. Cox agreed with the Comte de Paris that Miles could have offered more "stubborn resistance," even admitting that "Halleck ought to have ordered the place to be evacuated earlier, *as McClellan suggested* [emphasis added]." Nevertheless, Cox argued, "at noon of the 13th McClellan had it in his power to save the place and interpose his army between the two wings, of the Confederates with decisive effect on the campaign. He saw that it was an 'emergency,' but did not call upon his men for any extraordinary exertion. Harper's Ferry surrendered, and Lee united the wings of his army beyond the Antietam before the final and general engagement was forced upon him."[32]

Other writers at the turn of the twentieth century, such as Civil War veteran and Brevet Brig. Gen. Peter S. Michie, and British military officers Walter Birbeck Wood and Sir James Edward Edmonds, carried on the story of McClellan's absent

30 Jacob Dolson Cox, *Military Reminiscences of the Civil War, Volume I: April 1861-November 1863* (New York, NY, 1900), 277.

31 OR 19:2, 281. See Eugene D. Schmiel, *Citizen-General: Jacob Dolson Cox and the Civil War Era* (Athens, OH, 2014), 90-94 for a discussion of Cox's criticism of McClellan's decisions during the Maryland Campaign.

32 Ibid.

initiative along already well-established lines.[33] The critical treatment of Little Mac and the Lost Orders in Michie's work is perhaps the most surprising considering McClellan allies like Fitz John Porter endorsed the writer for producing an "impartial" biography of the general.[34] Michie trod familiar ground in recounting the events of September 13, writing

> The military situation presented exceptional advantages to McClellan, and threatened the gravest of disasters to Lee. The generalship displayed by each of these commanders, whereby the one failed to reap the legitimate fruit of the situation and the other extricated himself in a masterly manner from his critical position, is exceedingly characteristic of their abilities and capacity for command. Thirty minutes should not have elapsed after coming into possession of Lee's plans before orders should have been issued by McClellan for the immediate and speedy movement of his several corps to the South Mountain passes, and Pleasonton should have been at once informed of the situation, with the necessity of extreme vigor of attack upon the Confederate rear guard. But it was not till a quarter to seven that Couch, with the rearmost division, was ordered to move to Jefferson, not that night but the next morning, in order to join Franklin, whose orders, issued fifteen minutes earlier, and containing a complete review of the situation, directed him to move by Jefferson and Burkettsville [sic] upon Rohersville at daybreak the next morning. The remaining corps were also directed to move early on the 14th, and thus it was not until more than twenty-four hours after McClellan had come into possession of Lee's plans that the Army of the Potomac was in position to attempt the passage of the South Mountain Range.[35]

As of 1901, therefore, yet another former Federal officer had added the weight of his professional reputation to the Halleck-Swinton critique of Little Mac by simply repeating what others had written decades earlier. Then a former captain in the Army of the Potomac named Isaac Heysinger published a history of the Maryland and Virginia campaigns of 1862 intended to correct what he called the "inaccuracy of all the current histories."[36] Utilizing documents that no author had previously seen, Heysinger explained in detail how Lee's army had already

---

33 W. Birbeck Wood and Sir James Edward Edmonds, *A History of the Civil War in the United States, 1861-5* (New York, NY, 1905), 123-124.

34 Peter S. Michie, *General McClellan* (New York, NY, 1901), vi.

35 Ibid., 406-407.

36 Isaac W. Heysinger, *Antietam and the Maryland and Virginia Campaigns of 1862* (New York, NY, 1912), 19.

accomplished most of the objectives set out in Special Order No. 191 by September 13 when the lost copy came into McClellan's possession. It was therefore incumbent upon Dixon Miles to defend Harpers Ferry on his own, which the colonel could have done, in Heysinger's estimation, if he had not abandoned Maryland Heights. Doing so effectively trapped Miles's garrison at the bottom of a "soup-tureen" with no escape in sight.

McClellan, in the meantime, busily pushed cavalry and infantry toward Catoctin Mountain even before he read the Lost Orders. When he did read the orders he issued instructions for William Franklin to seize Crampton's Gap, advance into Pleasant Valley and trap McLaws's command against the Potomac River. McClellan, per Heysinger, then planned to break through at Turner's Gap and turn to support Franklin against the Rebels in Pleasant Valley. "Had Miles held Maryland Heights in force, nothing could have saved McLaws' whole command," argued the former army captain, "then Miles would have been court-martialed and shot, for abandoning what he was ordered to hold 'to the last extremity'."[37] Overall, "What McClellan got out of Lee's order was notice that Lee had actually embarked on a side enterprise full of peril for himself . . . McClellan saw [he could] attack Lee in Maryland instead of following and fighting him up through Pennsylvania, and would preserve our own State from the desolation and horror of invasion, to which McClellan's subsequent removal subjected it the next year."[38]

Heysinger's work began a revision of sorts when it came to evaluating McClellan's Maryland Campaign performance. The Dean of the Institute of Law at the University of Santa Clara, California, James Havelock Campbell, also offered a fresh perspective with the publication of his book on the general in 1916. Noticing a discrepancy between the nearly universal condemnation of McClellan in the historical literature and the praise of Little Mac offered by Robert E. Lee, Campbell's volume strove "to set forth clearly the services of General McClellan in the Civil War" in the form of a legal brief.[39]

Arguing along the same lines as Heysinger that despite more being "written about this subject than about any other within the realm of war except the campaigns of Napoleon," Campbell claimed

---

37 Ibid., 84-86.

38 Ibid., 86.

39 James Havelock Campbell, *McClellan: A Vindication of the Military Career of General George B. McClellan, A Lawyer's Brief* (New York, NY, 1916), Preface.

a comparison of what has been written with the facts will show that never before was any subject so little understood by those who undertook to discuss it. From what has been said by the majority of these authors one would conclude that McClellan was wholly devoid of military capacity. Yet General Lee, the most renowned leader of the South, emphatically proclaimed McClellan the ablest Northern General of the war; and von Moltke, the foremost chieftain of the nineteenth century, asserted that the war would have ended two years earlier than it did, if McClellan had been properly supported by the Government. . . . Certain facts hitherto ignored or insufficiently appreciated are iterated and reiterated for a purpose; but not often enough, I fear, in many instances, to penetrate the impervious armor of prejudice.[40]

Authors possessing less intestinal fortitude might fear Campbell had set an impossible goal for himself given the preponderance of books disparaging McClellan for his flaws. After all, in the five decades since the war only the Comte de Paris and little-known Isaac Heysinger had risen to defend Little Mac against the accusations leveled by Henry Halleck and William Swinton. Every other writer had either uncritically repeated those accusations or, in the case of Jacob Cox, added new details that cast the general in an even more deleterious light. Campbell rose to the occasion by dissecting each charge against McClellan and offering a meticulous rebuttal.

Concerning the Lost Orders specifically, Campbell deconstructed the alleged failure to order an advance on the evening of September 13 by closely examining the general's 6:20 p.m. dispatch to William Franklin. Closing with the admonition "I ask of you, at this important moment, all your intellect and the utmost activity that a general can exercise," this letter, argued Campbell, proved "beyond all power of questioning it that General McClellan was making an appeal to this brave, patriotic, and capable officer not merely to be quick but to exhaust every effort to reach the goal at the earliest moment possible."[41] Thus, "To fancy . . . that McClellan could have used greater energy seems either unfair or irrational" because it was Franklin, not Little Mac, who could have started off for Crampton's Gap that evening.

Why did the Sixth Corps' commander not proceed? Clearly it was because McClellan believed that Franklin required reinforcement, explained Campbell. "Consider these two sentences" from McClellan's order, he continued: "Couch

40 Ibid.

41 OR 19:1, 45-46 and Campbell, *McClellan*, 376.

has been ordered to concentrate his division and join you as rapidly as possible. Without waiting for the whole of that division to join you, you will move at daybreak in the morning by Jefferson and Burkittsville upon the road to Rohrersville." According to Campbell, this meant, "Your force at present is too small, so I am sending Couch to you. All his troops cannot reach you by daybreak, but haste is imperative, so go ahead at that time with what-ever you have."[42] In other words, McClellan hoped Couch would come up in time to support Franklin and so he requested Franklin wait until sunrise on September 14 to see if that occurred. If Couch did not come up McClellan ordered Franklin to march at daybreak. In addition, noted Campbell, McClellan sent three couriers to Col. Miles on September 14, one of them ordering him to, "Hold out to the last extremity. If it is possible, reoccupy the Maryland Heights with your whole force. If you can do that, I will certainly be able to relieve you." As things turned out, none of the couriers sent to Miles reached Harpers Ferry and the colonel instead surrendered his command one day before Franklin could get to him. McClellan could not be blamed for this, implied Campbell, because the responsibility rested squarely on the shoulders of Dixon Miles.

Campbell would prove until the 21st century to be the last person of any professional persuasion—historian, attorney, or otherwise—to offer a view of McClellan different from that initially put forward by William Swinton. One by one, scholars from Bruce Catton to James Murfin and Stephen Sears to James McPherson, continued echoing the tale of McClellan's ineptitude.[43] Sears in particular returned again and again to the drumbeat of McClellan's lost opportunity, his dawdling, and his overabundance of caution. Publishing on this for the first time in 1983, Sears concluded, "The record is clear that [on September 13] the Young Napoleon readily enough grasped the opportunity beckoning to him. He knew that Harper's Ferry still held out . . . and that Lee's army remained divided. 'No time shall be lost,' he promised in his noon wire to the president. But like the pledges of similar prompt action . . . this was empty posturing. A full

---

42 Campbell, *McClellan*, 377.

43 Bruce Catton, *The Army of the Potomac: Mr. Lincoln's Army* (New York, NY, 1951), 227-229; James V. Murfin, *The Gleam of Bayonets: The Battle of Antietam and the Maryland Campaign of September 1862* (New York, NY, 1965), 171-174; James M. McPherson, *Crossroads of Freedom: Antietam, The Battle that Changed the Course of the Civil War* (New York, NY, 2002), 109.

eighteen hours would pass before the first Yankee soldiers marched in response to the discovery of [the orders]."[44]

Five years later, Sears whistled the same tune, maintaining

The Lost Orders represented the opportunity of a lifetime . . . Had [McClellan] resolved to waste not a moment of his opportunity, seven hours of daylight were available on the thirteenth for Franklin's left wing to press forward ten miles to the base of South Mountain, to be in position to move against McLaws at dawn. At the same time, on his own front at Frederick, a ten mile march would put Hooker's First Corps alongside the Ninth Corps facing South Mountain, ready for an advance by the entire right wing toward Boonsboro in the morning. . . . Yet the afternoon hours of September 13 passed without a decision, and finally he ordered these movements to begin only the next day.[45]

And again in 2002:

Between his noon telegram to Lincoln and his evening conversation with [General] Gibbon, General McClellan deliberated on his response to this incredible good fortune. Characteristically, he made it into a thorny problem, to which answers did not come easily or quickly. During that Saturday afternoon he appears to have plunged from exuberance down into uncertainty and then back up to confidence, and the emotional journey required some six hours. Another twelve hours would pass before a single man of the Army of the Potomac advanced in response to the Lost Order. . . . Recipient of dazzling fortune, awarded an unparalleled opportunity to divide and conquer the Confederacy's main army, he . . . allowed the first eighteen hours of his good fortune to slip away.[46]

Of perhaps greater interest to those concerned with actual historical fact, Sears appears to have thought for some inexplicable reason that it was appropriate to fabricate certain portions of the "twisted tale," as he styled it. The most glaring example of this can be found in his repeatedly voiced insistence that a group of Frederick's leading citizens was present at army headquarters when the courier sent by Alpheus Williams arrived with the errant copy of Lee's orders. This idea, since repeated as fact by subsequent writers, first appeared in Sears's 1988 biography, *George B. McClellan: The Young Napoleon*. Writing in its pages that, "McClellan was meeting with a delegation of local citizens when he was handed

44 Stephen W. Sears, *Landscape Turned Red: The Battle of Antietam* (Boston, MA, 1983), 117.

45 Stephen W. Sears, *George B. McClellan: The Young Napoleon* (New York, NY, 1988), 283.

46 Sears, "The Twisted Tale," 58.

the paper and Williams's note," Sears claimed, "after a quick reading he threw up his hands and exclaimed (according to one of his visitors), 'Now I know what to do!'"[47]

Sears then repeated this claim in his brazenly titled 1992 essay "The Last Word on the Lost Order," which he republished several years later in 1999.[48] By 2002, with the publication of "The Twisted Tale of the Lost Order," Sears had apparently become so enamored of his embellishment that his earlier general statement now zeroed in on a specific timeframe. "It was about 11:30 a.m.," elaborated the suddenly omniscient Sears, "and McClellan was meeting with a group of local citizens regarding the Federal occupation of Frederick when his adjutant Seth Williams interrupted to hand him what proved to be the intelligence coup of the war."[49]

This enhancement stuck and Sears has retained it ever since.[50] The problem is that it is pure fiction. Just as no source exists stating that a delegation of Fredericktonians visited McClellan on September 13, there is also no document, comment, or other evidence indicating that the events described by Sears took place at 11:30 in the morning. The impossibility of McClellan receiving Lee's orders at noon will be dealt with later. For now it is sufficient to point out only that the source on which Sears based his contrivance is a statement made by Robert E. Lee to William Allan and Edward C. Gordon on February 15, 1868. According to Allan, Lee told them that, "Stuart informed him of a report of a Md. gentleman, who said he was at McClellan's H. Qr.s when the Lost Dispatch was found, and that he (McC) openly expressed his delight." Gordon, for his part, recalled Lee's comment with only slight differences in detail, recording afterward, "that he (Stuart) had learned from a gentleman of Maryland, who was in McClellan's head quarters when the dispatch from Genl. Lee to Gen. Hill was brought to

---

47 Sears, *George B. McClellan*, 281.

48 Stephen W. Sears, "The Last Word on the Lost Order," in Robert W. Cowley, ed., *Experience of War: An Anthology of Articles from MHQ: The Quarterly Journal of Military History* (New York, NY, 1992), 202 and Sears, "Last Words on the Lost Order," in *Controversies and Commanders: Dispatches from the Army of the Potomac* (Boston, MA, 1999), 115.

49 Sears, "The Twisted Tale," 54.

50 See, for example, Stephen W. Sears, "The Curious Case of the Lost Order" in *The Civil War Monitor*, Vol. 6, No. 4 (Winter 2016), 53. "At about 11:30 a.m. an aide interrupted to hand him the documents sent by Alpheus Williams from the XII Corps. By report, upon reading them McClellan threw up his hands and exclaimed, 'Now I know what to do!'"

McClellan."[51] Neither of these recollections of Lee's comment mentioned a delegation of Fredericktonians or a time when the event allegedly took place, but rather than be content with the available information and leave it at that, Sears instead thought it proper to manufacture a timeline of events and then repeatedly pass it off as fact without any subsequent scholar verifying the truth of his claims.

Sears's ceaseless repetition of the points previously made by William Swinton (i.e., McClellan slow and cautious to a fault) and Jacob Cox (i.e., the noon "trophies" telegram), might have been the twentieth century's last word on the lost orders had Joseph L. Harsh not published a voluminous study of the Maryland Campaign in 1999.[52] Although his work focused on the campaign from the Confederate perspective, Harsh cut his academic teeth studying Little Mac at Rice University, eventually producing a doctoral thesis in 1970 titled, "George Brinton McClellan and the Forgotten Alternative: An Introduction to the Conservative Strategy in the Civil War."[53] Reflecting his interest in McClellan, Harsh's work on the Confederate campaign included a more extensive treatment of the Federal commander than one might expect. Harsh offered, for example, a detailed exploration of the circumstances facing McClellan on September 13, showing how even before the general received Lee's orders he had sent Alfred Pleasonton's cavalry and a portion of Jesse Reno's Ninth Corps after Lee's army. "These operations brought the Federals by evening to the foot of South Mountain at both Turner's and Crampton's Gaps. These were movements that would panic Lee when he learned of them later that night. *And they were conceived before and pursued independently of the Federal discovery of a copy on S.O. 191 left behind in Frederick* [emphasis added]."[54]

Additionally, Harsh picked away at the claim that slow-marching had doomed Harpers Ferry. "Stuart's reports," wrote Harsh, "suggested [to Lee] that one reason the enemy advanced so slowly was that they had formed an 'extended front'

51 William Allan, "Memoranda of Conversations with General Robert E. Lee," in Gary W. Gallagher, ed., Lee the Soldier (Lincoln, NE, 1996), 8. For Edward C. Gordon's account see p. 26.

52 Joseph L. Harsh, *Taken at the Flood: Robert E. Lee and Confederate Strategy in the Maryland Campaign of 1862* (Kent, OH and London, 1999).

53 Harsh's thesis is available online at http://scholarship.rice.edu/bitstream/handle/1911/14610/7023520.PDF?sequence=1.

54 Harsh, *Taken*, 230.

to protect both [Washington and Baltimore] from attack."[55] In other words, the two phases of the campaign—the period leading up to the Army of Northern Virginia's departure from Frederick and McClellan's later pursuit after receiving the Lost Orders—should be treated as separate matters and not conflated as Halleck had done in his attempt to discredit Little Mac. Finally, Harsh explained how on the day that McClellan read S.O. No. 191 he believed Lee commanded a force larger than his own even though he did not know the size of the detached commands outlined in Lee's special orders. Weighing these factors added time to McClellan's planning of the attacks on the South Mountain gaps. "The finding of Special Orders, No. 191," concluded Harsh, "did not give McClellan a realistic opportunity to destroy Lee."[56] This re-interpretation of the events retained the traditional September 13 timeline, but it minimized the importance of the Lost Orders to Union operations, thereby undercutting the long-standing claim that McClellan had missed an extraordinary chance to strike a war-ending blow.[57]

Harsh's re-evaluation of McClellan and the Lost Orders opened the first modern crack in the edifice of McClellan criticism that had towered over the subject since 1864. Further cracks then appeared with the work of Ethan S. Rafuse (a student of Harsh's) in 2005 and, eventually, in Steven Stotelmyer's 2019 book *Too Useful to Sacrifice*. Like his mentor, Rafuse did not question the timeline of events. He agreed that, "After sending his message to Lincoln promising to 'send trophies,' McClellan more closely scrutinized what fate had brought him and found that the value of Special Orders No. 191 might not be what he had suggested to Lincoln."[58] McClellan decided, therefore, "not to make any rash deviations from his already well-developed operational plan for September 13" to put his army "in a position [to] force Lee to abandon his campaign north of the Potomac sooner rather than later."[59] That plan pushed Burnside's troops toward Turner's Gap and William Franklin's Sixth Corps toward Crampton's Gap. "Franklin was to deliver the decisive blow," concluded Rafuse, and if all went well, Burnside's command

---

55 Ibid., 150.

56 Ibid., 241.

57 Ibid. Harsh maintains that McClellan's plan to attack the gaps was "a good one" and "untypically bold" although overly ambitious.

58 Ethan S. Rafuse, *McClellan's War: The Failure of Moderation in the Struggle for the Union* (Bloomington, IN, 2005), 291. Rafuse did his Ph.D. training under Joseph Harsh so his sharing of Harsh's interpretation is understandable.

59 Ibid., 292.

and Franklin's corps could then either combine against the Confederate force thought to be in Boonsboro (per information in S.O. No. 191) or Franklin, with Burnside on his right flank, could turn south and rescue Harpers Ferry.[60]

Rafuse's book appeared in 2005, making it strange that he did not include new information about the timing of McClellan's "trophies" telegram to President Lincoln unearthed by Canadian researcher Maurice 'Moe' D'Aoust in 2002. "Perusing the Library of Congress's newly digitized online collection of Lincoln's papers," wrote D'Aoust, "I decided to search for Lincoln's received copy of the [trophies] message. Having pulled the document up, it was with some astonishment that I read the time designation: '12 Midnight'."[61] This bombshell information changed everything since Jacob Cox's history one hundred years earlier. If McClellan did not send his telegram to Lincoln at noon on September 13 it meant the entire timeline of events required re-examination.

Not only did McClellan not lose eighteen hours digesting what he had learned, the evidence now showed that he may have responded to the situation with uncharacteristic vigor. Timothy J. Reese, a resident of Burkittsville, Maryland, and specialist on the Battle of Crampton's Gap, recognized the implications of D'Aoust's find, mentioning it for the first time in a brief collection of essays on the Maryland Campaign that he published in 2004. Discussing the now-midnight telegram in an essay on McClellan's 6:20 p.m. orders to Sixth Corps commander William B. Franklin, Reese described how Little Mac urged his subordinate to advance on Crampton's Gap with the utmost speed. Reese also added a fascinating piece of previously overlooked information—a portion of McClellan's 6:20 p.m. orders to Franklin that did not make it into printed copies of the *Official Records* until 1897.

This fragment informed Franklin that he was "fully authorized to change any of the details of this order as circumstances may change, provided the purpose is carried out . . . to attack the enemy in detail and beat him."[62] To this McClellan

---

60 Rafuse, *McClellan's War*, 291-294.

61 Maurice D'Aoust, "Little Mac Did Not Dawdle," in Civil War Times (October 2012). Available online at https://www.historynet.com/little-mac-not-dawdle.htm. The D'Aoust quote used here comes from Dimitri Rotov, "Guest Post: Maurice D'Aoust on a famous telegram." Civil War Bookshelf, March 20, 2014. Online at http://cwbn. blogspot.com/2014/03/guest-post-maurice-daoust-on-famous.html.

62 Timothy J. Reese, *High-Water Mark: The 1862 Maryland Campaign in Strategic Perspective* (Baltimore, MD, 2004), 31. The additional text of McClellan's order appears in OR 51:1, Sec. 2, 826-827.

added recently received intelligence about a small Rebel force reported near the Potomac River. "If, with full knowledge of all the circumstances, you should consider it preferable to crush the enemy at Petersville before undertaking the movement I have directed, you are at liberty to do so," wrote McClellan,

> but you will readily perceive that no slight advantage should for a moment interfere with the decisive results I propose to gain. I cannot too strongly impress upon you the absolute necessity of informing me every hour during the day of your movements, and frequently during the night. Force your colonels to prevent straggling, and bring every available man into action. I think the force you have is . . . sufficient for the end in view. If you differ widely from me, and being on the spot you know better than I do the circumstances of the case, inform me at once, and I will do my best to re-enforce you.[63]

Reese remarked concerning this openly aggressive order to Franklin,

> Here McClellan literally granted Franklin a free hand to adjust his orders at will, a luxury rarely ever allowed any corps commander to such a degree. In effect McClellan entrusted Franklin with wholly independent offensive command and guaranteed him reserves plus reinforcements upon demand . . . McClellan thereby banked on the ability of a highly perceptive confidante to comprehend and seize the moment. In this he ironically mirrored the relationship common to Lee and Jackson.[64]

In the end, Franklin did not rise to the occasion, but neither did Little Mac make the most of his opportunity, declared Reese. Granting Franklin the freedom to advance as he chose, "plainly overreached Franklin's intellect and activity," and by not travelling to the Sixth Corps to personally direct Franklin's offensive McClellan also overreached his own.[65] This may well be, but the "missing" portion of the 6:20 p.m. orders discussed by Reese at least cast McClellan's September 13 activities in a new light, demonstrating that he responded forcefully to the information he had learned from reading Special Orders No. 191.

With the publication of Harsh's study, D'Aoust's revelation, and Reese's analysis the major pieces fell into place for a comprehensive revision of McClellan's handling of the Lost Orders. D. Scott Hartwig made an effort to provide this in his

---

63 OR 51:1, Sec. 2, 827.

64 Reese, *High-Water Mark*, 31.

65 Ibid., 33.

2012 book, *To Antietam Creek: The Maryland Campaign of September 1862.* Incorporating the information that McClellan had sent his trophies telegram to Lincoln at 12 midnight on September 13, Hartwig described how the errant copy of Special Orders No. 191 could not have reached Little Mac until after noon.

Details of timing now became critically important. Surmising that the Lost Orders, if found before noon per the long acknowledged timeline, did not reach army headquarters until sometime later, Hartwig concluded it was more likely that the courier sent by General Alpheus Williams, "delivered the orders to Marcy, or Seth Williams, [both members of McClellan's staff] and they may not have had the opportunity to show it to McClellan until nearly midafternoon."[66] Continuing a trend of integrating material from the Confederate side of the story first started by Sears, Hartwig also included the claim voiced by Robert E. Lee in 1868 that when the orders reached McClellan he blurted out "Now I know what to do" in front of a local secessionist sympathizer. This man, continued Hartwig, then reported the information to Jeb Stuart, who sent word of it to Lee late on September 13, allowing the Rebel general to bring Longstreet's command back to South Mountain in time to hold off McClellan's assault.[67]

The problems that exist with Lee's recollection of the events more than five years after they occurred will be dealt with later in this book. At this point it is important to note Hartwig's observation that within only one or two hours of reading S.O. No. 191, and perhaps even earlier, McClellan sent orders for the Ninth Corps divisions of Orlando B. Willcox and Samuel Sturgis to march on Middletown Valley and support the division under Jacob Cox that was already there. Aggressively pushing troops forward in pursuit of a two-pronged offensive against the South Mountain gaps, "even if McClellan's plan for September 14 had some shortcomings, it was still an offensive [and] represented a dramatic change .... from the excessive caution" of previous campaigns, concluded Hartwig.[68]

66 D. Scott Hartwig, *To Antietam Creek: The Maryland Campaign of September 1862* (Baltimore, MD, 2012), 284.

67 Edward C. Gordon, "Memorandum of a Conversation with General R. E. Lee, February 15, 1868," in Gallagher, ed., *Lee the Soldier*, 26. We do not accept the argument that Lee learned McClellan had his plans on Sept. 13, concluding instead that he learned only of the Army of the Potomac's rapid advance to the eastern base of South Mountain without understanding why it had occurred.

68 Hartwig, *To Antietam Creek*, 294.

With the publication of *To Antietam Creek*, it appeared that the rehabilitation of George B. McClellan's handling of the Lost Orders had begun in earnest.[69]

Beginning with Harsh and continuing through Hartwig, modern studies of McClellan's handling of Lee's orders have incorporated increasingly finer details on the Army of the Potomac's operations in an effort to better understand the history of the Maryland Campaign. As a result, scholars have documented McClellan's effort to push Franklin toward Crampton's Gap, they have shown that blame for the surrender of Harpers Ferry fell more on Dixon Miles than on Little Mac, and they have challenged the timing of incidents like the transmission of the "trophies telegram" to President Lincoln. But what of the accusation first leveled by Henry Halleck that McClellan advanced too slowly to rescue Harpers Ferry?

Steven Stotelmyer, a licensed battlefield guide and admirer of Joseph Harsh, addressed this subject in a re-evaluation of McClellan's generalship published in 2019. Examining multiple unit histories, Stotelmyer documented how, "On September 11, the Kanawha Division marched from Goshen through the hamlet of Damascus to Ridgeville, Maryland, a distance of 10-12 miles." He then showed that on "The next day, the same division marched from Ridgeville to Frederick, a distance of at least 12 miles. This brought the total distance for two days to between 22 and 24 miles." Also, "On September 9, the 16th Connecticut marched 19 miles and on the 12th tramped 14 miles more [and] on September 11, the 50th Pennsylvania marched 15 miles, and 10 miles the day after.[70] Thus, concluded Stotelmyer, Henry Halleck's comment that McClellan's army marched only 6 miles

---

69 None of this work has made a difference to Stephen Sears, who as of 2016 continued to defend the orthodox position of McClellan's overcautious ineptitude. Ignoring the detailed research and documented conclusions reached by D'Aoust, Harsh, and Hartwig, Sears called the 12 midnight 'trophies' telegram a "misread document" and insinuated Harsh had engaged in "unhistory." See Stephen W. Sears, "The Curious Case of the Lost Order," in *Civil War Monitor*, Vol. 6, No. 4 (Winter 2016), 40. This followed two online exchanges between Sears and Gene Thorp in 2012–2013 and Maurice D'Aoust in 2013. Sears claimed in the former concerning the midnight telegram, "D'Aoust did not discover this McClellan-to-Lincoln telegram. I found it 30 years ago, as had others before me. We long-since solved its puzzle." Despite "discovering" the telegram Sears never mentioned it in any of his many publications on the subject, rendering his claim disingenuous. See Gene Thorp, "McClellan Debate," Sept. 12, 2012–Apr. 27, 2013. Online at https://www.washingtonpost.com/wp-srv/special/artsandliving/civilwar/civil-war-email-exchange/. In the latter exchange, meanwhile, Sears wrote in reply to D'Aoust, "I find no factual, confirmable evidence disproving the telegram was sent at noon, so, obviously, the Lost Order reached McClellan *before* noon." See "Guest Post: A re-rebuttal from Stephen Sears on McClellan's telegram," Civil War Bookshelf, Mar. 30, 2014. A full compilation of the D'Aoust-Sears exchange from Mar.-Apr. 2013 is available here https://cwbn.blogspot.com/search?q=d%27aoust&max-results=20&by-date=true.

70 Stotelmyer, *Too Useful to Sacrifice*, 11-12.

per day, was "not only biased, but myopic in scope ... Nonetheless, the partisan report of the Harpers Ferry commission [had] become the 'official' source supporting the popular myth of the slow McClellan in the Maryland Campaign."[71] Little Mac did not have "the slows," as Lincoln styled it, the general's Ninth Corps troops had actually advanced at a speedier pace than anyone had imagined.

There is one additional development worth noting in relation to newer interpretations of McClellan's handling of the Lost Orders, This concerns the significance of learning what the orders contained within the grand sweep of the Maryland Campaign. As researchers from Harsh to Stotelmyer increasingly put context around the subject, a growing number of them reached the conclusion that, contrary to Stephen Sears's oft-repeated claim about the importance of the event, the discovery of Special Orders No. 191 did not amount to particularly much. Stotelmyer summed up this thinking as follows:

> The information in the Lost Orders did not materially affect the movements of the Union army on September 13, and it was those movements that logistically set the stage for the battle of South Mountain on September 14. . . . The fact that finding the Lost Orders coincided with these movements is what makes it such a 'spinable yarn,' as Harsh put it... Once he contacted Stuart's cavalry at Hagan's Gap early on the morning of September 13, Pleasonton was following orders by chasing the Confederates through the Middletown Valley to the foot of South Mountain. Had Mitchell or Bloss used the Lost Orders to light the cigars and smoke them, the operational situation in the Middletown Valley would not have changed at all. Ironically, if the Lost Orders had any effect at all it was to prompt a bit more caution and prudence on the Union leaders who knew about them. Finding them may have slowed McClellan's advance rather than sped it up.[72]

Mark Grimsley, an historian at Ohio State University, agreed with Stotelmyer that reading the Lost Orders had an unexpectedly negative impact on McClellan's thinking about how to get at Lee's army in western Maryland. The standard version of the story concerning the discovery of the Lost Orders by soldiers with the 27th Indiana is an interpretive "trap," argued Grimsley, "Because the . . . story is unsatisfactory unless McClellan used the order to secure a major advantage. But

---

71 Ibid., 14.

72 Ibid., 44-45.

was that the case? And did it substantially alter what McClellan would have done had he not got hold of Special Orders No. 191?"[73]

Hearkening back to the critique offered by Draper in the late 1860s, Grimsley claimed that McClellan, "ought to have known what to do already" on September 13 when he read the Confederate orders—that being to relieve Harpers Ferry as quickly as possible. However, thanks to the information he learned from the orders the Federal commander instead lunged at the detached and weakened main body of Lee's army at Boonsboro without sending William Franklin reinforcements. Doing so had three outcomes, according to Grimsley. It sealed the fate of Harpers Ferry, it enabled Lee to defend the gaps near Boonsboro, and it provided the time Lee needed to concentrate his army around Sharpsburg, resulting in the fight there on September 17. Had McClellan concentrated on rescuing Harpers Ferry, contended Grimsley, "Lee would have abandoned the Maryland Campaign then and there" without staying to fight. "Thus the finding of the Lost Order arguably worked to the detriment of McClellan's plans. But the story's entrenchment in the American Iliad ensures that it will ever be told in the more poetic way."[74]

From being considered a potentially war-ending opportunity to becoming little more than a distraction, the tale of the Lost Orders has twisted in new and unexpected directions. Historical examinations of the subject have in recent years become more detailed than ever and yet an interpretational consensus on the importance of the orders to the history of the Maryland Campaign remains elusive. Even determining the hour when the Lost Orders reached McClellan continues to raise debate. Within two years after Maurice D'Aoust announced finding the "12 Midnight" copy of the trophies telegram that McClellan sent to President Lincoln, descendants of Col. Samuel E. Pittman, the officer on Gen. Alpheus Williams's staff who verified the authenticity of Confederate Col. Robert Chilton's signature on the Lost Orders, donated Pittman's papers to Williams College in Massachusetts. This new collection contained letters written to and from Pittman, and others, by Ezra Carman of the Antietam Battlefield Board, and several of those missives described how the Lost Orders traveled from Twelfth Corps headquarters to McClellan on September 13, 1862.

One of these correspondents, a colonel from Indiana named Nathan Kimball, wrote to Carman that he had personally delivered Special Orders No. 191 to

---

73 Mark Grimsley, "The Impact of the Lost Order: Rethinking the Significance of the Discovery of Special Orders No. 191," in *Civil War Monitor*, Vol. 9, No. 2 (Summer 2019), 28.

74 Ibid., 74.

McClellan, and that the time he handed the orders to the general "was not later than 9:30 A.M." However, in his reply to Carman dated May 24, 1897, Pittman could not confirm if Kimball had indeed been the man selected by General Williams to deliver the orders to Little Mac. "From what Genl. Kimball writes you it would appear that the paper never came into either Genl. Williams hands or mine," puzzled Pittman, "some strange mist must have clouded Genl. Kimball's memory." His cloudy recollection notwithstanding, Pittman assured Carman concerning the time when he handled the Lost Orders, "I thought the hour earlier than noon, and from 9 to 10 A.M. has always been in my memory." This echoed more exactly the first occasion when Pittman had replied to Carman on May 7, 1897, to say the time General Williams forwarded the Lost Orders to McClellan "was somewhat earlier than noon . . . it certainly could not have been later."[75]

Two key participants in the story of the Lost Orders appeared to validate the claim that Little Mac had received the document before noon on September 13 and, therefore, that the general had more than enough time to write his "trophies" telegram. Carman, however, saw inconsistencies in Kimball's tale that did not match the other information he possessed, leading him in the end not to buy it. "I confess that I was somewhat surprised at Kimball's assertion that he handed the lost dispatch to McClellan in person and made no reference to Gen. Williams and yourself," Carman wrote to Pittman in May 1897. "He (Kimball) is a very old man, in failing health and liable, as you say, to be a little 'misty' in his recollections."[76]

If this review of the literature surrounding George McClellan's handling of the Lost Orders demonstrates anything it is that the smearing of the general's reputation first undertaken by Henry Halleck in autumn 1862 morphed into a full-blown character assassination by William Swinton soon after McClellan declared for president in late 1863. McClellan also did himself no favors by alienating powerful people in the army, the administration, and in Congress, both while and after he commanded the Army of the Potomac. Leaving behind a trail of enemies only too happy to see him ruined, Little Mac soon found himself in the unenviable position of defending his performance against a backdrop of escalating bloodshed. His conservative approach to waging the war had borne no fruit and

75 Charles Dew, "How Samuel E. Pittman Validated Lee's 'Lost Orders' Prior to Antietam: A Historical Note," in *The Journal of Southern History*, Vol. 70, No. 4 (Nov. 2004), 867-868.

76 Ezra Carman to Samuel Pittman, May 26, 1897, in the Civil War Papers of Samuel E. Pittman, Lt. Col., Am-Mss-Pittman, Box 1, Folder 17. Chapin Library, Williams College, Massachusetts. https://archivesspace.williams.edu/repositories/4/ archival_objects/18391. Cited hereafter as Pittman Papers.

now, well after he had shed his uniform, McClellan paid the price for challenging a national leader vindicated by battlefield victories paid for in blood. Lincoln's assassination then transformed the late president into a secular martyr, offering McClellan no realistic chance of defending his record. Persuading anyone to question the policies of a sainted president proved to be an insurmountable task.

Returning specifically to the Lost Orders, most of those writing about the subject have continued to perpetuate the derogatory wartime depiction of McClellan first peddled by Halleck and Swinton. There are many reasons for this. Some writers have without reflection or curiosity told the story as received. If Lincoln said McClellan had "the slows" then they accept it must have been the case. Others seem to possess an irrational anti-McClellan animus, seeking for some undisclosed reason to harm the general's reputation in every way possible. Although there are a few voices calling for a more favorable treatment of McClellan, they have remained lost in the wilderness until the last twenty years.

Their attempts to produce more objective studies of the general's record, particularly as it pertained to the Lost Orders, have proven more durable than earlier efforts, but in the process, they have split the field in two. Stephen Sears and those who agree with him continue to defend the orthodox interpretation of McClellan responding slowly to the potentially war-winning intelligence in Special Orders No. 191. Others influenced by Joseph Harsh challenge the time when McClellan received Lee's orders and minimize the benefit that reading the orders bestowed to the Federal commander.

The reading and viewing public, meanwhile, arguably as important to historical memory of the events as the writers seeking to shape that memory, continues to see the subject from the perspective first promoted by Swinton and defended for so long by Sears. The figure of a dawdling Little Mac even appeared in the award-winning Civil War documentary produced by Ken Burns in 1990, and it featured in the film shown for decades at the Antietam National Battlefield Visitors Center introducing guests to the Maryland Campaign.[77] To these many thousands of viewers and readers George McClellan remains the incompetent, timid, slow general who frittered away a once-in-a-lifetime opportunity to crush his opponent when he was most vulnerable. This interpretation persists despite being false and it is to proving just how incorrect it is that this study is dedicated.

---

77 For the segment in Ken Burns's documentary mentioning McClellan's "dawdling" see the 42:09 mark here https://www.youtube.com/watch?v=HMc5vg4LmPo. The National Park Service's "Antietam Visit" film from 1981 can be seen here https:// www.youtube. com/watch?v=_LNP_mMSFlA. Advance to the 6:50 mark.

Chapter 2

What McClellan Knew:
Harpers Ferry and the Army of the Potomac's
Advance to Frederick, Maryland

Any thorough analysis of George McClellan's actions on September 13, 1862, particularly those connected with the fate of the Union garrison at Harpers Ferry, must take three things into account: what the general knew of the Rebel army's movements before he read Special Orders No. 191, what steps he took in response to that information, and what the worn down and defeated forces handed to him eleven days earlier were capable of accomplishing by that date. Taking the last subject first, on the morning of September 2, Gen. McClellan, at that point without a formal command, found himself surprised at his home in Washington by an impromptu visit from President Lincoln and army General-in-Chief Henry Halleck. Of this meeting McClellan later recalled,

> the President informed me that . . . our affairs were in a bad condition; that the army was in full retreat upon the defenses of Washington; the roads filled with stragglers &c. He instructed me to take steps at once to stop and collect the stragglers, to place the works in a proper state of defense, and to go out to meet and take command of the army when it approached the vicinity of the works; then to place the troops in the best position—committing everything to my hands.[1]

1 OR 19:1, 37.

Initially, McClellan appears to have rejoiced at this return to prominence, writing to his wife, "Everything is to come under my command again!" And yet to this statement he added it is "a terrible and thankless task," suggesting he knew well the tremendous difficulty of the position into which he had been placed.[2] Caught in the twilight zone between commanding troops to defend the capital, but not authorized to take men into the field, the general went immediately to work consolidating, reorganizing, and resupplying the forces he had at hand; including his own Army of the Potomac, John Pope's Army of Virginia, Ambrose Burnside's command from the North Carolina coast, Jacob Cox's Kanawha Division from western Virginia, and tens-of-thousands of raw recruits that had been organized into regiments, but which had not yet been trained or received permanent assignments.

It is no exaggeration to say that McClellan faced a monumental task. Expected by the president to reconstitute a viable field army as rapidly as possible and then, as of September 7, to conduct a vigorous campaign against the victorious enemy, Little Mac found the various units he inherited in dreadful condition. Hard marching, critical supply disruptions, and bad management during the disastrous Second Bull Run campaign had left most Union veterans dejected and jaded.

John M. Gould of the 10th Maine attested to the depth of the morale problem as his regiment returned to the Washington fortifications. We "had been starved till we were sick and brutish," wrote Gould, "chafed and raw from lice and rough clothing; we were foot sore and lame; there was hardly a man of us who was not afflicted with the diarrhea; we had filled our clothes with dust and perspiration till they were all but rotten; our blood was 'thin' and heated, and now this fierce north wind searched our very marrow. We had been out-generaled and driven behind the defenses of Washington, we were demoralized and discouraged. *It was the darkest day and the darkest hour in our regimental history.*"[3]

McClellan's re-appearance on the scene changed much of this for men disheartened by recent events. As the troops coming into the city's defenses quickly found themselves transferred to his command, word of McClellan's return spread rapidly, leading even those who had not previously served in the Army of the Potomac to openly celebrate his return. George Kimball of the 12th Massachusetts Volunteers recalled, for example, that at the end of the retreat from Bull Run, his

---

2   George B. McClellan, *McClellan's Own Story: The War for the Union* (New York, NY, 1887), 566.

3   John M. Gould, *History of the First-Tenth-Twenty-Ninth Maine Regiment* (Portland, ME, 1871), 217-218. Emphasis is in the source.

men lay "scattered about in groups, discussing the events of their ill-starred campaign. . . . [When] suddenly . . . a mounted officer, dashing past our bivouac, reined up enough to shout, 'Little Mac' is back here on the road, boys!'" Elation promptly followed," wrote Kimball, and "From extreme sadness we passed in a twinkling to a delirium of delight. A Deliverer had come. A real rainbow of promise 'had appeared suddenly in the dark political sky.'"[4]

The sudden, even miraculous, recovery of morale among Union troops proved both heartening and perplexing to observers outside of the army. A columnist with the *Washington Evening Star* covering military matters endeavored to explain to the public what he had witnessed in an article published on September 4. Writing that despite the reverses McClellan had suffered in Virginia, the men "attribute his failure to other causes than that of not being an efficient and able General. They believe, also," the correspondent continued, "that the enemy fears him more than any other General in the field. . . . They have faith in him, and in no one else, whatever may be the opinion of politicians. Their recent experience, and the apparent design of the Government to set him aside, has increased their faith, and what was before enthusiasm has now become almost devotion and man worship."[5]

President Lincoln surely hoped that returning McClellan to command would improve morale, and indeed it did, but remedying the army's dire physical condition remained a difficult and even more pressing challenge. As John Gould recalled in his narrative on September 3, "Famished as we were, and though in sight of the dome of the Capitol, we received no rations during the entire day . . . when the sun went down on our regiment, we were as thoroughly discouraged as ever we were."[6]

Few men wearing a blue uniform would get the opportunity to rest at this moment of supreme national crisis. With Robert E. Lee's army threatening to enter Maryland, it became imperative that McClellan shore up the capital city's northern defenses before he could contemplate taking any further steps. On September 3, therefore, he moved the Second, Twelfth, and elements of the Ninth Corps across the Potomac River to take up defensive positions above Washington. The men in

4 Letter from George Kimball printed in George B. McClellan, "From the Peninsula to Antietam: Posthumous Notes by George B. McClellan," Robert Underwood Johnson and Clarence Clough Buel, eds., *Battles and Leaders of the Civil War*, 4 Vols. (New York, NY, 1887), 2:550.

5 *Washington Evening Star*, Sept. 4, 1862.

6 Gould, *History*, 222.

these commands marched without rest until they reached their destinations, a fact that further added to their discomfort. Major William Child, a surgeon with the 5th New Hampshire in the Second Corps, participated in this movement, writing that when he and his comrades finally halted they "were without rations, and had had nothing to eat for three or four days." That night they begged for food from homes in nearby Tennallytown and even approached members of the Irish Brigade for a few leftover loaves of bread that they possessed.[7] Only by September 6 did conditions for these leading regiments finally begin to improve, with Gould noting in his diary, "Rations still scarce, but we are by no means starving now."[8]

At the same time he shifted troops north, McClellan also began integrating dozens of newly-raised regiments into the army. These troops came to Washington in response to Lincoln's call for an additional 300,000 soldiers back in July. Each new regiment averaged 900 men and, as of the day McClellan took command, 43 of them had already reached the city.[9] None of them had been in service for more than four weeks and few received more than rudimentary training because most of their time in uniform so far had been spent traveling to the front from their muster locations up north.

The experience of the 125th Pennsylvania is instructive here. Assembled in Harrisburg on August 16 and placed under the command of Mexican War veteran Col. Jacob Higgins, these men from the central part of the state entered the Washington fortifications at the end of August, just in time to witness the disheartening flood of troops returning from the disaster at Second Bull Run. Some of the men in Higgins's command, "had been members of military organizations of the Commonwealth before the Rebellion [while] others had been in the late three months' service, but the great majority of its members had no previous military experience."[10]

Clad in clean uniforms with shiny brass buttons and spotless caps, these fresh recruits watched in mortification as the mud and blood-spattered veterans of the shattered Army of Virginia flowed past. "My God! Shall WE ever look like that?"

---

7 William Child, *A History of The Fifth Regiment New Hampshire Volunteers of the American Civil War, 1861–1865* (Bristol, NH, 1893), 108.

8 Gould, *History*, 223. Gould's account is only a sample of many throughout the army which describe the same dire conditions.

9 See Chart A: Arrival of New Troops in Washington, DC, Aug. 14 to Sept. 10, 1862, on page 38.

10 William W. Wallace, et al., *History of the One-Hundred and Twenty-Fifth Regiment Pennsylvania Volunteers, 1862-1863* (Philadelphia, PA, 1906), 34.

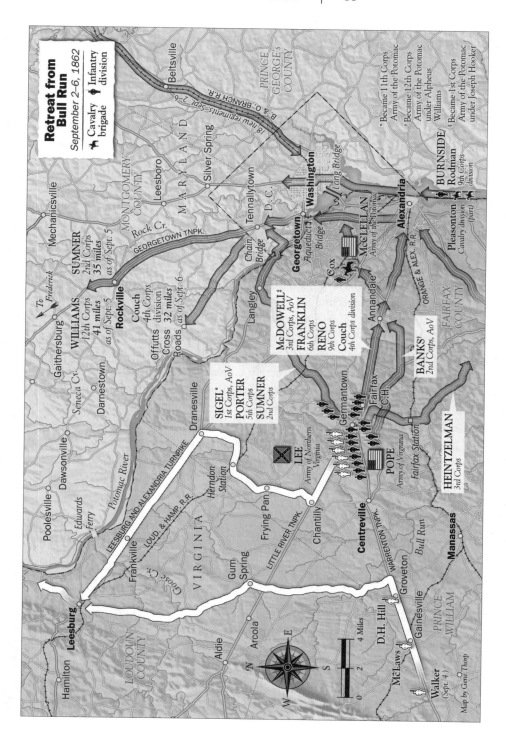

Retreat from Bull Run
September 2–6, 1862

Cavalry brigade
Infantry division

* Became 11th Corps Army of the Potomac
† Became 12th Corps Army of the Potomac under Alpheus Williams
‡ Became 1st Corps Army of the Potomac under Joseph Hooker

Map by Gene Thorp

declared one witness of the terrible sight, voicing the horror echoed by Sheldon Thorpe of the green 15th Connecticut:

> Alas, what a revelation! Could these blackened, bearded, tattered, begrimed veterans who swooped down upon the slop barrels of the cook houses 'like a wolf in the fold,' greedily clutching the contents in their hands and cups and ravenously devouring scraps of 'soft bread' and fresh beef; could these blackened and in many cases wounded men, shoeless, hatless, blanketless, be the army of the Union? Could these officers with dusty and battered equipments, scarcely a badge of rank discernible, weary and footsore, be their commanders? Where was all the pomp and panoply of war? But so it was. Humiliating as was the sight, it was none other than the torn and broken columns of Pope, fresh from the disaster at Bull Run, and now on swift march to withstand the invasion of Maryland.[11]

Shock and dismay shaped the experience of men new to the army, a difficult situation made worse by the disdain that many Army of the Potomac veterans expressed for the reinforcements. "The fresh troops are worse than useless," wrote Edgar Newcomb of the grizzled 19th Massachusetts, another regiment in the Second Corps. "They don't know how to fight, and the shadow of an enemy makes them run. No reliance whatever is put in them, and though doubtless in time they will become veterans, they are now only fit to garrison the forts about Washington. . . . The contempt of our men for these 'gingerbread soldiers' is as amusing as it is intense."[12] McClellan required their services in the field immediately, however, so garrison duty would not be the fate for many of these raw troops. Such was the desperation of the moment that 23,740 of these inexperienced men, marched with McClellan against the Army of Northern Virginia during the Maryland Campaign, amounting to some twenty percent of his attacking force.[13] Most of these same raw

11 Edward O. Lord, *History of the Ninth Regiment New Hampshire Volunteers In The War of the Rebellion*, (Concord, NH, 1895), 35 and Sheldon B. Thorpe, *The History of the Fifteenth Connecticut Volunteers in the War for the Defense of the Union* (New Haven, CT, 1893), 21.

12 Albert B. Weymouth, ed., *A Memorial Sketch of Lieut. Edgar M. Newcomb of the Nineteenth Mass. Vols.*, (Malden, MA, 1883), 84-85.

13 See OR 12:3, 780-782 for strength returns as of Aug. 31, 1862, and OR Ser. 3:3, 203-404 for the number of July 1862 volunteers. The first recruits arrived in Washington on Aug. 14 and from that date to Sept. 10 approximately 62,420 men arrived in total. Subtracting the 23,740 new recruits that marched with McClellan leaves approximately 39,695 recruits in the Washington defenses. This means that untrained troops made up more than half of the 73,000 men Maj. Gen. Banks reported to Halleck on Sept. 10. See OR 19:2, 264. Also see D. Scott Hartwig, "Who Would Not Be a Soldier: The Volunteers of '62 in the Maryland Campaign," in

troops fought at South Mountain and Antietam before they had even learned how to properly fire their muskets or follow combat commands from their officers.

In addition to dealing with vast numbers of inexperienced infantry, McClellan also entered the campaign in Maryland with virtually no cavalry; a fact overlooked by most studies. The rush to supply Pope's army with reinforcements before its fight at Bull Run had forced Col. Rufus Ingalls, the Chief Quartermaster of the Army of the Potomac, to make difficult logistical decisions. In order to get the most fighting men to Pope from the James River peninsula as quickly as possible, Ingalls sent infantry before cavalry, and even these foot soldiers arrived without animals to haul supplies, move artillery, or mount officers. Shipping cavalry and pack animals last meant that mounted units only began landing in squads, companies, and battalions on August 30.

When Gen. McClellan assumed command of the Washington defenses on September 2, portions of just four cavalry regiments had reached the vicinity of Washington, with another nine regiments still en route from the Peninsula. As fast as each unit arrived, McClellan hurried it across the Potomac "to the fords near Poolesville, to watch and impede the enemy in any attempt to cross in that vicinity."[14] Some regiments would be slow in coming up, too, with the last of the Army of the Potomac's cavalry arriving in Washington only on September 8. The dearth of mounted units created a material weakness in the Army of the Potomac that left McClellan with a serious lack of troopers for scouting, screening, and intelligence gathering in the first half of the campaign.

Turning to the matter of Harpers Ferry, McClellan found time to recommend the garrison's evacuation, despite shouldering the immense command and logistical burden of assimilating three armies into one, and the fact that he bore no responsibility for the garrison at the time. The evidence documenting this is clear, notwithstanding the petty accusation leveled by William Swinton that McClellan initially ignored the garrison's fate. Claiming, "There is no doubt that the moment Lee crossed the Potomac, the forces at Harper's Ferry were placed in a false position and should have been promptly withdrawn," Swinton pontificated in the heat of the 1864 presidential election that "we find no recommendation to this effect by General McClellan during the period in which it was possible to carry it

---

Gary W. Gallagher, ed., *The Antietam Campaign* (Chapel Hill, NC, 1999), 164, which provides a list of the green regiments engaged at Antietam.

14 OR 19:1, 38.

Arrival of new troops in Washington, *August 14 to September 10, 1862*

Date	Regiment	Men	Date	Regiment	Men
Aug. 14	107th N.Y. Inf.*	1,040		Recruits	450
Aug. 16	124th Penn. Inf.*	974	Aug. 29	136th Penn. Inf.	930
	126th Penn. Inf.*	984		19th Maine	1,000
	122nd Penn. Inf.	1,000		137th Penn. Inf.*	850
Aug. 17	129th Penn. Inf.*	950	Aug. 30	17th Mich. Inf.*	950
	34th Mass. Inf.	960		141th Penn. Inf.	950
Aug. 18	33rd Mass. Inf.	1,200		15th N.J. Inf.	800
	125th Penn. Inf.*	920	Aug. 31	149th Penn. Inf.	857
	128th Penn. Inf.*	900	Sept. 1	16th Conn. Inf.	1,015
	131st Penn. Inf.	1,010†		24th Mich. Inf.	1,000
Aug. 19	130th Penn. Inf.*	950		13th N.J. Inf.*	850
	Recruits	85	Sept. 2	118th Penn. Inf.*	1,000
	102nd Penn. Inf.	958	Sept. 3	68th Penn. Inf.	700
	132nd Penn. Inf.	985†		114th Penn. Inf.	700
Aug. 20	Recruits	363		142nd Penn. Inf.	772
	10th N.Y. Cav.	Ukn.		121st N.Y. Inf.*	1,000
	133rd Penn. Inf.*	1,000		119th Penn. Inf.	930
	134th Penn. Inf.	975†		139th Penn. Inf.*	935
Aug. 21	135th Penn. Inf.	933		122nd N.Y. Inf.*	980
	16th Maine Inf.	1,040		Recruits	600
	130th N.Y. Inf.	890	Sept.4	20th Mich. Inf.	950
	Recruits	Ukn.		116th Penn. Inf.	900
	Maine Regts.	95		Recruits	1,000
	12th U.S. Inf.	160	Sept. 5	Recruits	1,300
	25th Ohio Inf.	31	Sept. 6	150th Penn. Inf.	878
	Wis. battery	66		121st Penn. Inf.	700
Aug. 22	123rd Penn. Inf.*	1,030		155th Penn. Inf.*	780
	Recruits	1,018		20th Maine Inf.	961†
	7th Ind. Inf.	55	Sept. 8–9	39th Mass. Inf.	987
	10th N.J. Inf.	70		10th Vt. Inf.	1,023
	1st R.I. Cav.	35		124th N.Y. Inf.	930
	11th Penn. Inf.	54		123rd N.Y. Inf.	930
	32nd Mass. Inf.	335	Sept. 9	11th Vt. Inf.	991
Aug. 23	108th N.Y. Inf.*	950		130th N.Y. Inf.	980
	17th Maine Inf.	1,018		119th N.Y. Inf.	1,000
Aug. 24	35th Mass. Inf.*	1,018		Recruits	300
Aug. 25	107NY	1,000	Sept. 10	40th Mass. Inf.	1,035
	Keystone Bat.	151	**TOTAL**		**62,444**
Aug. 23–25	Recruits	200			
Aug. 26	11th N.J. Inf.	900			
	Recruits	148			
	120th N.Y. Inf.	975			
Aug. 27	18th Maine Inf.	1,140			
	9th N.H. Inf.*	975			
Aug. 28	14th Conn. Inf.	1,007			

Note: The 107th New York Infantry was the first regiment to arrive in Washington after Lincoln's July 1862 call for 300,000 men. New troops continued to arrive for weeks after September 10.

*New regiment which had joined the Army of the Potomac on the field by Sept. 18, 1862.

†Strength from OR Ser. 3, Vol. 3, 760.

‡Strength from OR Ser. 3, Vol. 3, 771.

Source: Arrival dates and strength *The Washington Evening Star*, Aug.–Sept. 1862 unless otherwise noted.

out."[15] This statement by Swinton amounted to little more than an outright lie, made worse by the fact that he failed to mention the responsibility for Col. Miles's garrison belonged to Maj. Gen. John E. Wool of the Middle Department's Eighth Corps, and not to George McClellan. Wool, who also outranked McClellan, reported directly to Henry Halleck.

McClellan first recommended the evacuation of Harpers Ferry after an inquiry made by Secretary of State William H. Seward into the safety of the garrison. Seward had returned to Washington from New York City late on September 3 and proceeded immediately to the Soldier's Home north of the city to consult with Lincoln about what occurred in his absence.[16] We do not know what Seward learned that night, or throughout the next day, but the isolation of the Harpers Ferry garrison appears to have greatly concerned him.

Already on September 4, a Washington area journalist had reported "that the rebels are making a demonstration up the river, and that some of them have already reached Leesburg." He further added that "Winchester has been evacuated, the rebels having appeared in force in the valley."[17] Reports like these caused great concern in the capital city because the roughly 14,000 infantry, artillery, and cavalry under Col. Dixon S. Miles occupied Harpers Ferry between Winchester and the Army of Northern Virginia at Leesburg.[18] Short-term men whose three-to six-month terms were about to expire, and raw troops sent to the ferry only a week earlier to learn the basics of soldiering, made up about half of Miles's command, meaning, in effect, that Miles commanded only a marginally-capable combat force, especially if circumstances forced it to face the veteran ranks of Lee's army.

Seward understood the precariousness of Miles's situation, which prompted him to make an impromptu call on McClellan, whose headquarters sat adjacent to his house in Washington.[19] During this visit, Seward asked McClellan his opinion

15 Swinton, *McClellan's Career Reviewed and Exposed*, 30.

16 Frederick W. Seward, *Seward at Washington as Senator and Secretary of State: A Memoir of His Life, With Selections from His Letters, 1861-1872*, Vol. 2 (New York, NY, 1891), 127.

17 See the Sept. 3 report from Washington, DC, published in the *New York Herald*, Sept. 4, 1862.

18 Halleck telegraphed Brig. Gen. Julius White, the commander of 3,000 men posted at Winchester, to remove his post to Harpers Ferry on Sept. 2 out of fear that Lee's army might advance into the Shenandoah Valley. This addition of soldiers brought Miles's command to about 14,000 men. See Carman, *The Maryland Campaign*, I:211.

19 Seward, *Seward at Washington*, 127. "General McClellan is re-established in his old quarters, on the corner of the Avenue next to our house."

"of the condition of affairs at Harper's Ferry, remarking that he was not at ease on the subject." Little Mac replied that while he did not exercise any control over the garrison he "regarded the arrangements there as exceedingly dangerous [and] that in [his] opinion the proper course was to abandon the position and unite the garrison . . . to the main army of operations." The general's thoughts on the matter so impressed Seward that he asked McClellan to visit Halleck at that very moment to discuss the subject. The two men roused the General-in-Chief from his bed so that McClellan, at Seward's urging, could tell Halleck his opinion. "Halleck received my statement with ill-concealed contempt," recalled McClellan, arguing "everything was all right as it was; that my views were entirely erroneous, etc., and soon bowed us out, leaving matters at Harper's Ferry precisely as they were."[20]

The available evidence suggests that this exchange occurred on the night of September 4, one day before Halleck sent a telegram to Maj. Gen. Wool in Baltimore declaring, "I find it impossible to get this army in to the field again in large force for a day or two. In the mean time Harper's Ferry may be attacked and overwhelmed. I leave all dispositions there to your experience and local knowledge. I beg leave, however, *to suggest the propriety of withdrawing all of our forces in that vicinity to Maryland Heights* [emphasis added]. I have no personal knowledge of the ground, and merely make the suggestion to you."[21]

The tactical recommendation offered by Halleck makes this telegram of special interest because it repeated almost verbatim a suggestion offered by McClellan for saving the Federal garrison. Noting in his official campaign report from October 1862, "Before I left Washington, while it was yet time, I recommended to the proper authorities that the garrison of Harper's Ferry should be withdrawn, via Hagerstown, to aid in covering the Cumberland Valley, or that, taking up the pontoon bridge and obstructing the railroad bridge, *it should fall back to the Maryland Heights and . . . hold its own to the last* [emphasis added]."[22] Then, in a statement he made before the Joint Committee on the Conduct of the War in early March 1863, McClellan specified for a second time, "some days before I left Washington . . . I

20 McClellan, *Own Story*, 549-550.

21 *OR* 19:2, 189.

22 *OR* 19:1, 26.

recommended that the garrison at Harper's Ferry should either be withdrawn entirely *or withdrawn to Maryland Heights* [emphasis added]."[23]

Although Halleck rebuffed McClellan, he nevertheless appears to have taken the general's counsel and wired it to Wool. McClellan, after all, knew the ground around the Ferry intimately, and could offer expert guidance, while Halleck admitted he knew nothing of it; and if he knew nothing it seems highly unlikely he would have suggested Miles move his command to Maryland Heights without hearing the idea from someone else. On this final point we can only speculate, but it could be that animosity toward McClellan may have prevented Halleck from openly accepting the general's advice as far as Col. Miles was concerned.[24] General Wool, in the interim, wired Miles on September 5 to say he should "not abandon Harper's Ferry without defending it to the last extremity," making a fateful decision that Henry Halleck fully endorsed even though it ended up sealing the garrison's fate.[25]

Unable to convince Halleck to take more decisive action to save Miles's command, McClellan returned to preparing the army for the upcoming campaign. From September 6 to September 10, while Lee rested his men around Frederick, Little Mac consolidated his forces, digested intelligence reports on Rebel positions, and pushed columns into Maryland to blunt any possible Confederate advance on Washington or Baltimore. Typically overlooked in studies of the Maryland Campaign, and certainly not taken into account by Halleck when he uttered his six miles per day comment, is the fact that most of McClellan's troops were still in Virginia at the outset of the campaign.

This situation forced them to make long, tedious marches to the new front line in Maryland. Halleck's claim about slow marching appears to have come from a review of only the movements of McClellan's center column *after* it had arrived in Maryland. This is what makes the General-in-Chief's comment so misleading. By September 5, the center "wing" of Edwin Vose Sumner's Second Corps and Alpheus Williams's Twelfth Corps had already marched 35 to 41 miles practically non-stop from Centreville, Virginia, to beyond Rockville, Maryland. But since

---

23 *JCCW*, 440. The general repeated this claim a third time in McClellan, *Report on the Organization and Campaigns of the Army of the Potomac*, 356-357.

24 See Rafuse, *McClellan's War*, 269 for details surrounding Halleck and Edwin Stanton's complaints about McClellan in connection with the defeat and humiliation of Maj. Gen. John Pope.

25 OR 19:1, 520.

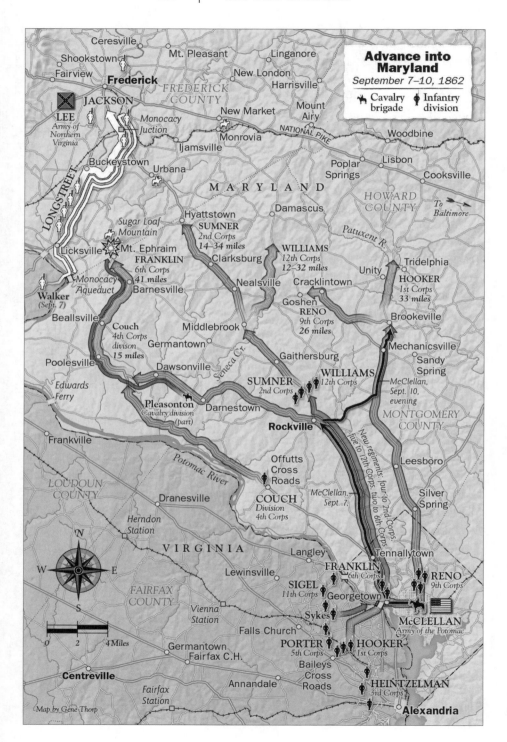

Map by Gene Thorp

most Maryland Campaign studies only begin on the 5th, the grueling marches of the previous days are ignored. The shorter marches of Sumner's and Williams's men from Rockville to Hyattstown are counted instead as the campaign's beginning and it is these marches that totaled only thirteen miles over five days.

Even this slower pace must be studied carefully, however, because McClellan considered the center wing his army's main column and he purposely measured its advance to allow the rest of the army—especially the Ninth and First Corps under Ambrose Burnside and William Franklin's Sixth Corps—to catch up and take position on either flank. Securing the flanks is a textbook military decision that any competent commander would have made under the same circumstances, especially when that commander does not know the enemy's intentions. Not only did Maj. Gen. J. E. B. Stuart's cavalry spread false information stating that Baltimore was their intended target, leading federal officials also feared an advance by Lee toward that city, which would have put the Army of Northern Virginia on McClellan's right flank. For a senior officer allegedly as intelligent as "Old Brains" Halleck to have condemned McClellan for not advancing rapidly under these circumstances makes the General-in-Chief's comment highly suspicious.

After the army's new center wing reached Rockville, McClellan rushed nine new regiments of infantry to its support. Five of these regiments joined the Twelfth Corps, while four went to the Second Corps. Unaccustomed to hard marching, these raw recruits tramped fifteen to twenty miles on their first day of campaigning.[26] During their march, "many of the green troops were prostrated with sunstroke, and stretched along the highway," wrote one of these new soldiers.[27] Another from the 14th Connecticut Volunteers recalled the despair of a death in their ranks from fatigue: "Just as the regiment turned into company streets at the Rockville camp, James McVay of Company K, an old man, died of exhaustion incident of the days march. He had two sons in the same company, who wailed bitterly, touching the hearts of all who beheld their grief."[28] Although these 9,000 new men were now part of the center wing, the disingenuous Halleck left their hard, and for a few individuals terminal, marching out of his calculations.

---

26 These distances derive from detailed research on many sources carried out for the maps with this project. See "Map 2: Advance into Maryland, September 7-10, 1862" of this study for a cartographic depiction.

27 Edward W. Spangler, *My Little War Experience* (York, PA, 1904), 22.

28 Charles D. Page, *History of the Fourteenth Regiment, Connecticut Vol. Infantry* (Meriden, CT, 1906), 26.

Regarding the army's left wing, comprised of the Sixth Corps under William Buel Franklin and the Fourth Corps infantry division of Darius Couch, it took position covering the Potomac River crossing points near Poolesville in case the army should need them, or in the event that the Confederate forces thought to be lurking in Virginia attempted a flanking movement against the Army of the Potomac's left and rear.

Couch crossed his men into Maryland on September 5. Working his way up the left bank of the Potomac to Poolesville, he left half of his force scattered in regimental detachments to guard fords along the route.[29] Franklin's corps also did not enter Maryland until it left the outskirts of Alexandria, Virginia, on a night march on September 6. In the four days from after dark on September 6 to September 10 these men marched 41 miles to Barnesville, Maryland, where the column came under artillery fire from a detachment of Col. Thomas Munford's Confederate cavalry at the base of Sugar Loaf Mountain.[30]

At the same time that Franklin and Couch advanced, McClellan formed an army right wing out of Irwin McDowell's Third Corps, Army of Virginia, and Burnside's recently formed Ninth Corps. Replacing McDowell with Joseph Hooker after the latter had been relieved from command in John Pope's now defunct Army of Virginia, McClellan returned the corps to its original designation

---

29 McClellan ordered Couch on Sept. 10 to "watch all the fords in his vicinity." See *OR* 19:2, 238. The 61st and 102nd Pennsylvania of Couch's command guarded Offutt's Cross-Roads, the 23rd Pennsylvania and 36th New York guarded Conrad's Ferry, the new 122nd New York picketed the mouth of the Monocacy River. The sources are unclear which unit(s) guarded Edwards' Ferry and Seneca, but the 61st Pennsylvania is noted as picketing the Potomac, so it was probably at one of these fords. Presumably, another as yet unidentified regiment guarded the other ford. The new 139th Pennsylvania was burying the Union dead at Bull Run and did not join the division until Sept. 17. As a result, 8 regiments of the fifteen listed in Couch's order of battle were not present with him at Licksville on Sept. 13. See *OR* 19:1, 174. Couch's return for his full division on Sept. 20 totaled 7,219 present for duty. See *OR* 19:2, 336. Logically, then, more than half of that number (3,600) would not have been with Couch at Licksville. Since two of these absent regiments were new and full strength, Couch likely had even less than 3,600 men immediately at hand.

30 Robert S. Westbrook, *History of the 49th Pennsylvania Volunteers* (Altoona, PA, 1898), 123-4: "We marched at 9 A. M., passed through Dawsonville, and camped about 3 P. M. in the wood near Barnesville; the rebels are in sight, and the pickets went out; a little shelling was done this afternoon" Also see G. G. Benedict, *Vermont in the Civil War, A History of the part Taken by the Vermont Soldiers and Sailors in the War for the Union, 1861–5*, Vol. 1 (Burlington, VT, 1886), 318: "Here, at the foot of Sugar Loaf Mountain, on the 11th, distinct proof of the presence of the enemy in the vicinity was afforded by a skirmish in front with a reconnoitering force of Confederate cavalry *and infantry* (i.e., Walker's Division), which retired before the Union advance."

as First Corps, Army of the Potomac.[31] Burnside then assumed command of this new wing, an assignment officially acknowledged in writing on September 14. Major General Jesse Reno, another veteran from the Army of Virginia, subsequently replaced Burnside as commander of the Ninth Corps in accordance with a direct order from President Lincoln.[32] To Reno's three divisions McClellan also added the Kanawha Division, a unit filled with veteran Ohio troops under Jacob Dolson Cox that had recently arrived from western Virginia.[33]

As reports of the Rebel army entering Maryland in strength continued to arrive on September 7, McClellan ordered Burnside to gather his wing and march north to threaten the flank of any Confederate force that might advance down the National Pike toward Baltimore.[34] Robert E. Lee never planned such a movement, but, as was mentioned previously, the public and many in the army feared that the Rebel general had the city in his sights.[35] Accordingly, McClellan took no chances. Unaware of Lee's objectives, but awake to the possibility that he could indeed target Baltimore, McClellan wisely ordered Burnside north.

Reality, however, soon impeded the right wing commander's ability to fulfill his orders as Reno found his Ninth Corps divisions scattered across northern Virginia. Two divisions remained in position near Alexandria, while one camped at

31 *OR* 19:2, 197-198.

32 Burnside's orders may be found in *OR* 19:2, 290. Reno's assignment is in *OR* 19:2, 197.

33 Cox, *Military Reminiscences*, I:264.

34 *OR* 19:1, 25: "The disappearance of the enemy from the front of Washington and their passage into Maryland enlarged the sphere of operations, and made an active campaign necessary to cover Baltimore." See also *OR* 19:2, 222-3: "The object of these movements was to feel the enemy—to compel him to develop his intentions—at the same time that the troops were in position readily to cover Baltimore or Washington." On Sept. 9 at 10:00 p.m. McClellan wrote Burnside, "Should the enemy make any demonstration toward Baltimore, let his column get well in motion, and then attack him vigorously on the flank, sending immediate information to the major-general commanding, who will support you with all his available force."

35 Gov. Curtin wrote to McClellan on Sept. 10: "I have letter from clergyman, dated Taneytown, Md., Sunday night, in which he says: One of my elders, a reliable man, traveled 7 miles through their camps on Sunday. Their force around Frederick is not less than 120,000 men, and the part under Lee had not joined that army. He conversed with many officers and men. They appeared to believe their whole army in Maryland would exceed 200,000 men, and their intention was to march either upon Harrisburg or Baltimore, probably the latter." See *OR* 19:2, 248. According to the *Baltimore American*, Sept. 8, 1862, "a meeting of the citizens [of Frederick] was called on Saturday evening at which an address was delivered by Bradley Johnson, who used the most conciliatory language and made great predictions as to the power of the Confederate army not only to hold Western Maryland but to capture Baltimore and Washington."

Upton's Hill in Arlington, and a fourth even occupied Fredericksburg.[36] All of these divisions eventually united north of Washington by September 7, where they proceeded to the vicinity of the upper Patuxent River, but reaching their destination had required that they march thirty to forty miles from their various positions south of the Potomac. Joseph Hooker faced a similar situation, too, marching the men of his First Corps 33 miles from the vicinity of Bailey's Cross Roads, Virginia, to Mechanicsville, Maryland.

These marches through the dense camps outside of Washington, and the crowded streets of the city itself, took a heavy toll on the men. Hooker's troops, for instance, started their brutal trek north shortly before midnight on September 6 and kept going all through the night without a stop. As one soldier from Cortland, New York, recalled, "When morning came we thought we would halt and rest, but we did not. The day was very hot and the dust four inches deep. The word was always 'Forward! Forward!' During the whole day we did not stop long enough to take a real meal or make a cup of coffee. . . . We did not halt until 7 p.m., having marched 24 hours."[37]

Colonel William Rogers, commanding the 21st New York, another First Corps regiment, remembered this march as "one of the most fatiguing and harassing of the campaign." Finding the road to Washington "blocked with trains [which made] our march a very tedious and disagreeable one," Rogers's regiment crossed the aqueduct bridge before plodding "through Georgetown and Washington about

36 Cox, *Military Reminiscences*, I:264. Burnside's three division expeditionary force of Brig. Gen. Isaac P. Rodman, Brig. Gen. Jesse L. Reno and Brig. Gen. Isaac I. Stevens moved by water from Newport News to Fredericksburg from Aug. 1-7, 1862. See Matthew J. Graham, *The Ninth Regiment New York Volunteers, Being A History of the Regiment and Veteran Association, From 1860 to 1900* (New York, NY, 1900), 249, and William A. Croffut and John M. Morris, *The Military and Civil History of Connecticut During The War of 1861–65* (New York, NY, 1868), 257, Reno's and Steven's divisions marched inland and joined Pope's army near Culpeper in mid-August while Rodman's division of six regiments remained behind in Fredericksburg and Falmouth to keep the railroad line open to Aquia landing on the Potomac. Following Pope's defeat at the Second Battle of Bull Run, Reno's and Stevens's divisions retreated with the Army of Virginia to Alexandria, Virginia. Stevens was killed at Chantilly on Sept. 1, opening the door for Brig. Gen. Orlando B. Willcox to assume command of Stevens's division on Sept. 8. Halleck ordered Burnside to move Rodman's division from Fredericksburg and Falmouth to Alexandria on Aug. 31. See OR 12:3, 774. At 5:00 p.m. on Sept. 4, Burnside reported that by morning the next day he would have all of Rodman's troops embarked for Washington. See OR 19:2, 175. Rodman's division arrived in Washington during the two days from Sept. 3–5 and marched to Meridian Hill. See Graham, *The Ninth Regiment, 250 and Croffut and Morris, The Military and Civil History of Connecticut*, 259.

37 Uberto A. Burnham, "76th NY," in *The National Tribune* (1928). Available online at https://www.76nysv.us/burnham-somtn.html.

daylight on Sunday morning, and turning into Seventh street, took the road to Leesboro, Maryland, which place we reached the following day."[38] Making matters worse, Hooker's men found no rations waiting for them when they finally reached their destination. Why were we "started so abruptly upon this march without rations, and not followed immediately by a supply train?" puzzled an incredulous member of James Ricketts's division.[39] Forced to seek help from the local inhabitants, or gather what they could from nearby cornfields, Hooker's troops did the best they could to supply themselves.

For his part, McClellan took command of the reconstituted Army of the Potomac in the field on September 7, leaving Washington that same evening with his staff.[40] Riding fifteen miles to Rockville, Maryland, the general established his new headquarters with his army still in significant disarray. Brigadier General George Sykes's division of U.S. Army regulars, serves as a case in point. It also marched to Rockville from Tennallytown on September 7, but whereas the division officially belonged to the army's Fifth Corps, the leadership of that corps remained unfilled thanks to controversy surrounding the role of Fitz John Porter in allegedly undermining the Second Bull Run campaign of John Pope.[41]

In the meantime, two other divisions of Fifth Corps troops, those under George Morrell and Andrew Humphreys, stayed in the Washington fortifications

38 J. Harrison Mills, *Chronicles of the Twenty-First Regiment New York State Volunteers* (Buffalo, NY, 1887), 278.

39 Isaac Hall, *History of the Ninety-Seventh Regiment New York Volunteers ("Conkling Rifles") in the War for the Union* (Utica, NY, 1890), 82.

40 In a bizarre turn of events indicating the administration's disorganization at the time, Halleck and Lincoln each claimed the other had authorized McClellan's return to field command. McClellan claimed, however, that he never received any authorization for field command and so took it upon himself to lead the army in Maryland. See "From the Peninsula to Antietam: Posthumous Notes by George B. McClellan," Johnson and Buel, eds. *Battles and Leaders*, 2:552: "As the time had now arrived for the army to advance, and I had received no orders to take command of it, but had been expressly told that the assignment of a commander had not been decided, I determined to solve the question for myself, and when I moved out from Washington with my staff and personal escort I left my card with P. P. C. written upon it, at the White House, War Office, and Secretary Seward's house, and went on my way. I was afterward accused of assuming command without authority, for nefarious purposes." For further discussion of the controversy see Stotelmyer, *Too Useful to Sacrifice*, 161-164.

41 Although Lincoln had ordered Porter relieved of command it never happened due to McClellan's request to keep him in place. Porter remained formally in command of the Fifth Corps from Sept. 1 to Sept. 20. See Halleck's order, and McClellan's response in Stephen W. Sears, ed., *The Civil War Papers of George B. McClellan: Selected Correspondence, 1860-1865* (New York, NY, 1989), 437.

in case a Rebel attack on the city developed in northern Virginia.[42] Samuel P. Heintzelman's Third Corps and Franz Sigel's Eleventh Corps, along with unassigned new regiments, and heavy artillery units joined these men under the overall command of Maj. Gen. Nathaniel P. Banks.

By September 10, George McClellan could count approximately 86,000 men as his effective offensive force to confront Lee, while 73,000 or so remained behind to defend Washington against any surprise attack the Confederates might muster. McClellan also received the remaining portion of his missing cavalry on that day, putting some twelve regiments in front of the army to scout for the enemy. One week after he had assumed command of the Washington defenses, and three days after he took command of the Federal field army, McClellan finally had eyes on the Confederates.

With a substantial force now at hand, new units coming up, secure lines of supply forming, and his cavalry out in front, McClellan revisited the Harpers Ferry situation with Halleck. Penning a second request for the garrison's evacuation on September 10, even though he still bore no official responsibility for its safety, Little Mac wrote, "I would . . . advise that the force of Colonel Miles, at Harper's Ferry, where it can be of but little use, and is continually exposed to be cut off by the enemy, be immediately ordered here."[43] Shortly afterward, McClellan rode ten miles north to consult with Burnside at Brookeville before returning to Rockville at 3:00 a.m. that same night.

McClellan communicated his request for a third time the next morning, writing from his headquarters at 9:45 a.m., "Colonel Miles is at or near Harper's Ferry, as I understand, with 9,000 troops. He can do nothing where he is, but could be of great service if ordered to join me. I suggest that he be ordered to join me by the most

---

42 OR 19:1, 369. Brigadier General Andrew Humphreys's division consisted of eight new regiments. Halleck placed these regiments under Humphrey's command on Sept. 12, 1862, while at the same time assigning him to McClellan's army.

43 OR 19:2, 254. Two days earlier, McClellan had also communicated the following to Gen. Wool in Baltimore, demonstrating that the fate of Harpers Ferry continued to occupy his attention: "It seems to me of great importance that we should co-operate fully . . . I should be especially gratified to learn everything that you can get regarding the movements of the enemy in the direction of Harper's Ferry and above. OR 19:2, 212.

practicable route."[44] Yet for reasons that remain a mystery, Halleck stubbornly refused to move Miles's men or to place Miles under McClellan's command. Responding on September 11, "There is no way for Colonel Miles to join you at present," Halleck claimed, "His only chance is to defend his works till you can open communication with him." Once McClellan had done so, Halleck assured him in a case of doing too little too late, Miles "will be subject to your orders."[45]

Consequently, on the afternoon of September 11, with Miles still dangerously isolated, McClellan started northwest to Middleburg. The following morning, Col. David Hunter Strother, a topographer from Martinsburg, (West) Virginia, who had recently joined McClellan's staff, recorded in his diary, "Tents struck at eight o'clock and the staff took the road early."[46] Riding along the Georgetown Pike, McClellan stopped to visit a resident of Clarksburg at 9:30 a.m., before updating Halleck with the latest intelligence some thirty minutes later. "My columns are pushing on rapidly to Frederick," he wrote. "I feel perfectly confident that the enemy has abandoned Frederick, moving in two directions, viz, on the Hagerstown and Harper's Ferry roads."[47]

McClellan added that the latest information from Burnside's command indicated "four regiments of cavalry and six pieces of artillery" under the Confederate general Fitzhugh Lee had shifted north from New Market to Liberty, Maryland, with Federal cavalry in pursuit. McClellan's knowledge of the Rebel departure from Frederick originated in a message he had received from Pennsylvania Gov. Andrew Curtin at 8:00 p.m. on September 11. "We have advices that enemy broke up whole encampment at Frederick yesterday morning, 3 o'clock, and marched in direction of Hagerstown with over three hundred pieces artillery, large bodies of infantry and cavalry, Stonewall Jackson leading," wrote the governor. Adding incorrectly that "Jackson is now in Hagerstown," Curtin explained that the "Man who gives information said rebel army marching 5 a.m. to

44 George McClellan to Henry Halleck, 9:45 a.m., Sept. 11, 1862, George Brinton McClellan Papers: Letterbooks and Telegram Books, Telegram book, 1862; Sept. 8 – Oct. 25, 1862. Library of Congress, Manuscript/Mixed Material. Available online at: https://www.loc.gov/resource/mss31898.mss31898-065_0436_0739/?sp=60&r=-1.265,0.033,3.53,1.635,0. Cited hereafter as McClellan Papers.

45 OR 19:1, 44, 758.

46 Cecil D. Eby, Jr., ed., *A Virginia Yankee in the Civil War: The Diaries of David Hunter Strother* (Chapel Hill, NC, 1961), 105.

47 OR 19:2, 270-271.

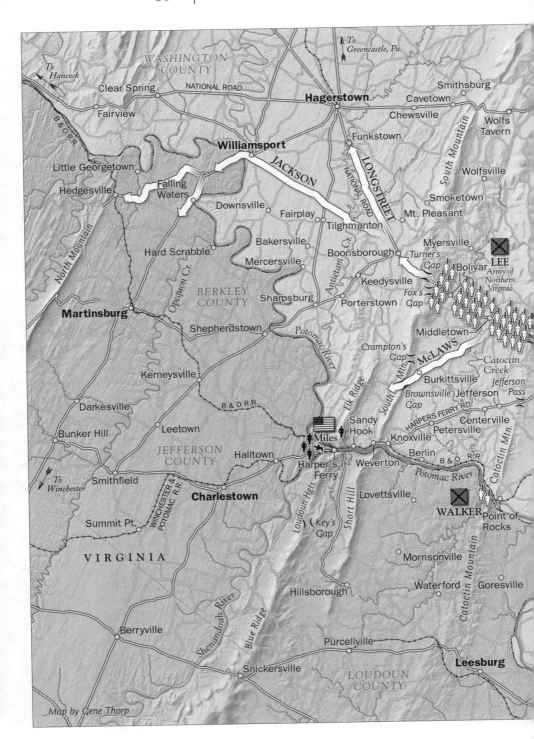

Map by Gene Thorp

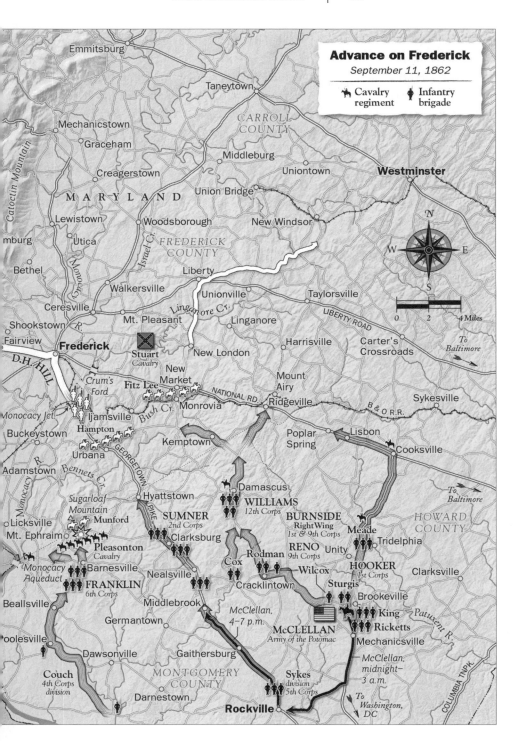

Advance on Frederick
September 11, 1862

Cavalry regiment | Infantry brigade

9 p.m. yesterday out of their camps at Frederick. Men all believed they were going to Pennsylvania."[48]

The governor's message echoed information coming in from other sources as well, one of those being Brig. Gen. Jacob Cox, the commander of the Kanawha division in Jesse Reno's Ninth Corps. Notifying McClellan on the evening of September 11 that a newly-arrived informant from Frederick City "reports that place evacuated by the rebels except pickets," Cox explained, "there is no force but cavalry pickets of small numbers anywhere on the road between Frederick and Ridgeville; saw only 30 or 40 cavalry at New Market. [Informant] dodged their pickets through the woods. His report is confirmed by several partial accounts received by me from citizens in the neighborhood, and I think it reliable. . . . The rebels in leaving Frederick are reported to have gone on the Hagerstown road."[49]

The 10:00 a.m. dispatch sent by McClellan on September 12 shows that confusion never clouded the general's knowledge of the enemy. Contrary to decades of erroneous claims to the contrary, McClellan had a sound grasp of Lee's movements within hours of their occurrence.[50] Less than one day after the Army of Northern Virginia had left Frederick City, McClellan knew not only that it had gone, he also knew the directions that its columns had taken, even though the information he received concerning one of those routes (i.e., down the Harpers Ferry Road from Frederick) proved to be only partially correct. As for McClellan's claim that his own columns "were pushing on rapidly to Frederick," the evidence shows them doing exactly that. Already by 10:00 p.m. on September 11, McClellan responded to the news of Lee's movement by ordering Burnside to "advance to-morrow, if possible, to Frederick and occupy it," requiring a march of between fifteen and twenty miles from the Ninth Corps' positions near Damascus and Ridgeville.[51] Little Mac simultaneously instructed Edwin Sumner's wing and

---

48 *OR* 19:2, 269.

49 *OR* 19:2, 256-257. Newspapers in Pennsylvania also reported on Sept. 11, "We hear that General McClellan is satisfied that the force of the Rebels that have crossed the Potomac were yesterday massed in the vicinity of Frederick," illustrating the extent to which local informants kept authorities apprised of Rebel movements in Maryland. See *Philadelphia Inquirer*, Sept. 11, 1862.

50 For example, see Sears, *McClellan*, 278-279.

51 *OR* 19:2, 255 and *OR* 51:1, 818. McClellan wrote to Burnside at 10:00 p.m. on Sept. 11: "Our information is that enemy has abandoned Frederick and is moving toward Hagerstown. If the information you gain tends to confirm this, push on toward Frederick by the National pike and the railroad as rapidly as possible. We will do the same from Urbana. Keep your

William Franklin's Sixth Corps to converge on Urbana, located some seven miles southeast of Frederick.[52]

Accounts of the marching done by various regiments with the Ninth Corps demonstrate the celerity with which the Army of the Potomac's vanguard advanced to Frederick even before Robert E. Lee found it less than convenient. Historians have long cited an unfortunate comment made by McClellan in his Maryland Campaign report as evidence that the general did not advance rapidly enough to meet the Confederate threat. Writing that until September 10 he had "not imposed long marches" on his columns due to "The absolute necessity of refitting and giving some little rest to troops worn down by previous long-continued marching and severe fighting," McClellan added, "together with the uncertainty as to the actual position, strength, and intentions of the enemy, [circumstances] rendered it incumbent upon me to move slowly and cautiously until the headquarters reached Urbana."[53]

These words, reflecting a modesty on McClellan's part for which he is never given credit, did the general and his army a great disservice because the evidence shows clearly and irrefutably that the location of his troops in Virginia following Second Bull Run required McClellan to march his men as far as forty miles during the first few days of the Maryland Campaign. The general then slowed the advance of his center wing from September 7-10 to allow for other columns to cover the Potomac River crossing points on his left flank and block the route to Baltimore on his right.

Typically overlooked in the general's report is his comment that the men given to him at the outset of the campaign had been "worn down by previous long-continued marching." These words accurately reflected the army's condition as its various portions moved out to confront Lee's Army of Northern Virginia. Once he had accomplished his initial objective of ensuring the safety of Baltimore and Washington, and once he had given the fatigued divisions of his army's center wing a brief opportunity to rest, and allowed time for new regiments to arrive, McClellan resumed the steady marching rate that had marked his army's early

---

flankers and cavalry well out to the right toward Liberty, Westminster, &c. Be extremely cautious in your advance. Watch your front and flanks with care, and be careful to communicate fully with headquarters and the troops on your left. It is thought that the enemy has abandoned Frederick and moved toward Hagerstown. In any event, occupy Frederick to-morrow if you can possibly do so without too much exposing your command."

52 *OR* 19:2, 255.

53 *OR* 19:1, 26.

September advance. This push began at approximately the same time as incoming information confirmed the Rebel army's withdrawal from Frederick. As David Thompson of the 9th New York, a regiment with the Ninth Corps put it, from September 10 "on our purpose seemed to grow more definite."[54] After receiving orders to advance on September 11, the four divisions of Reno's Ninth Corps marched around thirty miles in two days to reach Frederick from the vicinity of Brookeville. Hooker's First Corps also marched 25 miles from the vicinity of Mechanicsville to various positions east of Frederick along the National Pike.

Oliver Bosbyshell of the 48th Pennsylvania, a regiment belonging to the Ninth Corps' Second Division, recorded that "At 3 o'clock a.m. of the eleventh the regiment . . . left camp at daylight . . . the night's camp was located some two miles north of Damascus . . . the Forty-eighth . . . made thirteen miles. . . . Seven o'clock the next morning [September 12] found the regiment on the go. The march was slow and easy . . . the bivouac made on the west side of the Monocacy, near the large stone bridge, and in sight of Frederick City" for a march that day of roughly 15 miles.[55] Charles F. Walcott, a captain in the 21st Massachusetts, also with the Second Division, wrote similarly of this advance,

> September 11th. We started at seven A. M., and *after a day's march of eighteen miles* [emphasis added], through a rich and fertile country, halted in a lovely spot near New Market at five o'clock. Heavy showers fell at intervals during the day, but it was the first rain for several days and was not unwelcome. September 12th. Starting at seven A. M., we crossed the Baltimore and Ohio Railroad, and after a slow march crossed the high stone bridge over the beautiful little river Monocacy, [a distance of 10 miles] and went into bivouac in sight of Frederick City, about sundown.[56]

54 David L. Thompson, "In the Ranks to the Antietam," in Johnson and Buel, eds., *Battles and Leaders*, 2:557.

55 Oliver C. Bosbyshell, *The 48th in the War, Being a Narrative of the Campaigns of the 48th Regiment Infantry Pennsylvania Veteran Volunteers, During the War of the Rebellion* (Philadelphia, PA, 1895), 73-74.

56 Charles F. Walcott, *History of the Twenty-First Regiment Massachusetts Volunteers in the War for the Preservation of the Union, 1861-1865* (Boston, MA, 1882), 187. Also see the Sept. 12 and 13 entries of Elisha J. Bracken, Civil War Diary, 100th Pennsylvania Volunteer Infantry, Pennsylvania State University. Special Collections Library; available online at https://digital.libraries.psu.edu/digital/collection/ejb/id/57/, and the Sept. 21 letter of Capt. Wolcott P. Marsh, Co. F, 8th Connecticut Volunteers. Available online at http://8cv.home.comcast.net/~8cv/).

Even the Kanawha division of Jacob Cox, who later recalled inaccurately in his memoir that his men "moved forward by very short marches of six or eight miles," actually marched from Ridgeville to the western outskirts of Frederick on September 12, a distance of more than fifteen miles. Hooker, in the meantime, "had been ordered further to the right on the strength of rumors that Lee was making a circuit towards Baltimore," wrote Cox, "and his corps reached Cooksville and the railroad some ten miles east of my position," culminating a march that put the First Corps 25 miles from Frederick.[57] The evidence is clear, therefore, that on September 11 and 12, Ninth Corps troops marched an average of fourteen miles per day, or more than double the six miles per day conjecture volunteered by Halleck that William Swinton repeated in 1864, and which Stephen Sears and others have relied upon repeatedly to condemn McClellan's supposed lethargy.[58]

After-action reports often garble details about what commanders knew at the time, and in this case McClellan's post-campaign report of October 15, 1862, did him no favors. Writing "uncertainty as to the actual position" of the enemy was one of the reasons that compelled him to advance slowly in Maryland, students of the campaign have made a habit of using McClellan's words against him. Yet, twice in the same document the general admitted that he knew full well Lee's army occupied the "line of the Monocacy," and by September 11 he had already moved the Second, Twelfth, Ninth, and First Corps, as well as George Sykes's Second Division, to confront Lee if his army advanced from that position toward Washington or Baltimore.

Concerning Franklin's Sixth Corps, McClellan ordered it "to support the center should it have been necessary (as was supposed) to force the line of the Monocacy."[59] He then repeated this idea, conceding that while he had maneuvered his army to cover Baltimore and Washington he had also tried to ensure "that the troops were in position . . . to attack him (the enemy) should he hold the line of the

57 Cox, *Military Reminiscences*, I:267-268.

58 See Sears, *McClellan*, 280: "His advance on September 12 averaged six miles;" Sears, "Last Words on the Lost Order," 113: "On that day, as on previous days, the average march in the Army of the Potomac was just six miles."

59 OR 19:1, 26. McClellan wisely assumed that Lee might choose to fight along the Monocacy. Jackson is said to have suggested it to Lee while the army camped near Frederick and there is evidence that the Rebel commander had chosen the river as a potential line of defense. See Alexander B. Rossino, *Their Maryland: The Army of Northern Virginia from the Potomac Crossing to Sharpsburg in September 1862* (El Dorado, CA, 2021), 90, Note 34.

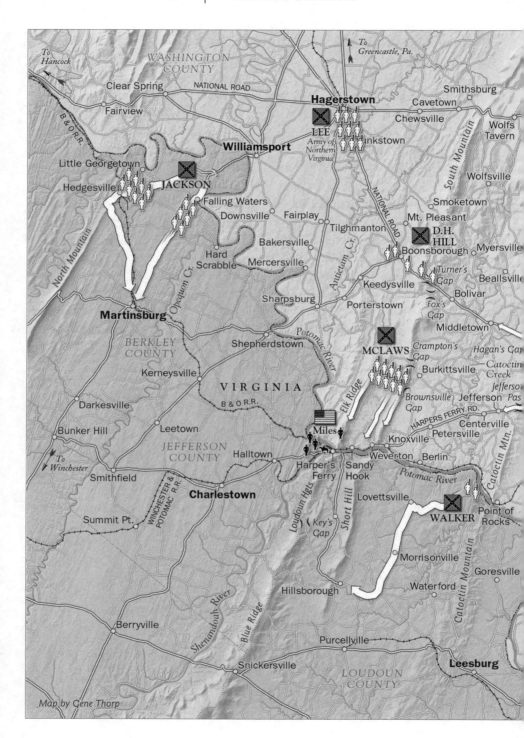

Map by Gene Thorp

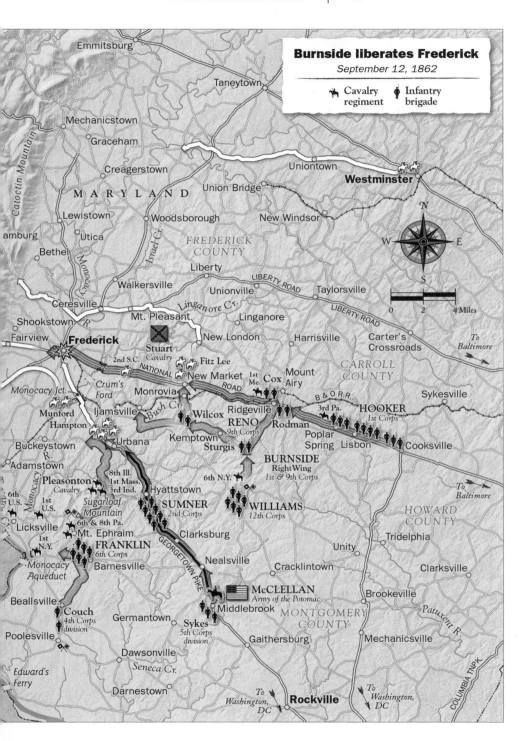

Burnside liberates Frederick
September 12, 1862

Monocacy."[60] That McClellan updated the information he had on this subject is obvious in his second official report on the Maryland Campaign from August 1863. This time he replaced the claim that he did not know the position of the enemy with the statement, "Uncertainty as to *the intentions of the enemy* [emphasis added] obliged me . . . to march cautiously."[61]

This statement more accurately reflected the situation as it existed during the campaign. The sources demonstrate that from the afternoon Robert E. Lee's forces first traversed the Potomac River at Noland's Ferry to the day Indiana troops found Special Orders No. 191, McClellan did not have a "decidedly cloudy" picture of the enemy.[62] He knew definitively as of September 8 that Jackson's command had reached Frederick, although it is likely he had learned this information even earlier since Col. Strother of his staff wrote in his diary on September 6, "five thousand men of the Rebel advance marched into Frederick."[63] McClellan also knew that no sizeable Rebel force other than cavalry had advanced toward Baltimore from the Army of Northern Virginia's encampments around Frederick.[64]

On September 9, for example, he telegraphed Halleck from Rockville, "The latest information from the front indicates the enemy in large force near Frederick. . . . I do not think they have yet left Frederick."[65] In short, as of September 10, only Lee's ultimate objective in Maryland remained unclear to McClellan. Even then, Little Mac had clarified the situation by blocking the routes east.[66] With moving in that direction out of the question for Lee, unless he desired to bring on a general engagement, the options open to him included marching north toward Gettysburg,

---

60 *OR* 19:1, 25-26.

61 *OR* 19:1, 39. McClellan likely altered his report in response to criticism that slow-marching had prevented him from rescuing Harpers Ferry.

62 Sears, "The Twisted Tale," 57.

63 Eby, Jr., ed., *A Virginia Yankee*, 102.

64 *OR* 19:2, 211. Two of Stonewall Jackson's divisions and other portions of the Army of Northern Virginia camped along the eastern bank of the Monocacy, but they did not advance in the direction of Baltimore or Washington, rendering McClellan's belief that Lee's army remained near Frederick correct. For a detailed analysis of the Confederate encampments around Frederick see Rossino, *Their Maryland*, Chapter 3.

65 *OR* 19:2, 219.

66 We agree with Thomas Clemens's observation in Ezra Carman's history of the Maryland Campaign that "McClellan was still unsure of Lee's direction and intent." See Carman, *The Maryland Campaign*, I:190, Note 57.

retreating south to Virginia, or moving northwest into Washington County, Maryland. When news arrived on the evening of September 11 that the Army of Northern Virginia had marched out of Frederick on the National Road toward Hagerstown, it confirmed that Lee had taken the path of least resistance. This movement opened the door for an unopposed advance to Frederick by the Army of the Potomac, which McClellan promptly ordered and which Burnside rapidly executed.[67]

At 3:00 p.m. on September 12, the army's headquarters group stopped "in a lovely grove surrounded by grass fields like shaven lawns" near Little Bennett Creek one mile southeast of Urbana. "Here camp was pitched," recalled Col. Strother, allowing McClellan the opportunity to jot a few lines to his wife, Mary Ellen, using his photo album as a lap desk.[68] "The place selected for our camp tonight . . . [is] in a beautiful grove on the summit of a hill," wrote the general, and is "one of the prettiest camps we have yet had." He then told her what he suspected of Lee's movements, stating, "From all I can gather secesh is skedadling, and I don't think I can catch him unless he is really moving into Pennsylvania. In that case I shall catch him before he has made much headway towards the interior. I am beginning to think he is making off to get out of the scrape by recrossing the river at Williamsport, in which case my only chance of bagging him will be to cross lower down and cut into his communications near Winchester."[69]

This letter accurately reflected the military situation at the moment. McClellan knew that once the Rebel army had moved into Washington County only two options for fighting and two for maneuver remained open to Lee. He could either defend the South Mountain passes or fight west of the mountains, or he could march north into Pennsylvania, or retire south to Virginia. According to Strother, the prevailing belief at headquarters favored the latter. "Telegrams from divers[e] points . . . [show] that a movement *en masse* had been commenced [by the enemy] toward Hagerstown and the points in front (east) of the Monocacy had been abandoned," confided the topographer to his journal. "[General] McClellan suspected from this news that Lee had elected to retreat to Virginia rather than face

---

67 Sears, *McClellan*, 278 either deeply misrepresented or incorrectly interpreted the actual state of McClellan's knowledge on Sept. 11–12, claiming that reports showing "Confederate troops were sighted at virtually every other point on the compass, south, west, and north" practically paralyzed the Federal army's advance to Frederick.

68 Eby, Jr., ed., *A Virginia Yankee*, 105.

69 McClellan, *Own Story*, 570.

the Army of the Potomac. . . . The retrograde movement on Hagerstown . . . meant a retreat into the Valley of the Shenandoah by way of Williamsport. This seemed to be the received opinion."[70] As McClellan himself put it in an unusually colloquial turn of phrase to his wife, Lee "evidently don't want to fight me, for some reason or other."[71]

At 4:10 p.m. on September 12, McClellan received a brief message from Lincoln, originally sent twelve hours earlier, asking "How does it look now?" McClellan did not initially reply because news coming in from the recently re-established signal station on Sugarloaf Mountain reported that Reno's Ninth Corps had just fought its way into Frederick along the National Road. With the town now in Federal hands, and Brig. Gen. Wade Hampton's Rebel cavalry brigade pushed back to a defensive position atop Catoctin Mountain, McClellan directed his attention to informing Halleck about Frederick's capture. Cognizant of the fact that Lincoln read all of Halleck's incoming telegrams, McClellan knew he could forego responding to the president's earlier missive first.[72]

"I have just learned, by signal from Sugar Loaf Mountain, that our troops are entering Frederick," reported Little Mac at 5:30 p.m. "The remainder of Burnside's troops are between Frederick and New Market.[73] Sumner is near Urbana, with our advance guard thrown out to the Monocacy; Williams [is] on his right; Franklin on his left; Couch at Barnesville." Then McClellan noted that "Cavalry has been sent toward Point of Rocks to ascertain whether there is any force of the enemy in that direction," demonstrating he still accounted for Halleck's odd fear that a large Confederate force might be operating on his left near Leesburg, and that he would order no advance unless he felt his army's flanks were secure. Finally, he concluded, "Burnside has cavalry in pursuit of Fitzhugh Lee, toward Westminster."[74]

---

70 Eby, Jr., ed., *A Virginia Yankee*, 104.

71 McClellan, *Own Story*, 570.

72 According to War Department telegraph office manager David Homer Bates, "Lincoln's habit was to go immediately to the drawer each time he came into our room, and read over the telegrams, beginning at the top, until he came to the one he had seen at his last previous visit." See David H. Bates, *Lincoln in the Telegraph Office: Recollections of the United States Military Telegraph Corps during the Civil War* (New York, NY, 1939), 41. McClellan revealed that he knew Lincoln's telegram reading habits in his 9:00 p.m., Sept. 12 wire found in *OR* 19:2, 272. It states, "You will have learned by my telegram to General Halleck ..."

73 McClellan could only have been referring to the Ninth Corps, as portions of Hooker's First Corps still stretched all the way back to Mounty Airy.

74 *OR* 19:2, 271.

Turning to the movements he planned for the next day, McClellan repeated what he had written to his wife, clarifying the notion that while he knew where the Army of Northern Virginia could be found he did not know where Lee intended to lead it. "Should the enemy go toward Pennsylvania I shall follow him," declared McClellan. "Should he attempt to recross the Potomac I shall endeavor to cut off his retreat. My movements to-morrow will be dependent upon information to be received during the night. The troops have marched to-day as far as it was possible and proper for them to move." Confident that Lee's army no longer posed a threat to Washington, or to the Army of the Potomac's rear, McClellan added a postscript which did not sit well with Halleck, who remained obsessed with the possibility that a large Rebel force could advance on the capital from Virginia. Informing the General-in-Chief, "I have ordered [Maj. Gen. Nathaniel] Banks to send eight new regiments to relieve [the] parts of [Darius] Couch's command left at Offutt's Cross-Roads, Seneca, and Conrad's and Edwards Ferries," McClellan asked, "How soon may I expect these troops?"[75]

Satisfied that the whole Rebel army occupied Maryland ahead of him, and that his request to consolidate Couch's command would prompt no complaints, McClellan settled into the business of issuing orders for the next day's march. His primary aim at this point involved pushing his army across the Monocacy River and securing Frederick City. At 5:45 p.m. on September 13, McClellan directed Franklin to depart at daylight the next day for Buckeystown from a short distance west of Urbana. Adding that the Sixth Corps' commander should await further orders once he arrived at his destination, Little Mac told him to be "ready to move either to Frederick or Harper's Ferry" as the situation warranted.[76]

A telegram from Halleck sent earlier in the day at 1:45 p.m. then interrupted McClellan. Informing the general that the two remaining divisions of the Fifth Corps had started their march from Washington to join the army in the field, Halleck inquired, "Have you any reliable information of enemy's force south of the Potomac?" Here again the General-in-Chief hinted at the concern about a Confederate attack from that quarter which haunted the War Department. Then Halleck asked, "Is it not possible to open communication with Harper's Ferry, so that Colonel Miles' forces can co-operate with you?"[77]

75 OR 19:2, 271.

76 Ibid.

77 Ibid.

Receiving this missive must have been maddening for McClellan considering the advice he gave on September 4 that Dixon Miles should abandon Harpers Ferry before Lee blocked his opportunity to retreat. Little Mac had also urged in the strongest possible terms on September 11 the necessity of "uniting all our disposable forces" in response to the numerous estimates showing that Lee's army amounted to "not less than 120,000 men."[78] Accusations that the general habitually overinflated the enemy's strength have shadowed McClellan ever since William Swinton's vilification in 1864. At the time, however, the idea that Lee commanded a very large army appeared quite real to everyone involved in repelling the Rebel offensive.[79] Governor Curtin, for example, assured Halleck on September 10 and Lincoln on September 11 that "The enemy will bring against us not less than 120,000, with a large amount of artillery;" and even the military commission investigating the Harpers Ferry debacle concluded at the end of its proceedings, "97,000 [men comprised] . . . the whole of Lee's army."[80] Neither of these overestimates had anything to do with George McClellan and yet they were considered realistic by high-ranking political and military officials at the time.

Halleck had of course agreed on September 11 that Miles's command could join McClellan only if he managed to "open communication with Harpers Ferry." Now, one day later, with the garrison's options rapidly running out, the General-in-Chief changed his tune, ordering Col. Miles to unconditionally "obey such orders as General McClellan may give you. You will endeavor to open communication with him and unite your forces to his at the earliest possible moment. His army is now near the line of the Monocacy."[81] Unfortunately for both Col. Miles and Henry Halleck, telegraphic communications between Washington

---

78 *OR* 19:2, 254-255.

79 Gene Thorp, "In Defense of McClellan at Antietam: A Contrarian View," in *The Washington Post* (Sept. 2012) Rebel Strength section, available online at: https://www. washingtonpost.com/wp-srv/special/artsandliving/civilwar/mcclellan-graphic/?tab=1&tid =a_inl_manual, estimates the Army of Northern Virginia's numerical strength totaled about 77,769 at the start of the campaign. Thorp's analysis is deeply-sourced, providing a sound, statistically-based estimate of Lee's strength. In his own statistical analysis of the subject Harsh, *Taken*, 39 concluded that the Rebel army's strength at the beginning of the campaign was around 75,500. Meanwhile, Hartwig, *To Antietam Creek*, 679-680 placed the ANV's strength on Sept. 2 at 75, 305.

80 *OR* 19:2, 248, 268 and *OR* 19:1, 800.

81 *OR* 19:1, 758.

and Harpers Ferry went dead on September 11, making it unlikely that Miles ever received these instructions.[82]

It is therefore only with the enemy threat to the garrison becoming obvious, and with communications to Harpers Ferry cut, that Halleck finally saddled McClellan on September 12 with the task of rescuing Miles's command.[83] Prior to this point McClellan had borne no responsibility, officially or otherwise, for the fate of Harpers Ferry, which is a fact that critics of the general have repeatedly ignored.

Responding at 6:00 p.m. on September 12 to Halleck's questions about Rebels below the Potomac River, and opening communication with Miles, McClellan wrote, "I learn nothing reliable as to the enemy south of the Potomac. I this morning ordered [the 6th U.S.] cavalry to endeavor to open communication with Harper's Ferry, and in my orders of movement for to-morrow have arranged so that I can . . . send [Franklin and Couch] to his relief, if necessary." To be clear, McClellan had "heard no firing in that direction," believing if Miles "resists at all, I think I can not only relieve him, but place the rebels who attack him in great danger of being cut off. Everything moves at daylight tomorrow. Your message to him this moment received. Will forward by first opportunity."[84]

Fifteen minutes later, a flurry of orders dictating the army's September 13 advance began issuing from McClellan's headquarters. One of these directed Burnside to mass his troops at Frederick. Reno's four divisions would spend the

---

82 Evidence for Miles not receiving Halleck's order comes from the testimony of Maj. Charles Russell before the Harpers Ferry Military Commission on Oct. 16, 1862. According to Russell, Col. Miles asked on Sept. 13 "if I could not go with two or three men, and pass the enemy's lines, and try to reach somebody that had ever heard of the United States Army, or any general of the United States Army, or anybody that knew anything about the United States Army, and report the condition of Harper's Ferry. I told Colonel Miles that I was willing to make the trial, and he told me that if I could get to any general of the United States Army, or to any telegraph station, or, if possible, get to General McClellan, whom he supposed was at Frederick—he thought he must be at Frederick." It is doubtful Miles would have issued such vague instructions if he was aware at the time that he reported to Gen. McClellan. See OR 19:1, 720.

83 The last telegram received from Miles at the War Department was timestamped 1:50 p.m. on Sept. 11. President Lincoln then noted in a telegram to McClellan sent at 5:45 p.m. on Sept. 12 that the War Department had received "nothing from Harper's Ferry or Martinsburg to-day." See OR 19:2, 266, 270. Halleck's post-campaign report is decidedly vague on the subject of McClellan commanding the garrison at Harpers Ferry, stating "As this campaign was to be carried on within the department commanded by Major-General Wool, I directed General McClellan to assume control of all troops within his reach, without regard to departmental lines." Halleck naturally neglected to mention that he only made this decision on Sept. 12 after rebuffing repeated warnings from McClellan about the safety of the garrison. See OR 19:1, 4.

84 OR 19:2, 271–272.

night of September 12 camped on the outskirts of the city guarding the roads into town while Hooker's three divisions would bivouac along the National Pike from east of the Monocacy to Mount Airy. At 6:30 p.m., McClellan ordered Darius Couch to advance at daylight across the Monocacy River to the hamlet of Licksville, near Noland's Ferry, where he should wait for further instructions. General Sumner's orders went out at 7:00 p.m. directing him to have Alpheus Williams's Twelfth Corps march "by Ijamsville and Crum's Ford to Frederick, halting one mile this side of town." At 8:30 p.m., McClellan then directed Burnside to have the two corps of his wing ready "to move in any direction that may be required," adding proactively, "Should you hear very heavy firing in the direction of Harper's Ferry you will move toward it at once with your command, and report your departure to these headquarters."[85]

Finally, around 9:00 p.m., McClellan found time to reply to Lincoln's earlier "How does it look now?" telegram with a summary of the situation. Confirming he knew that the president read dispatches directed to his General-in-Chief, McClellan stated, "You will have learned by my telegram to General Halleck that we hold Frederick and the line of the Monocacy. I have taken all possible means to communicate with Harper's Ferry, so that I may send to its relief if necessary. Cavalry are in pursuit of the Westminster party [of Rebels while] . . . The main body of my cavalry and horse artillery are ordered after the enemy's main column, with orders to march as much as possible, that I may overtake it." McClellan then tried to reassure the president that "If Harper's Ferry is still in our possession, I think I can save the garrison, if they fight at all. If the rebels are really marching into Pennsylvania, I shall soon be up with them. My apprehension is that they may make for Williamsport, and get across the river before I can catch them."[86]

The mention of Williamsport referred to a telegram sent by Lincoln stating that Jackson's command had been seen crossing the Potomac there. Adding that he had received no recent information from either Harpers Ferry or Martinsburg, Lincoln suggested the silence from that quarter reinforced "the idea that the enemy is recrossing the Potomac." To this the president added, "Please do not let him get off without being hurt."[87]

Although McClellan shared the president's suspicion that Lee might make for Virginia, he also continued to entertain the possibility that either a portion of the

85 *OR* 51:1, Sec. 2, 821-823.

86 *OR* 19:2, 272.

87 Ibid., 270.

Confederate army, or the entire Rebel force itself, might advance into Pennsylvania. Should that occur, McClellan informed Gov. Curtin, he expected the 50,000 militia troops assembling in Harrisburg, and soon to be under the command of Brig. Gen. John F. Reynolds, "to hold the enemy in check until I can overtake him."[88] Achieving this would be simpler said than done, however, as closing with Lee's force involved traversing the two mountain ranges that separated the armies. Surmounting the less imposing Catoctin Range would need to be accomplished first. At 11:00 p.m., therefore, McClellan directed Burnside to move "cautiously" at daylight toward Catoctin Mountain and take the pass there "if possible" to allow Alfred Pleasonton's cavalry to move through it. "Should you gain this pass, you will hold it for the purpose specified and report for further orders," asserted McClellan. "The commanding general desires to impress upon you that he does not wish you to run too great a risk with your own command in taking the pass referred to." Pressing onward would be the responsibility of General Pleasonton, "who will co-operate with you as far as may be necessary."[89]

To ensure that cooperation, McClellan sent Pleasonton orders at 11:30 p.m. directing him to search north of Frederick the next day in case "any force of the enemy has moved in that direction with a view of getting into our rear," revealing his ongoing concern about the security of the army's flanks. Furthermore, explained Little Mac, "General Burnside has been directed to march at daylight . . . [and] to take possession, if possible, of the pass . . . through the Catoctin range of mountains, so as to enable your cavalry to debouch into the Catoctin Valley beyond. Please communicate and co-operate with him."[90] As for Harpers Ferry, McClellan charged Pleasonton with ascertaining the "state of affairs" there if he could and communicate back to headquarters. So much the better if the cavalry could also confirm that Jackson's command had crossed back into Virginia.

---

88 Ibid., 269. At 8:30 p.m. on Sept. 11, Curtin communicated to McClellan, "we will add all the militia forces possible, and I think in a few days we can muster 50,000 men." See OR 19:2, 268. The belief that poorly trained militia could keep the veteran troops of Lee's army in check was a pipe dream, but McClellan did have confidence that if anyone could put backbone into militiamen it was John Reynolds, whom Halleck ordered to Harrisburg on Sept. 12. See OR 19:2, 273, 277. Curtin, in the meantime, communicated to McClellan on Sept. 13, "we are assembling militia rapidly at Chambersburg," illustrating the cooperation going on to slow a possible northward advance by Lee. Curtin then reported the occupation of Hagerstown, Maryland, by militia on September 15. See OR 19:2, 287, 306.

89 OR 51:1, Sec. 2, 823–824.

90 Ibid., 824–825.

The orders to Burnside and Pleasonton contained no ambiguity. Instructing Burnside to seize and hold Hagan's Gap (known as Braddock Heights today) over the Catoctins, but not to proceed from there without receiving further orders, McClellan directed Pleasonton to push into Middletown Valley ahead of Burnside once the way was clear in order to confirm the Rebel army had moved in that direction. This part of McClellan's orders can be attributed to prudence because while all of the intelligence reaching him placed Lee's army near Hagerstown and Williamsport, he wanted to be sure that significant numbers of Rebel troops, said on September 10 to have taken the road to Harpers Ferry, were not waiting to attack him from just behind the Catoctin range.

With Burnside's and Pleasonton's orders sorted for the next day, instructions began going out to the other parts of the army. At 11:45 p.m., the general ordered Edwin Sumner to march his Second Corps for Frederick on the following morning.[91] Another order went out for the remaining two divisions of the Fifth Corps—still near Washington—to march for Frederick as well.[92] Being thirty to forty miles away, McClellan did not expect these two divisions to be in the area until the day after next at the earliest. The general then sent a message to Gen. Wool in Baltimore requesting him to use a portion of his 20,000 troops protecting the city to guard the Baltimore and Ohio Railroad.[93]

When Burnside replied to McClellan at 1:00 a.m., he described the advance into and capture of Frederick, followed by a note on the "programme" to carry out the next day's orders that he had agreed upon with Pleasonton earlier in the evening. Pleasonton, explained Burnside, would "detail in his dispatch" their agreement.[94] Word then arrived from Pleasonton a half an hour later elaborating on the accord. "I have arranged with Gen. Burnside the following program," wrote the cavalry chief. "I shall push forward at day-break with the 8th Illinois, 1st Mass and 3rd Indiana and a battery toward Hagerstown. The 1st New York, 8th Pennsylvania, and 12th Pennsylvania with a section of artillery will proceed to Adamsville and scout the road to Gettysburg—sending out scouts toward Liberty

91 *OR* 51:1, Sec. 2, 826.

92 Ibid., 822.

93 *OR* 19:2, 276.

94 Ambrose Burnside to George McClellan, 1:00 a.m., Sept. 13, 1862, McClellan Papers, LOC, Microfilm Box A79, Reel 31.

and Westminster. The Lancers will [proceed] to Jefferson and follow up the road to Harpers Ferry communicating with [Captain] Sanders."[95]

Pleasonton's horsemen could reach and assault Hagan's Gap more quickly than Burnside's infantry, so if the cavalry met no resistance, it could ride into Middletown Valley to search for the enemy. Pleasonton and Burnside's plan did not alter McClellan's previous orders, other than to allow the cavalry to lead the advance. Burnside would still be obligated to hold the heights if they were taken and wait for further instructions, an adjustment that fell entirely within the scope of McClellan's 11:30 p.m. instructions.

Having issued orders into the early morning hours of September 13, McClellan retired for what remained of the night. As this analysis of the events leading up to September 11 and 12 shows, the general displayed no signs of indecision, confusion, or timidity in the days before his army's occupation of Frederick City. Not only did he secure Baltimore and Washington from the suspected danger of a Rebel attack, he also drew his army close enough to Lee's to threaten the Confederate supply line through the Shenandoah Valley if Lee moved farther north. All of the intelligence that had reached McClellan as of September 12 indicated that the Army of Northern Virginia probably remained in Washington County, Maryland, although prudence dictated that the Federal commander confirm no significant force of Rebel troops lurked in the Middletown Valley between the Catoctin Range and South Mountain. No information from Gov. Curtin, the War Department, or any other source had yet placed the Rebel army in southern Pennsylvania, so for the time being Little Mac could be confident that the Keystone State remained free of Confederate troops. If Lee did move north, McClellan hoped that Gen. Reynolds and his militia could hold him in check long enough for the Army of the Potomac to come up and attack the Army of Northern Virginia from behind. Confronting veteran troops with militia would not be ideal, but it might slow Lee's advance, and it was all that McClellan had to rely on at the time.

The records show without ambiguity that as of early on September 13 George McClellan did not know the enemy's tactical dispositions in detail, or where Lee intended to march his force. They also show that McClellan recognized the danger in which Henry Halleck had left Harpers Ferry, a situation he only received the authority to address a few hours earlier on September 12. Yet even at that late date

---

95 Alfred Pleasonton to George McClellan, 1:30 a.m., Sept. 13, 1862, McClellan Papers, LOC, Microfilm Box A79, Reel 31.

Little Mac did not know for certain Lee had the garrison in his sights. To wit, a message sent from army headquarters to Alfred Pleasonton at 8:45 p.m. on September 12 stated, "Captain Sanders [of the 6th U.S. Cavalry] seemed to be under the impression that Jackson is marching on Harper's Ferry. It is important to ascertain if this is so. The commanding general desires you to send out scouts to-night to endeavor to get information regarding this."[96] Confirmation of Jackson's unfolding siege, and many other things then hidden behind the mountainous terrain of western Maryland, would become crystal clear to McClellan on the next day, after the discovery of Special Orders No. 191.

96 *OR* 51:1, Sec. 2, 824.

Chapter 3

Early Morning to Noon on
September 13, 1862:
George McClellan, the Army of the Potomac's
Movements, and the Discovery of Lee's Orders

Getting an early start at his headquarters near Urbana on September 13, George McClellan fired off two messages to subordinates between sunrise and 7:30 a.m. The first of these went to Brig. Gen. George Sykes, commander of the 3,820 man strong Second Division in Fitz John Porter's Fifth Corps, instructing him to march from the vicinity of Hyattstown to the road bridge over the Monocacy River on the Georgetown Pike. The second order directed the 1st Rhode Island Cavalry, then near Rockville, to ride west and "watch all the fords from Seneca to the mouth of the Monocacy." This latter missive indicated the ongoing concern McClellan felt about the safety of his army's left flank, as well as sensitivity to Gen. Halleck's fears that only a part of Lee's army had crossed into Maryland. As Little Mac wrote concerning this in his second post-campaign report, "a portion of [the Rebel] army had crossed into Maryland; but whether it was their intention to cross their whole force with a view to turn Washington by a flank movement down the north bank of the Potomac . . . we had no means of determining."[1]

With these arrangements complete, McClellan mounted his dark bay horse, Dan Webster, and rode out of the encampment before 9:00 a.m. with his staff and

---

1 OR 19:2, 195; OR 51:1, Sec. 2, 826 and 830; OR 19:1, 39. Also see Frederic Denison, *Sabres and Spurs, The First Regiment Rhode Island Cavalry, In the Civil War, 1861–1865* (Central Falls, RI, 1876), 157.

personal guard in tow.[2] Traveling the Georgetown Pike (roughly today's Maryland State Route 355) northwest for five miles before reaching the Monocacy, Little Mac descended the ridge east of the river and crossed the road bridge near the grounds of John T. Best's rented farm four miles southeast of Frederick.

There he encountered the troops of Maj. Gen. Edwin Vose Sumner's Second Corps massed in line on the road leading into the city. Sumner had marched his men in advance of the general that morning, crossing the Monocacy, recalled Thomas Aldrich of the 1st Rhode Island Artillery, at "about ten o'clock . . . where we halted for over an hour."[3]

Lieutenant Edgar M. Newcomb of the 19th Massachusetts Volunteers observed at the time that "The railroad bridge had been burned by the rebels, though strangely enough the highway bridge across the same stream (the Monocacy) remained intact." Earl Fenner, also of the 1st Rhode Island Artillery, remembered marching "through Monocacy Mills, a thriving little village, situated on the Monocacy River . . . [before making] a halt of two hours. At noon we resumed our onward march." Veterans of the Army of the Potomac's original incarnation, these troops greeted McClellan "with the most enthusiastic cheers" while parting ranks to let him pass.[4]

---

2   Robert S. Robertson, 93rd New York Infantry, Sept. 13, 1862, entry in "Diary of the War," *Old Fort News*, Vol. XXVIII, No. 1 (Jan.-Mar. 1963), 53. Also see Eby, Jr., ed., *A Virginia Yankee*, 105 where Col. Strother wrote that the general and his entourage "started early" that morning, reaching Frederick by 10:00 a.m. A member of McClellan's security. escort noted incorrectly that the general "left Urbana for Frederick at about 7 o'clk A.M." See Joseph S. C. Taber, *The Civil War Diary of Private Jos C. Taber, dating from July 15, 1861 to August 16, 1863*. Transcribed by Frank and Denise Marrone (Frederick, MD, No Date), 9.

3   Thomas M. Aldrich, *The History of Battery A, First Regiment Rhode Island Light Artillery, In the War to Preserve the Union, 1861–1865* (Providence, RI, 1904), 120. The "Diary of Jonathan Stowe, Sept. 13, 1862," in *Civil War Times Illustrated* Collection, Item No. 76.162, U.S. Army Heritage and Education Center, Carlisle, PA, also recorded: "Arrive at RR Junction at 10 A.M. . . . Gen. Mack and staff pass us on road near city." Cited hereafter as CWTI, USAHEC.

4   Albert B. Weymouth, ed., *A Memorial Sketch of Lieut. Edgar M. Newcomb of the Nineteenth Mass. Vols.* (Malden, MA, 1883), Letter of Sept. 18, 1862, 89. Earl Fenner, *The History of Battery B, First Regiment Rhode Island Light Artillery, In the War to Preserve the Union, 1861-1865* (Providence, RI, 1894), 132. If Fenner resumed his march at noon after a two hour rest, then the original halt time would have been 10 a.m. Andrew E. Ford, *The Story of the Fifteenth Regiment Massachusetts Volunteer Infantry in the Civil War, 1861-1864* (Clinton, MA, 1898), 189. A newspaper reporter who witnessed McClellan's ride by Sumner's men published the following account on Sept. 15: "On our way hither this morning from Urbanna, after crossing the Monocacy, Gen. McClellan and staff passed through Gen. Sumner's Corps, who opened their ranks for that purpose." See the *Washington Evening Star*, Sept. 15, 1862.

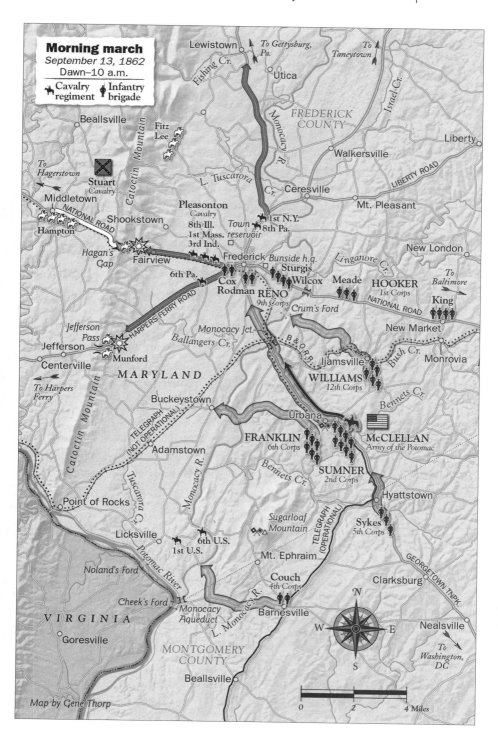

Morning march
September 13, 1862
Dawn–10 a.m.

Cavalry regiment   Infantry brigade

Lewistown

To Gettysburg, Pa.

To Taneytown

Fishing Cr.

Utica

FREDERICK COUNTY

Beallsville

Fitz Lee

Monocacy R.

Walkersville

Liberty

To Hagerstown

Stuart Cavalry

L. Tuscarora

Ceresville

LIBERTY ROAD

Mt. Pleasant

Middletown

NATIONAL ROAD

Shookstown

Pleasonton Cavalry

8th Ill.
1st Mass.
3rd Ind.

Town reservoir

1st N.Y.
8th Pa.

New London

Hampton

Hagan's Gap

Fairview

Frederick

Burnside h.q.

Sturgis

Linganore Cr.

To Baltimore

6th Pa.

Cox
Rodman

RENO
9th Corps

Wilcox

Meade

HOOKER
1st Corps

NATIONAL ROAD

King

HARPERS FERRY ROAD

Crum's Ford

Jefferson Pass

Monocacy Jct.

Ballangers Cr.

B. & O. R.R.

New Market

Jefferson

Munford

MARYLAND

Ijamsville

Bush Cr.

Monrovia

Centerville

WILLIAMS
12th Corps

To Harpers Ferry

Catoctin Mountain

Buckeystown

Bennets Cr.

TELEGRAPH (NOT OPERATIONAL)

Urbana

FRANKLIN
6th Corps

McCLELLAN
Army of the Potomac

Adamstown

Monocacy R.

Bennets Cr.

SUMNER
2nd Corps

Tuscarora Cr.

Point of Rocks

Sugarloaf Mountain

Hyattstown

TELEGRAPH (OPERATIONAL)

Sykes
5th Corps

Licksville

6th U.S.
1st U.S.

Mt. Ephraim

GEORGETOWN TNPK.

Potomac River

Noland's Ford

Couch
4th Corps

Clarksburg

Cheek's Ford

Monocacy Aqueduct

Barnesville

N

VIRGINIA

L. Monocacy R.

W   E

Nealsville

Goresville

MONTGOMERY COUNTY

S

To Washington, DC

Beallsville

Map by Gene Thorp

0   2   4 Miles

Witnesses also recalled forming up for an informal review, which surely slowed McClellan's pace as he traversed the final three miles to the city. When at last he entered Frederick on South Market Street (also called Main Street at the time) the hour had progressed to around 11:00 a.m. A salient detail worth noting at this point is that according to the previously mentioned Lt. Newcomb, the telegraph line from Monocacy Junction to Frederick was "down the whole way along," meaning electronic messages to and from the city would need to travel by mounted courier eight miles back to Urbana, or be sent by signal station through the post atop Sugarloaf Mountain, until the wires could be restrung.[5]

From the moment he departed his headquarters until his arrival in Frederick City, Gen. McClellan must have heard the fighting going on atop Catoctin Mountain. The engagement at Hagan's Gap (Braddock Heights) began soon after sunrise as the mounted regiments under Alfred Pleasonton clashed with Maj. Gen. J. E. B. Stuart's rear-guard defending the route into Middletown Valley. Per McClellan's September 12 orders that Pleasonton "take possession ... of the pass ... through the Catoctin range of mountains, so as to enable your cavalry to debouch into the Catoctin Valley beyond," the army's cavalry chief had directed the 8th Illinois, 3rd Indiana, and 1st Massachusetts, along with assorted guns, up the National Road until they met resistance.

At roughly the same time, Pleasonton sent two more cavalry regiments "in the direction of Gettysburg" with a section of artillery to look for Confederate cavalry reported to be there, as well as Col. Richard Rush's 6th Pennsylvania Cavalry to support William Franklin's Sixth Corps at Jefferson. The clash at Hagan's Gap erupted soon after daybreak with an exchange of small-arms fire that continued until between 8:00 and 9:00 a.m. when both sides brought up artillery and began blasting away. The telegraph operator at Poolesville, Maryland, wired the War

---

5 Eby, Jr., ed., *A Virginia Yankee*, 105. Strother recorded in his diary that McClellan, "entered Frederick City at about ten o'clock." The *Washington Evening Star* reporter referenced above noted, "Gen. McClellan and his staff entered, at 11 o'clock," and Lewis Steiner, a Sanitary Officer and Frederick resident with the U.S. Sanitary Commission estimated McClellan's arrival time at "about 9 o'clock." See Lewis H. Steiner, *Report of Lewis H. Steiner, Inspector of the Sanitary Commission Containing a Diary Kept During the Rebel Occupation of Frederick, MD, and an Account of the Operations of the U.S. Sanitary Commission During the Campaign in Maryland, September, 1862* (New York, NY, 1862), 24. McClellan could not have entered Frederick at 9:00 a.m. because Aldrich, Rhodes, and Stowe's accounts show McClellan did not reach the Monocacy, three miles from Frederick, before 10:00 a.m. No mention of McClellan's arrival is made either by men of Isaac Rodman's division from Reno's Ninth Corps, who filled South Market Street at 9 a.m. Weymouth, ed., *A Memorial Sketch*, 89. It is not clear what time a signal station was established that morning in Frederick.

Department at 11:05 a.m. that he had "heard cannonading for last 2 1/2 hours in direction of Frederick, at least that way and to the left of it. Operator at Rockville [also] says he hears firing." The telegraph station established by Ambrose Burnside at Damascus, Maryland, roughly thirty miles to the east, reported the same, with Operator Doyle wiring Washington at 9:20 a.m., "For 20 minutes past we have heard rifled shelling in direction of Frederick. We still hear it. It is about one shot every five seconds." Doyle then further cemented the time when he filed another message a few hours later. Informing the War Department that "A courier … left Burnside's headquarters at Frederick at 8 o'clock this morning," Doyle noted, "as the courier was leaving Frederick, our artillery was shelling the woods briskly." The signal station on Sugarloaf Mountain, some twelve miles away, also noted the artillery fire and "at once reported [it] to General McClellan," who was still "near Urbana" at that time, according to Maj. Albert Myer, the army's Chief Signal Officer.[6]

By the time McClellan arrived in Frederick, the Hagan's Gap fight had been underway for almost four hours with rising volume, but no progress made by Pleasonton's troopers. Frustrated by the stubborn Confederate resistance, Pleasonton fell back onto the "programme" he and Maj. Gen. Burnside had agreed upon the night before and called for infantry support shortly before 9:00 a.m. Burnside quickly sent Brig. Gen. Isaac Rodman's two infantry brigades to Pleasonton from their encampment on the grounds of the old Hessian Barracks just south of the city, filling downtown Frederick with a column of marching troops.[7] The sight of Rodman's men brought out the city's Unionist population, which packed the sidewalks to cheer. McClellan himself then arrived in town as the final ranks disappeared down West Patrick Street, catching the attention of the townspeople as he rode to the intersection of Market and Patrick Streets. The

6 OR 19:1, 209. See "Operator Doyle from Damascus, MD, and Col. Anson Stager to Lincoln," Library of Congress, Manuscript Division, Abraham Lincoln Papers, Series 1. General Correspondence 1833-1916, Sept. 13, 1862, No. 18393. Cited hereafter as Lincoln Papers. Also see OR 19:2, 285 and OR 19:1, 119-120.

7 According to Burnside, "[Pleasonton] called upon me for infantry support . . . [and] General Rodman's division was sent." OR 19:1, 416. For information on the deployment of Rodman's division see George H. Allen, Forty-Six Months with the Fourth R.I. Volunteers in the War of 1861 to 1865 (Providence, RI, 1887), 140: "At 9 o'clock the next morning, the line started on again, marching through the city of Frederick." Also see Graham, The Ninth Regiment, 263: "Almost as soon as coffee had been prepared and disposed of the Ninth was ordered out to the support of "Rush's Lancers" who, striving to drive back the rebel rear guard, found a detachment of them so strongly posted that infantry was required to dislodge them."

Gen'l Geo B McClellan passing through Fredrick City Myd at the head of the Army. of the Potomac Sept 12th 1862.

Pursuit of Gen'l Lee.

spectators already gathered there quickly recognized Little Mac and the throng exploded into a jubilant mob.

According to a reporter from *Harper's Weekly* traveling with McClellan, "The General rode through the town on a trot, and the street was filled six or eight deep with his staff and guard riding on behind him." With his head uncovered in honor of the crowd's greeting, McClellan "received gracefully the salutations of the people. Old ladies and men wept for joy, and scores of beautiful ladies waved flags from the balconies of houses upon the street, and their joyousness seemed to overcome every other emotion."[8]

A resident of Frederick named Anne Schaeffer witnessed these events, describing in her diary how "Leaping down the steps we ran to the square and were among the first ladies to grasp [McClellan's] hand—Shouts and deafening cheers! People seemed beside themselves and forced him to stop—to receive their greetings—He sat as one confounded—the enthusiasm so unexpected—while ladies hung upon his horse's neck—patting his head—stuck a flag in the gearing." The tumultuous welcome McClellan received in Frederick (one staffer remembered the general and his horse being "absolutely covered with wreaths and bouquets") delayed him for an undetermined period of time before "at length" he broke away from the crowd and rode east on Patrick Street toward Burnside's headquarters, then located along the Baltimore Pike on the eastern outskirts of the city. At this point, recalled Schaeffer, the crowd began to disperse, suggesting that for the moment, now well after 11:00 a.m., no troops from the Army of the Potomac occupied the streets of town.[9]

Sources clarifying how long McClellan visited with Burnside are yet to be found, but the available evidence suggests that he lingered long enough to discuss Pleasonton's fight at Hagan's Gap and how the two corps under Burnside's army wing should advance now that Sumner's Second Corps and Williams's Twelfth Corps had moved within close supporting distance. We can infer this because soon after McClellan's visit Jacob Cox received orders to advance his two brigade Kanawha division from the west side of Frederick, where it had camped the night

8 *Harper's Weekly*, Oct. 4, 1862.

9 Entry for Sept. 13, 1862, in *Records of the Past: Ann R. L. Schaeffer Civil War Diary, September 4–23, 1862*. Transcribed by Kira Vaughan (Frederick, MD, No Date). "At length he (General McClellan) galloped away and when the streets cleared I hurried to the P-Office which had just opened." Eby, Jr., ed., *A Virginia Yankee*, 105.

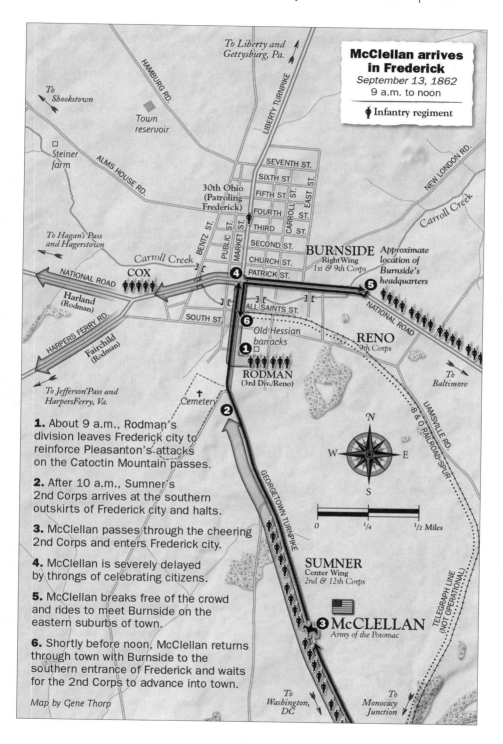

McClellan arrives in Frederick
September 13, 1862
9 a.m. to noon

♦ Infantry regiment

To Liberty and Gettysburg, Pa.

HAMBURG RD.

To Shookstown

Town reservoir

LIBERTY TURNPIKE

NEW LONDON RD.

Steiner farm

ALMS HOUSE RD.

SEVENTH ST.

SIXTH ST.

30th Ohio (Patroling Frederick)

FIFTH ST.

EAST ST.

CARROLL ST.

Carroll Creek

FOURTH ST.

THIRD ST.

To Hagan's Pass and Hagerstown

BENTZ ST.

PUBLIC ST.

MARKET ST.

SECOND ST.

CHURCH ST.

BURNSIDE
Right Wing
1st & 9th Corps

Approximate location of Burnside's headquarters

Carroll Creek

COX

PATRICK ST.

4

NATIONAL ROAD

5

Harland (Rodman)

ALL SAINTS ST.

SOUTH ST.

6

NATIONAL ROAD

RENO
9th Corps

HARPERS FERRY RD.

Fairchild (Rodman)

Old Hessian barracks

1

To Baltimore

To Jefferson'Pass and HarpersFerry, Va.

Cemetery

2

RODMAN
(3rd Div./Reno)

N

W   E

S

B & O RAILROAD SPUR

LIAMSVILLE RD.

1. About 9 a.m., Rodman's division leaves Frederick city to reinforce Pleasanton's attacks on the Catoctin Mountain passes.

2. After 10 a.m., Sumner's 2nd Corps arrives at the southern outskirts of Frederick city and halts.

3. McClellan passes through the cheering 2nd Corps and enters Frederick city.

4. McClellan is severely delayed by throngs of celebrating citizens.

5. McClellan breaks free of the crowd and rides to meet Burnside on the eastern suburbs of town.

6. Shortly before noon, McClellan returns through town with Burnside to the southern entrance of Frederick and waits for the 2nd Corps to advance into town.

Map by Gene Thorp

GEORGETOWN TURNPIKE

0   1/4   1/2 Miles

SUMNER
Center Wing
2nd & 12th Corps

3 McCLELLAN
Army of the Potomac

TELEGRAPH LINE (NOT OPERATIONAL)

To Washington, DC

To Monocacy Junction

of September 12, to support Pleasonton's attack.[10] The orders to Cox arrived at his headquarters "about noon," suggesting that McClellan and Burnside must have conferred before 11:30 a.m. at the absolute latest in order for the directive to be written out and carried by courier through town.

Burnside also issued orders around this time (or possibly before he met with McClellan) for Joseph Hooker to get his First Corps on the road from locations east of the Monocacy as far out as Ridgeville, some fourteen miles away. That the First Corps and Ninth Corps had become so far detached from one another attests to the speed with which Reno's men had descended on Frederick one day earlier. Now the First Corps needed to catch up. As the author of the regimental history of the 13th Massachusetts Infantry, a part of the Second Division in Hooker's corps, put it, "We started at 1 p.m. and marched twelve more miles toward Frederick." Private John Vautier of the 88th Pennsylvania (Second Division, First Corps) recorded similarly in his diary that his regiment "Resumed the line of march at noon."[11]

Comparable orders reached the Second Corps before noon, too, suggesting that McClellan also sent Sumner's instructions while he was at Burnside's headquarters. According to Earl Fenner of the 1st Rhode Island Light Artillery, "At noon we resumed our onward march [from Monocacy Junction] . . . and entered Frederick." This timeframe is supported by Charles Willoughby of the 34th New York Infantry, a part of the Second Division in Sumner's corps, who noted in his diary, "We passed through Frederick City about 12 o'clock." More importantly, in the context of McClellan's handling of the Lost Orders, Sgt. Stowe of the 15th Massachusetts recorded in his diary that the regiment, "Pass[ed] in review of Gens. Mack and Burnside at noon."[12]

General McClellan, accompanied by Burnside, had traveled back into the city just before noon to review the passage of Sumner's troops, explaining Stowe's

---

10 Cox recalled after the war that he received his instructions at "About noon," with McClellan's order later being "put into writing by Chief of Staff Marcy at 3:35 p.m." See Cox, *Military Reminiscences*, I:274. For a copy of the order see OR 51:1, Sec. 2, 827.

11 Charles E. Davis, Jr., *Three Years in the Army. The Story of the Thirteenth Massachusetts Volunteers from July 16, 1861, to August 1, 1864* (Boston, MA, 1894), 133 and "Civil War Daily Diary of John D. Vautier," Philadelphia, Pa, transcribed by Phyllis Weaver Bickley, Civil War Library in Carlisle, PA. Available online at: https://www.wikitree.com/wiki/Vautier-28# Transcript_of_John.27s_Civil_War_Diary.

12 Fenner, *The History of Battery B*, 120. Charles Willoughby quoted in *Fifth Annual Report of the New York Chief of the Bureau of Military Statistics* (Albany, NY, 1868), 531. Stowe Diary, Sept. 13, 1862.

sighting of the commander there at midday. The Unionist Frederick diarist, Anne Schaeffer, spotted McClellan's return to the downtown area as well, writing, "Again McClellan and Burnside passed through town and now indeed came an army—[which] began passing at noon—[and] *continued marching as rapidly as possible until night* [emphasis added]."[13] From all of these activities it is thus possible to conclude that by noon on September 13 George McClellan had begun concentrating the elements of four army corps around Frederick. He had also set William Franklin's Sixth Corps early in the morning on the path to Buckeystown south of the city to establish a bridgehead on the Monocacy and support the capture of Jefferson Pass over Catoctin Mountain by the 6th Pennsylvania Cavalry and the Ninth Corps infantry brigade of Col. Harrison Fairchild.[14]

The army's Twelfth Corps remained the one large formation approaching Frederick to be accounted for at noon. Then temporarily under the command of Brig. Gen. Alpheus S. Williams, the Twelfth Corps had advanced sluggishly on September 12 along a rain-battered secondary road to the rural crossroads of Ijamsville, located some seven miles southeast of Frederick. The general roused his command at 3:30 a.m. on September 13, getting them back onto the same shabby thoroughfare at around 7:00 a.m. Sticky mud and the narrowness of the road made the passage difficult for wagons and artillery so Williams's infantry took to the fields to keep moving.[15] Although fences and other obstacles slowed their advance, Williams's command made steady progress and approached the Monocacy several hours later. The men waded across a shallow portion of the river at Crum's Ford and climbed the western bank to the fields that covered the southeastern approach to Frederick. Finally, around noon, the 27th Indiana Volunteers, under the command of Col. Silas Colgrove, whose skirmishers led the Twelfth Corps' advance, received orders to fall out and rest within sight of the city.

13 Schaeffer, *Records of the Past*, Sept. 13, 1862.

14 Franklin's Sixth Corps arrived at Buckeystown in the morning. In the afternoon, Irwin's brigade advanced from Buckeystown to aid the 6th Pennsylvania cavalry and Fairchild's infantry brigade in capturing Jefferson. In the evening, Hancock's brigade with part of Brooke's brigade, both of Smith's division, advanced to their support. See David W. Judd, *The Story of the Thirty-Third N. Y. S. Vols. or Two Years Campaigning in Virginia and Maryland* (Rochester, NY, 1864), 180; Robert S. Westbrook, *History of the 49th Pennsylvania Volunteers* (Altoona, Pa.: 1898) 124; and William F. Smith to William B. Franklin, 4:00 p.m., Sept. 13, 1862, McClellan Papers, LOC Microfilm, Box A79, Reel 31.

15 Gould, *History*, 224. "Reveille at 3:30; marched at 7; passed over the railroad at Ijamsville, and then took the fields on the right of the road."

General Williams's men reaching the vicinity of Frederick around noon has become a matter of some unnecessary, and, frankly, misleading, debate thanks to Stephen Sears's oft-repeated claim that Federal troops found the Lost Orders before midday. The fact is that all of the accounts written before 1892, most importantly those written on September 13 itself, note that the Twelfth Corps halted around noon. A letter sent by Gen. Williams himself bearing the location stamp "Camp near Frederick" stated, for example, "I reached [Frederick] this noon, having forded the Monocacy with my corps." Wilder Dwight of the 2nd Massachusetts recalled likewise in a letter he composed on September 13, stating that "soon after noon [we] reached the vicinity of Frederick." These accounts corroborate the September 13 diary entries of Lt. Col. Newton T. Colby of the 107th New York Infantry, who wrote, "We forded the Monocacy, arrived in the afternoon and encamped about a mile east of the city," and Sgt. C.D.M. Broomhall of the 124th Pennsylvania Infantry, who observed that his regiment "halted about a mile from Frederick City at 1 p.m." These contemporary sources substantiate the time offered by Col. Colgrove himself, who wrote in a short 1886 essay on the discovery of Lee's orders that "the Twelfth Army Corps arrived at Frederick, Maryland, about noon." Last, but not least, the grandfather of Maryland Campaign studies, Col. Ezra Carman, concluded, "accounts generally agree that Williams' Corps arrived near Frederick and halted about noon, [or] very near noon, and this agrees with the recollection and papers of the writer," who himself served in the Twelfth Corps.[16]

Returning to the men of the 27th Indiana, when First Sgt. John M. Bloss and Pvt. Barton W. Mitchell of Company F settled back to relax, Mitchell spotted what he thought was a long envelope lying in a patch of tall grass. Rising to fetch it, he found not an envelope, but a two-page document wrapped around two cigars. Mitchell glanced at the contents of the document before handing it over to Bloss, who read through it and immediately recognized its importance. Taking the document to Col. Colgrove, Bloss handed it over. The colonel read the orders himself and then carried them to his superior, Brig. Gen. George Henry Gordon,

---

16 Milo M. Quaife, ed., *From the Cannon's Mouth: The Civil War Letters of General Alpheus S. Williams* (Lincoln, NE, 1995), 120–121; Eliza Amelia Dwight, *Life and Letters of Wilder Dwight, Lieut.-Col. Second Mass. Inf. Vols.* (Boston, MA, 1868), 291; William E. Hughes, ed., *The Civil War Papers of Lt. Colonel Newton T. Colby, New York Infantry* (Jefferson, NC, 2003), 139; Diary of Sgt. C. D. M. Broomhall, 124th Pennsylvania, Sept. 13, 1862. Transcribed by Carolyn Ivanoff (Janes family papers); Silas Colgrove, "The Finding of Lee's Lost Order," in Johnson and Buel, eds., *Battles and Leaders*, 2:603; and Carman, *The Maryland Campaign*, I:280.

Gen. Alpheus S. Williams to Gen. George B. McClellan
Cover letter announcing that a lost copy of Lee's orders is enclosed

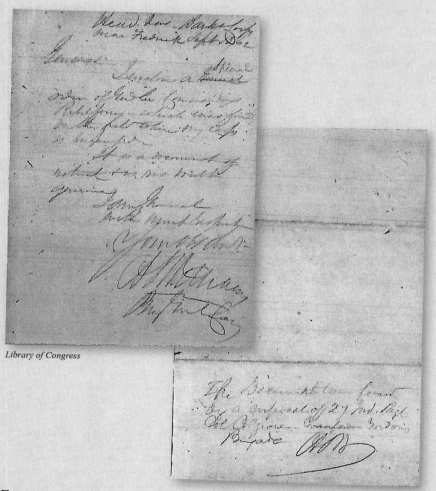

Library of Congress

Front page:
"General, I enclose a General Special Order of Gen. Lee commanding Rebel Army which was found on the field where my corps is encamped. It is a document of interest & is genuine."

Reverse side:
"The Document was found by a corporal of 27 Ind. Regt. Col. Colgrove [Commanding] Gordon's Brigade."

who exclaimed they were "worth a mint of money" after he too had reviewed them.[17]

Gordon directed Colgrove to deliver the orders to Gen. Williams, and upon arriving at Twelfth Corps headquarters, the colonel handed the document to Col. Samuel E. Pittman, Williams's Adjutant General.[18] Pittman played a key role at this point by claiming to recognize the signature of Col. Robert H. Chilton, Gen. Lee's Assistant Adjutant General, from business dealings that he and Chilton had before the war. This testimony satisfied Williams (who also read the document) that the orders were authentic and, after adding a brief accompanying note, he urged Pittman to forward them to McClellan.[19] Pittman attempted to scratch out a quick copy of the orders for posterity, but Williams instructed him to stop writing and send the orders to army headquarters immediately.[20]

Each man in this sequence of events—Mitchell, Bloss, Colgrove, Gordon, Pittman, and Williams—took time to read some or all of Lee's two-page dispatch. Considering the time that reading the orders would take, and the fact that they traveled some distance between four of the six readers before being forwarded to Gen. McClellan, it must have required at least an hour for the orders to travel up the chain of command. Multiple Twelfth Corps sources attest to the fact that the Lost Orders were not discovered until around noon because the leading regiments

17 Most histories of the Lost Orders claim that Mitchell found three cigars. Bloss, "Letter written from the barn hospital at Antietam," in Bloss Family Papers, Sept. 25, 1862, confirmed finding only two and is the source written chronologically closest to the event.

18 Colgrove recalled, "within a very few minutes after halting the order was brought to me by First Sergeant John M. Bloss and Private (actually, Corporal) B. W. Mitchell . . . I immediately took the order to his (i.e., General Williams's) headquarters, and delivered it to Colonel S. E. Pittman, General Williams's adjutant-general." See Colgrove, "The Finding of Lee's Lost Order," in *Battles and Leaders*, 2:603.

19 Williams's note read: "General, I enclose a General Special Order of Gen. Lee commanding Rebel Army which was found on the field where my corps is encamped. It is a document of interest & is no doubt genuine." Writing on the reverse side, Williams added, "The Document was found by a corporal of 27 Ind. Regt. Col. Colgrove [Commanding] Gordon's Brigade." See Alpheus S. Williams to George B. McClellan, Sept. 13, 1862, McClellan Papers, LOC Microfilm, Box A79, Reel 31.

20 "After writing a brief note to Genl. McClellan's Asst. Adgt. Genl. to accompany the order I commenced a hurried copy, as I could easily see that the finding such an important paper was likely to become a fact of history, but before I could get two lines copied Genl. Williams enquired whether the paper had gone forward to Genl. McClellan and would not consent to the delay of even a few moments and I had to go without the much-coveted copy." See Samuel Pittman to Ezra A. Carman, May 28, 1897, Pittman Papers, Lt. Col., Am-Mss-Pittman, Box 1, Folder 17. Chapin Library, Williams College, Massachusetts. Available online at https://archivesspace.williams.edu/repositories/4/archival_objects/18392.

of the corps reached the outskirts of Frederick at that time. Given the approximate time of their discovery and the chain of custody outlined above, the orders could not realistically have been placed in a courier's hands before 1:00 p.m. We must keep in mind as well that the courier then had to ride through the jammed and unfamiliar streets of Frederick in search of McClellan, who was himself probably on the move at that hour after receiving word that Pleasonton's men had finally taken Hagan's Gap. Even without the "12 midnight" copy of the telegram discovered by Maurice D'Aoust, there is simply no way McClellan could have sent a noon telegram about Lee's plans before he had even received them.

The final piece of the puzzle to unravel before putting the noontime McClellan telegram fallacy fully to rest is the postwar testimony of Col. Nathan Kimball, who claimed decades after the war that he took the copy of Special Orders No. 191 to McClellan before 9:30 in the morning. The first mention of Kimball's alleged involvement in finding the Lost Orders appeared in 1892 when John Bloss read a paper before the Kansas Commandery of the Military Order of the Loyal Legion of the United States (MOLLUS) claiming, "I saw General Kimball start with . . . [the Lost Orders] . . . to McClellan's headquarters; he had a good horse, understood the importance of the dispatch, and he has since told me that he carried it directly to General McClellan"[21]

Five years later, in 1897, Kimball stated in a letter to Twelfth Corps veteran Ezra Carman of the Antietam Battlefield Board that he had indeed been involved in the finding of the Lost Orders. Coincidentally, Carman was at the same time in contact with Samuel Pittman, the officer who validated Chilton's signature. Carman recounted to Pittman that Kimball

> says he carried the order 191 of Gen. Lee to McClellan and delivered it to him personally, and that this time was not later than 9:30 a.m. Kimball says he was in conversation with Colgrove on the [Georgetown] turnpike, waiting for McClellan and his escort to pass by when Capt. Bloss came up with the paper, that he, Colgrove and others present read it, and all seeing the importance, he, Kimball, mounted his horse and rode forward to meet with McClellan and give it to him. In your (i.e., Pittman's) letter you say you did not take the order but sent it. Have you any recollection of Kimball's taking the order? I think he must

---

21 *War Talks in Kansas, A Series of Papers Read before the Kansas Commandery of the Military Order of the Loyal Legion of the United States* (Kansas City, MO, 1906), 88. The MOLLUS published Bloss's paper in 1906, but Bloss first read it publicly in Kansas on Jan. 6, 1892. See p. 77 of *War Talks in Kansas*.

have done so, for he says so and Bloss writes me, also that he did, but I want your recollection to make it more binding, as one would say.[22]

Kimball's account, as summarized by Carman, raises many questions about its veracity. How reliable was Kimball's recollection of the details 35 years after the event? How could Kimball have delivered the Lost Orders to McClellan before 9:30 a.m. when neither his own corps, McClellan, nor the soldiers who found it, arrived in the area until after 10:00? How could Colgrove and Bloss's thin skirmish line have been on the Georgetown Turnpike one mile southwest of the Frederick-Ijamsville road when it was supposed to be screening for the Twelfth Corps coming up the road from Crum's Ford? How could Kimball claim he was waiting for McClellan to pass by and yet write that after he read the Lost Order he "rode forward" to meet with the general? More important still, why did Kimball not recount going to Alpheus Williams's headquarters to receive the orders when William's cover letter to McClellan proves the Lost Orders passed through the Twelfth Corps commander's hands?

Taken aback by Kimball's claim, Pittman responded to Carman as follows: "From what Genl. Kimball writes you it would appear that the paper never came into either Genl. Williams hands or mine, so that some strange mist must have clouded Genl. Kimball's memory."[23] Carman agreed with Pittman, writing of Kimball in his reply, "He is a very old man, in failing health and liable, as you say to be a little 'misty' in his recollections."[24] As for the pre-10:00 a.m. time mentioned by both Kimball and Bloss, Carman concluded, "Sergeant Bloss states that he found the paper not later than 10 o'clock, he thinks it was really an hour earlier, in this he is evidently mistaken."[25]

22 Ezra A. Carman to Samuel Pittman, May 21, 1897, Ezra Ayers Carman Genealogical Research Papers, Manuscripts and Archives Division, The New York Public Library. Cited hereafter as Carman Papers, NYPL. Our thanks to Tom Clemens for the source.

23 Samuel Pittman to Ezra A. Carman, May 7, 1897, Pittman Papers, Lt. Col., Am-Mss-Pittman, Box 1, Folder 17. Available online at https://archivesspace. williams.edu/repositories/4/archival_objects/18387. Pittman took care in his response not to tarnish Kimball's reputation, explaining in the same correspondence, "I remember General Kimball as a valiant colonel at Shields 'Winchester' when he saved the day. From his subsequent career also one must regard him as a man whose statements would be well founded. Under such impressions then, your letter must have been a surprise equal to that of an ambuscade."

24 Ezra A. Carman to Samuel Pittman, May 21, 1897, Carman Papers, NYPL.

25 Carman, *The Maryland Campaign*, 1:280.

Bloss is the only person other than Kimball himself to mention the colonel in the process of finding the Lost Orders. However, his second account of finding the orders, written thirty years after the event, strongly contradicted the earlier account he provided on September 25, 1862. Stating at that time, "I seen its importance and took it to the Col. (i.e., Colgrove). He immediately took it to General Gordon, he said it was worth a Mint of Money & sent it to General McClellan." Bloss made no mention of Kimball only two weeks after the event, a fact that renders his later account highly suspicious. Enough years had passed by 1892 for Kimball and Bloss to square their accounts, a possibility strengthened by the fact that Kimball had wed the niece of Bloss's wife on September 7, 1865, making the two men family.[26]

Finally, in a Ladies Evening talk on the 'Famous Lost Dispatch' before the MOLLUS Michigan Commandery on March 5, 1903, Samuel Pittman made no mention of Kimball, strongly implying that he continued to reject Kimball's claim even after being made aware of it years earlier by Ezra Carman.[27] Unless new accounts come to light, McClellan's own recollection of receiving Lee's orders must provide the final word. When McClellan wrote to the son of Barton Mitchell in 1879, "there was handed to me by *a member of my staff* [emphasis added] a copy (original) of one of General Lee's orders of march," he unintentionally refuted Kimball's claim that he had delivered the Lost Orders to McClellan personally. Nathan Kimball was, after all, a brigade commander in the Second Corps and not a part of the general's staff.[28]

Summing up, then, an analysis of the available documents demonstrates that George McClellan entered Frederick, Maryland, late in the morning on September 13. After being mobbed in the street by jubilant local Unionists, he rode to Burnside's headquarters and rapidly began coordinating the advance of four army corps on and through Frederick, as well as the advance of elements of William Franklin's Sixth Corps toward the pass over the Catoctin Mountains near Jefferson. McClellan then spent an hour or so—from roughly noon to around 1:00 p.m.—in

26 John McKnight Bloss, "Letter written from the barn hospital at Antietam, Sept. 25, 1862," Bloss Family Papers, Monocacy National Battlefield Park. R. Richard Bloss, *Bloss Genealogy, Edmund and Mary Bloss and Their Descendants in North America* (Beaumont, TX, 1959), 51.

27 Samuel W. Pittman, "Story of the 'Famous Lost Despatch'," Ladies Evening, Michigan Commandery Military Order of the Loyal Legion of the United States, Mar. 5, 1903, Pittman Papers, Box 1, Folder 8. Available online at https://archivesspace.williams.edu/repositories/4/archival_objects/18382 Our thanks to Wayne Hammond and Charles Dew for the source.

28 George McClellan to W. A. Mitchell, Nov. 18, 1879, in *The Century Illustrated Monthly Magazine*, Vol. 33, No. 1 (November 1886), 135.

Frederick viewing the march of Second Corps troops (and part of the Ninth Corps) through town.[29]

All of this took place at the same time that Alpheus Williams's Twelfth Corps marched from Ijamsville to its encampment one mile east of Frederick, where soldiers from the 27th Indiana discovered the errant copy of Special Orders No. 191 around noon. After some time had passed for the orders to make their way up the chain of command, Williams sent them to McClellan around 1:00 p.m. The telegraph line to Frederick remained down through all of this, making electronic communications with Washington impossible unless messages passed by signal before being wired. The available sources make it clear that McClellan did not remain in one location long enough to receive, read, and digest the content of Lee's orders before composing his famous telegram to President Lincoln marked "12 M." They also make clear that there was no means by which a wired message could be sent to Washington around noon. In short, the reading public has been fed a lie about McClellan's alleged "noon" message to Lincoln for more than 100 years. This lie may have originated innocently enough in a misreading of the evidence by Jacob Cox, but writers more intent on condemning George McClellan than they have been on establishing the truth have repeated it *ad nauseum* to the present day.

---

29 A prominent New York newspaper described the scene in print a few days later, writing "General Burnside at once pushed on after the rebels with his whole force, occupying every road . . . to come up with them." *New York Herald*, Sept. 15, 1862. Readers will recall that the Ninth Corps divisions of Cox and Rodman had already moved through Frederick as of noon on Sept. 13.

Chapter 4

Noon to Early Evening on September 13, 1862:
How McClellan Responded to
Reading Lee's Orders

As the mislaid copy of Lee's orders made its way to Gen. McClellan, he stood at the corner of Market and Patrick Streets watching Jesse Reno pass through town with a brigade from his Ninth Corps. While observing the march of Sumner's Second Corps north on Market Street, McClellan had ordered Burnside to get the remainder of Reno's command (Rodman and Cox's divisions had already passed through the city) moving west along Patrick Street.[1]

One soldier with the 21st Massachusetts Volunteers, a regiment with the Second Division of Reno's Ninth Corps, recalled of this march, "Our gallant brigadier (Gen. Ferrero) couldn't let us part [from the town] without at least a salute in honor of our reception; so the brigade was halted in the street, and the regiments faced to the front; but before arms were presented, General Reno, displeased at the block of the marching column, gave him an emphatic order to right face his men, and attend to business."[2]

---

1 According to the history of the 14th Connecticut Volunteers, Third Division, Second Corps, "The men were well received [in Frederick] and as they passed up the main street were greeted with loyal cheers.. . . . The regiment then marched about two miles beyond the town and bivouacked in a field near the reservoir." Charles D. Page, *History of the Fourteenth Regiment, Connecticut Vol. Infantry* (Meriden, CT, 1906), 27. Locals in the nineteenth century often referred to Market Street as "Main Street." The reservoir was located northwest of Frederick near the grounds of the Steiner Farm where McClellan made his headquarters. Cox's division had passed through Frederick the evening of Sept. 12 while a small part of the Second Corps had yet to pass through town.

2 Walcott, *History of the Twenty-First Regiment Massachusetts Volunteers*, 188 also mentions seeing McClellan, "On our passage through town we witnessed General McClellan's enthusiastic reception: as he appeared, the people gave themselves up to the wildest demonstrations of joy."

While all of this was going on a telegraph repair crew arrived at Monocacy Junction, located some four miles south of Frederick, around 1:00 p.m. Having just fixed the line from Washington to that point, they now planned to run a wire across the Monocacy River to reconnect Harpers Ferry and Frederick. Upon his arrival, telegraph operator F. T. Bickford reported to Washington that the rail bridge over the river was a "total wreck" and that the telegraph line running alongside the railroad tracks was "down as far as [one] can see." Bickford added that "Gen. McClellan is reported to have passed beyond Frederick about a half hour ago. Heavy firing apparently at Harper's Ferry. As soon as can run wire will proceed to Frederick."[3]

The timestamp on the War Department's copy of Bickford's telegram reads 12:55 p.m., so the message arrived very soon after it was sent, indicating no delay in the line. Bickford's message makes two things clear. First, there was still no functioning telegraph line from Frederick to Washington as of 1:00 p.m. of September 13, and, second, Bickford's work crew did not possess sufficient wire at that moment to run it the final four miles from Monocacy Junction.[4] Combine the lack of a working telegraph line to Frederick with the lengthy process of communicating by signal flag discussed earlier and the argument that Gen. McClellan could have sent Lincoln a dispatch marked "12 M" becomes completely untenable.

Returning to Bickford, his mention of McClellan passing beyond Frederick confirms rumors circulating at the time that the commanding general had departed the city limits. The receipt of a message from Alfred Pleasonton stating that his men had finally driven off the Rebel rear-guard atop Catoctin Mountain is likely what prompted McClellan to leave his spot in the city center watching the passing troops. Historians have long relied on the campaign report of J. E. B. Stuart, written more than a year after events in Maryland had passed, for the time when the

---

3 Operator Bickford to Col. Stager, 12:55 p.m., Sept. 13, 1862. National Archives and Records Administration, Record Group 107, Microcopy 473, Roll 18, No. 36. Cited hereafter as NA. Also see OR 19:2, 284. See Appendix A.

4 In fact, the telegraph line to Frederick would not be repaired until Sept. 14. As Operator Caldwell in Frederick wrote to Seth Williams at McClellan's headquarters in Middletown Valley, "I am told that the line towards Hagerstown is in good condition for eight miles from this place. We will push on to the end of the wire and try and open an office near Hd Qrs tonight. The line is working from here to Washington and operators will be left here. A building party will be here shortly to put the wire up and follow Hd Qrs. Please send orderlies to meet us tonight." A. H. Caldwell to Seth Williams, Sept. 14, 1862, McClellan Papers, LOC Microfilm, Box A79, Reel 31, Number 16159.

Confederate horsemen retreated. Writing that at "About 2 p.m. we were obliged to abandon the crest, and withdrew to a position near Middletown," Stuart mistakenly recalled his command being pushed back an hour later than it actually was. Pleasonton's message itself, timestamped 1:00 p.m., read "Have carried the rebel [position] with my cavalry and artillery. Infantry too late." A correspondent in Frederick from the *Washington Evening Star* also reported the 1:00 p.m. time of Pleasonton's victory in a story he filed for publication on September 15. Explaining that "The artillery duel yesterday [sic] . . . continued till one o'clock, between Pleasonton's force and the rear guard of the rebels," the reporter confirmed the earlier time mentioned in Pleasonton's dispatch and not the later hour claimed by Stuart.[5]

Assuming it took Pleasonton's courier thirty minutes or so to make his way four miles down the crowded National Road from Hagan's Gap to the center of town, it is safe to conclude that the message probably reached McClellan no earlier than 1:30 p.m.[6] With Federal cavalry now flowing into Middletown Valley per Little Mac's September 12 orders, the evolving situation compelled the general to focus on the next phase of his army's advance. He therefore rode west out of town at roughly the same time that Gen. Williams's courier entered Frederick from the east to deliver the recently discovered copy of Lee's orders.

We know for certain that McClellan moved west of Frederick between 1:30 and 2:00 p.m. because Capt. Andrew H. Boyd of the 108th New York Infantry noted marching past McClellan in the center of town at 1:30.[7] Jacob Cox then recalled that "McClellan himself met me as my column moved out of town" around 2:00. Cox's Kanawha division got a very slow start that day despite receiving orders from Burnside at around noon to support Pleasonton. Provost duties in town for part of Cox's command appear to have contributed to the delay, according to

---

5 *OR* 19:1, 817. Wade Hampton's report from Oct. 1862 also stated "the fight was kept up until 2 p.m.," which likely provided the source for Stuart's estimate. See *OR* 19:1, 823. Alfred Pleasonton to George McClellan, 1:00 p.m., Sept. 13, 1862, McClellan Papers, LOC Microfilm, Box A79, Reel 31, Number 16142. *Washington Evening Star*, Sept. 15, 1862.

6 It is possible, but not provable, that Pleasonton transmitted his message to McClellan in less than thirty minutes because Lt. N. H. Camp and Lt. G. J. Clarke of the Signal Corps were with Pleasonton at Hagan's Gap and in communication with Lt. W. H. Hill, who was with Gen. Burnside in Frederick. See *OR* 19:1, 120.

7 "We marched through Frederick City at 1:30 p.m. . . . [and] came through with all the pride of a conquering army; General McClellan and Sumner we passed in the street; each company cheered as they passed." See George H. A. Washburn, *Complete Military History and Record of the 108th Regiment N. Y. Vols., From 1862 to 1894* (Rochester, NY, 1894), 107.

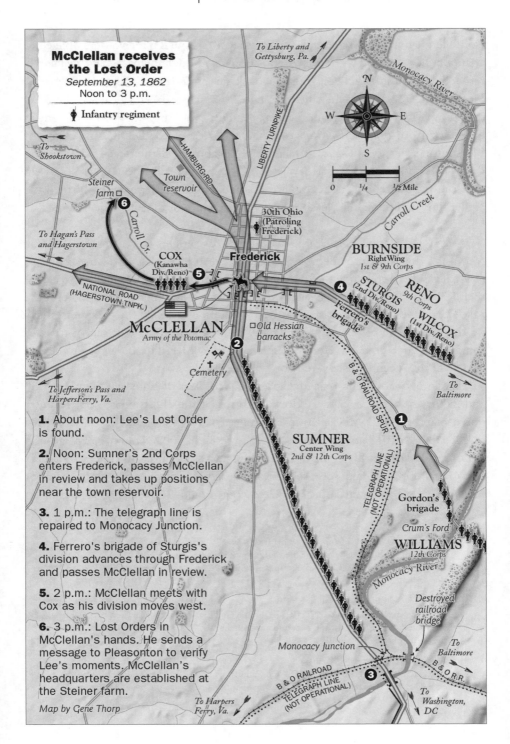

McClellan receives the Lost Order
September 13, 1862
Noon to 3 p.m.

Infantry regiment

To Liberty and Gettysburg, Pa.

Monocacy River

To Shookstown

Steiner farm

Town reservoir

HAMBURG RD.

LIBERTY TURNPIKE

N
W — E
S

0 — 1/4 — 1/2 Mile

Carroll Creek

Carroll Cr.

6

To Hagan's Pass and Hagerstown

30th Ohio (Patroling Frederick)

COX (Kanawha Div./Reno)

Frederick

5

NATIONAL ROAD (HAGERSTOWN TNPK.)

McCLELLAN
Army of the Potomac

□ *Old Hessian barracks*

2

BURNSIDE
Right Wing
1st & 9th Corps

STURGIS
(2nd Div./Reno)

Ferrero's brigade

4

RENO
9th Corps

WILCOX
(1st Div./Reno)

To Baltimore

B & O RAILROAD SPUR

TELEGRAPH LINE (NOT OPERATIONAL)

To Jefferson's Pass and Harpers Ferry, Va.

† Cemetery

SUMNER
Center Wing
2nd & 12th Corps

1

Gordon's brigade

Crum's Ford

WILLIAMS
12th Corps

Monocacy River

Destroyed railroad bridge

Monocacy Junction

3

B & O RAILROAD

TELEGRAPH LINE (NOT OPERATIONAL)

To Harpers Ferry, Va.

To Baltimore
B & O R.R.

To Washington, DC

1. About noon: Lee's Lost Order is found.

2. Noon: Sumner's 2nd Corps enters Frederick, passes McClellan in review and takes up positions near the town reservoir.

3. 1 p.m.: The telegraph line is repaired to Monocacy Junction.

4. Ferrero's brigade of Sturgis's division advances through Frederick and passes McClellan in review.

5. 2 p.m.: McClellan meets with Cox as his division moves west.

6. 3 p.m.: Lost Orders in McClellan's hands. He sends a message to Pleasonton to verify Lee's moments. McClellan's headquarters are established at the Steiner farm.

Map by Gene Thorp

Edward Schweitzer of the 30th Ohio. Recalling in his diary that "On the 13th I patrolled the town . . . [and] I left the city at 1 o'clock P.M.," Schweitzer returned to the division just as his "regt. was falling in to leave." Martin Sheets of the 11th Ohio remembered the same, writing "we did not move until about 2 P.M., [when] we took the road to Hagerstown," confirming Cox's own recollection of when his division finally got underway.[8]

As for George McClellan, he and his staff made their way to the farm of Lewis H. Steiner, located west-northwest of Frederick, to set up the army's headquarters in a field of clover at some point after 2:00 p.m. Steiner, a member of the U.S. Sanitary Commission, saw the encampment soon after it its establishment, recalling, "In the afternoon I found McClellan with a large portion of his army encamped on my farm, west of Frederick. The nature of the camp ... prevented one from forming any other conclusion than that it was a bivouac and only intended for temporary occupation."[9]

Either while he was on route out of Frederick, or once he had arrived at his new headquarters, McClellan finally received the lost copy of Lee's orders sent by Gen. Williams. The only primary account of McClellan receiving the orders comes from the general himself and his recollection of the incident was decidedly vague. Writing to the son of the 27th Indiana's B. W. Mitchell in 1879, the aging general remembered, "there was handed to me by a member of my staff a copy (original) of one of General Lee's orders of march directed to General D. H. Hill, which developed General Lee's intended operations for the next few days, and was of very great service to me in enabling me to direct the movements of my own troops accordingly."[10]

General Williams's cover note on the document promised that the orders from Lee were genuine based on the testimony of Col. Pittman, but after reading the dispatch, McClellan proved unwilling to immediately commit his army to a full-fledged advance without further confirmation. Little Mac knew from the experience of the last ten days that Stuart's riders and other Rebel troops had spread copious amounts of misinformation across Maryland ahead of the Army of

---

8 Cox, *Military Reminiscences*, I:274. Diary of Edward E. Schweitzer, Sept. 13, 1862, *CWTI*, USAHEC, Item 76.152. Diary of Pvt. Martin L. Sheets, Co A, 11th Ohio Volunteer Infantry, Dec. 2, 1861–Jul. 14, 1863, *CWTI*, USAHEC and Diary of Michael Deady, Sept. 13, 1862, Rutherford B. Hayes Presidential Center. Our thanks to Steve Stotelmyer for these sources.

9 Steiner, *Report*, 25.

10 McClellan to Mitchell, Nov. 18, 1879, *The Century Magazine*, 33:135.

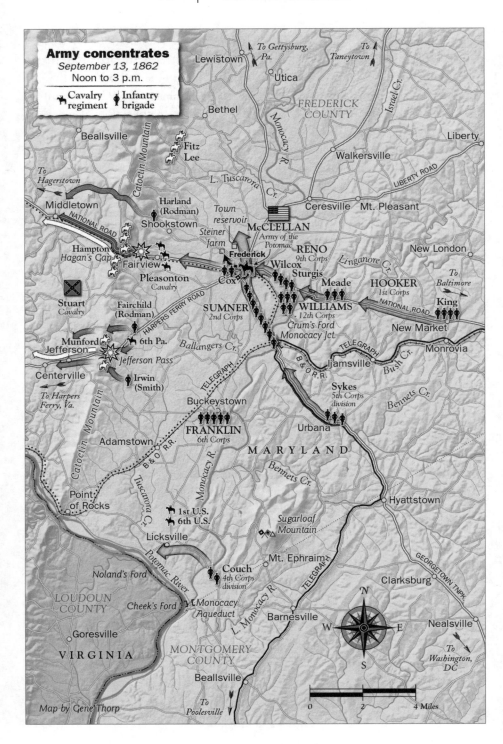

Army concentrates
September 13, 1862
Noon to 3 p.m.

🐎 Cavalry regiment   ↟ Infantry brigade

To Gettysburg, Pa.
To Taneytown
Lewistown
Utica
FREDERICK COUNTY
Bethel
Israel Cr.
Monocacy R.
Beallsville
Fitz Lee
Liberty
Walkersville
L. Tuscarora Cr.
LIBERTY ROAD
Catoctin Mountain
To Hagerstown
Harland (Rodman)
Town reservoir
Ceresville   Mt. Pleasant
Middletown
NATIONAL ROAD
Shookstown
Steiner farm
McCLELLAN
Army of the Potomac
RENO
9th Corps
Linganore Cr.
New London
Hampton
Hagan's Gap
Fairview
Frederick
Wilcox
Cox
Sturgis
Meade
HOOKER
1st Corps
To Baltimore
Pleasonton
Cavalry
SUMNER
2nd Corps
WILLIAMS
12th Corps
NATIONAL ROAD
King
Stuart
Cavalry
Fairchild (Rodman)
Crum's Ford
Monocacy Jct.
TELEGRAPH
New Market
Munford
Jefferson
6th Pa.
Ballangers Cr.
B. & O.R.R.
Ijamsville
Bush Cr.
Monrovia
Centerville
Jefferson Pass
Irwin (Smith)
TELEGRAPH
Bennets Cr.
To Harpers Ferry, Va.
Sykes
5th Corps division
Buckeystown
Urbana
Catoctin Mountain
FRANKLIN
6th Corps
M A R Y L A N D
Adamstown
B & O R.R.
Bennets Cr.
Tuscarora Cr.
Monocacy R.
Hyattstown
Point of Rocks
1st U.S.
6th U.S.
Sugarloaf Mountain
GEORGETOWN TNPK.
Licksville
Mt. Ephraim
Clarksburg
Noland's Ford
Potomac River
Couch
4th Corps division
TELEGRAPH
Nealsville
Cheek's Ford
Monocacy Aqueduct
Barnesville
To Washington, DC
LOUDOUN COUNTY
Goresville
L. Monocacy R.
N
W   E
S
V I R G I N I A
MONTGOMERY COUNTY
Beallsville
Map by Gene Thorp
To Poolesville
0   2   4 Miles

the Potomac's advance. McClellan also needed time to plan the best response to this windfall of new intelligence. In order to verify the authenticity of the orders he therefore ordered a copy of the document made and sent to Pleasanton with the following message: "General McClellan desires you to ascertain whether this order of march has thus far been followed by the enemy. As the pass through the Blue Ridge may be disputed by two columns, he desires you to approach it with great caution."[11]

Major Albert V. Colburn, McClellan's Assistant Adjutant General and, based on the handwriting of the original message, also likely the man to whom McClellan dictated the dispatch, timestamped it 3:00 p.m. and sent it off. Private Joe Taber, a member of McClellan's security escort, accompanied the courier, Lt. Nicholas Bowen, on the journey, which Taber described as a "sharp ride of about 8 miles" to Pleasonton's location west of Middletown.[12] To sum up, then, with Williams's courier departing to find McClellan no earlier than 1:00 p.m. and McClellan's message to Pleasonton timestamped 3:00 p.m., it is possible to conclude that the lost copy of Lee's orders reached the general at some point within that two-hour time frame.

When Bowen and Taber rode off to find Pleasonton they likely encountered the men of Brig. Gen. Orlando B. Willcox's division, who had "moved at 2 p.m." for Middletown in accord with Burnside's effort to support the army's cavalry.[13]

---

11 George McClellan to Alfred Pleasonton, Sept. 13, 1862, McClellan Papers, LOC Microfilm, Box C18, Reel 65.

12 "When we arrived at camp about 3 o'clk P.M., I received orders to go with Lieut. Bowen out to Genl. Pleasonton's Hd Qrs who was in the advance." Taber, Civil War Diary, Sept. 13, 1862. The average walking speed of a horse is 4 mph. The average trotting speed is 8 to 12 mph. Climbing the slope of Catoctin Mountain must be taken into consideration. Pleasonton responded to McClellan in a dispatch timestamped 6:15 p.m., indicating he had sufficient time to receive McClellan's message, review his latest intelligence, and compose a response. See www.speedofanimals.com for horse speed estimates.

13 Itinerary of the First Division, Ninth Army Corps, Sept. 1–Oct. 31, 1862. Addendum attached to Willcox's official report for the Maryland Campaign dated Sept. 21, 1862. OR 19:1, 432. While Cox's Kanawha Division took up the pursuit of Stuart's rear-guard once Pleasonton seized the summit of Catoctin Mountain at 1:00 p.m., Isaac Rodman had split his division in the morning to support Pleasonton's attacks on two Catoctin Mountain passes, sending Col. Harrison Fairchild's brigade to help Col. Rush's 6th Pennsylvania Cavalry seize the Jefferson Pass, and a second brigade under Col. Edward Harland around the Rebel left flank at Hagan's Gap via Shookstown Road northwest of Frederick. Unbeknownst to McClellan or Cox, Harland's brigade arrived in Middletown just after Pleasonton's troopers drove Stuart's cavalry through the town, and well before Cox's division showed up. See the Saturday morning entry

"Toward evening of the 13th we left Frederick City and marched out on the National Turnpike toward South Mountain," recalled David Lane of the newly-mustered 17th Michigan. Corporal Frederick Pettit of the 100th Pennsylvania echoed the departure time in a letter home, stating that "In the evening we took up our march through Frederick toward Middleton."[14]

Willcox's command moved out so rapidly, in fact, that members of the 79th New York, on picket duty since the night before, found themselves unable to catch up. "On returning to our bivouac, at four o'clock the following afternoon," wrote William Todd, "we found the army had moved forward.... We had marched a long distance out of our way in returning from picket duty, and when, at nightfall, we approached Frederick, the men were tired and hungry.... Passing through the city we bivouacked for the night a short distance beyond."[15] The regiment would not catch up to the rest of the division until 9:00 the following morning.

Brigadier General Samuel D. Sturgis's other brigade marched up the National Road in the wake of Willcox's command. The First Brigade of Reno's Ninth Corps, under the command of Brig. Gen. James Nagle (Sturgis's Second Division), began making its way through Frederick from the vicinity of the Monocacy River. As the regimental history of the 48th Pennsylvania recorded, "The start on the thirteenth was not made until 3:30 p.m., and the tramp through Frederick was a perfect ovation."[16] A writer serving with the recently arrived 9th New Hampshire of the same brigade also noted that, "at four o'clock the Ninth [Regiment] showed up in brigade line for the first time," before marching west down Patrick Street.[17] This procession continued on well after dark, recalled Ninth Corps Surgeon Thomas Ellis one year later, "For hours the long lines of men, horses, and artillery, kept

---

by Capt. Wolcott Marsh, Co. F, 8th Connecticut Volunteers dated Sept. 21, 1862. Available online at http://www.8cv.org/ant140/8cv-antietam-wolcott-marsh.html.

14 David A. Lane, *A Soldier's Diary: The Story of a Volunteer, 1862–1865* (Jackson, MI, 1905), 10. The term "evening" in nineteenth century parlance can refer to any time after 12:00 p.m. (noon). William G. Gavin, ed., *Infantryman Pettit, The Civil War Letters of Corporal Frederick Pettit, Late of Company C, 100th Pennsylvania Veteran Volunteer Infantry Regiment, "The Roundheads," 1862–1864* (Shippensburg, PA 1990), 23.

15 William Todd, *The Seventy-Ninth Highlanders New York Volunteers in the War of Rebellion, 1861–1865* (Albany, NY, 1886), 229-230.

16 Bosbyshell, *The 48th in the War*, 74.

17 Lord, ed., *History of the Ninth Regiment*, 58. Lord also wrote that the Second Corps marched through Frederick before the Ninth Corps. The Second Corps marched from south to north up Market Street while the Ninth Corps moved from east to west on Patrick Street.

passing through the town. It was not until near midnight that the monster military procession had drawn to a close."[18]

By late afternoon on September 13, Sumner's Second Corps had settled in near the town reservoir northwest of Frederick after an easy eight mile march, while Reno's Ninth Corps took the lead in pursuing Lee's Confederates up the National Road. The remaining portion of Burnside's right army wing had also finally converged on Frederick from the east. James B. Ricketts's division, the farthest away of Hooker's First Corps, finished its fourteen mile march from Ridgeville to come up at nightfall and halt east of the city while George Sykes's Fifth Corps division joined the Second Corps northwest of Frederick after a thirteen mile march from Hyattstown.[19] Prior to the Rebel retreat at 1:00 p.m., Maj. Heros von Borcke of J. E. B. Stuart's staff recalled seeing a sea of Federal troops massing below his observation point at Hagan's Gap. Attesting to the efficiency with which McClellan marshalled his forces west of Frederick, von Borcke described, probably with some exaggeration, how "the valley beneath, stretching away from the immediate base of the mountain . . . [was] literally blue with the Yankees."[20]

The Twelfth Corps, meanwhile, remained in place southeast of Frederick, not for a lack of orders, but rather because the other corps around Williams blocked his way forward. Readers will recall that it had taken Lee's army more than a day to march through the bottleneck of Frederick's streets when it pulled out on September 10–11. McClellan's larger army would now require an even longer time to make the same journey. As for Franklin's Sixth Corps, it made better progress on September 13 than historians have acknowledged, pushing some of Maj. Gen. William F. 'Baldy' Smith's Second Division over the Catoctin Mountains and into Middletown Valley before midnight.

---

18 Thomas T. Ellis, M.D., *Leaves from the Diary of an Army Surgeon; or, Incidents of Field Camp, and Hospital Life* (New York, NY, 1863), 253.

19 "At 6:30 p.m. camped on the banks of the Monocacy." Lt. Col. Benjamin E. Cook, *History of the Twelfth Massachusetts Volunteers (Webster Regiment)* (Boston, MA, 1882), 67; "Crossing the Monocacy, and encamping within a mile or so of the town, on the night of Saturday the 13th." Charles S. McClenthen, *A Sketch of the Campaign in Virginia and Maryland of Towers Brigade of Ricketts Division From Cedar Mountain to Antietam by a Soldier of the 26th N. Y. V.* (Syracuse, NY, 1862), 29; "Marched along the national road twelve miles on the afternoon of the 13th, and at nightfall crossed over the Monocacy on a new stone bridge and bivouacked in a field a little below." Isaac Hall, *History of the Ninety-Seventh Regiment New York Volunteers ("Conkling Rifles") in the War for the Union* (Utica, NY, 1890), 85.

20 Heros von Borcke, *Memoirs of the Confederate War for Independence*, Vol. I (London, 1866), 206. Von Borcke also recalled seeing a "mighty moving mass of blue" winding down the west side of Catoctin Mountain into Middletown Valley later in the day.

A soldier with the 49th Pennsylvania of Winfield Scott Hancock's brigade, Smith's division, recorded in his diary on that day, "we remained here [at Buckeystown] one hour, and went into camp in the meadow [before receiving] orders to march at 8 o'clock this evening and marched over the ridge and camped at Jeffersontown, at 10 o'clock to tonight." General Smith himself also wrote to Gen. Franklin from Jefferson at 4:00 p.m., "I have . . . ordered the 3 Regts of the 3rd Brigade, Col. Stoughton [of the 4th Vermont] & the Battery here [at Jefferson] where I await further orders from you."[21] By the late afternoon of September 13, Gen. McClellan had massed his army west of the Monocacy River and begun sending portions of it over the Catoctins into Middletown Valley. Not once that day had Federal troops ceased moving forward, either before McClellan received Lee's orders, or in the hours after he read them.

Around three-and-a-half hours of daylight remained for McClellan to act after Lee's errant dispatch fell into his hands, and contrary to nearly 160 years of criticism, the general did not waste a moment of that time. Maryland Campaign studies since Joseph Harsh's *Taken at the Flood* (1999) have made much of the fact that reading Lee's orders did not provide McClellan with information about the size of the separated Confederate commands confronting him, or even their true locations, since Lee had altered the orders by marching Longstreet's command to Hagerstown on September 11. They have cited this, along with McClellan's pre-Lost Orders instructions for Pleasonton and Burnside to advance into Middletown Valley, as evidence of the Lost Orders' relative unimportance. To quote Harsh, "The watershed of the campaign occurred on the evening of September 12 and the morning of September 13, when the Federals entered Frederick, and McClellan set in motion the pursuit to the foot of South Mountain. The information in the lost orders did not materially affect the movements of the Federal army on the 13th, except to cause Pleasonton and Burnside to approach Turner's Gap with greater caution."[22]

21 Robert S. Westbrook, *History of the 49th Pennsylvania Volunteers* (Altoona, PA, 1898), 124. A surgeon with the 5th Wisconsin Infantry named Alfred Castleman wrote of this movement, "At 9 o'clock last night (September 13) we took up our march across Catochtin Mountain, and we bivouacked in Middletown Valley . . . in the suburbs of the pleasant and flourishing little village of Jefferson." Alfred L. Castleman, *The Army of the Potomac: Behind the Scenes* (Milwaukee, WI, 1863), 222–223. William F. Smith to William B. Franklin, 4:00 p.m., Sept. 13, 1862, McClellan Papers, LOC Microfilm, Box A79, Reel 31.

22 See Harsh, *Taken*, 239 and 252; Stotelmyer, *Too Useful to Sacrifice*, 30.

This perspective is too narrow in scope. McClellan did indeed already have Pleasonton, Franklin, and Burnside's command on the move before he read Lee's orders, but while some have declared the Lost Orders unimportant for this reason, their judgments do not accurately reflect the opinion of the general himself. Rebel movements observed by Pleasonton's men up to September 13, as well as the numerous reports from Washington and Gov. Curtin in Harrisburg, appeared to indicate that Lee had set his sights on Col. Miles's garrison, but they did not confirm it. The reported presence of Confederate troops near Hagerstown also forced McClellan to consider that Lee might still be intent on entering Pennsylvania. McClellan's understanding of the situation thus remained fluid until seeing Special Orders No. 191 clarified the operational picture. Reading Lee's orders provided Little Mac with key pieces of information, including multiple enemy targets and confirmation that Col. Miles's force, not Chambersburg or points beyond it, faced the more immediate Rebel threat.

Not knowing these details before seeing Lee's orders forced McClellan to plan for multiple contingencies, whether it be pursuing the Rebel army into Pennsylvania, advancing directly against it in Washington County, or attempting to push through Harpers Ferry to arrest a retreat by Lee toward Winchester.[23] Upon reading Lee's orders, the slightly murky picture that McClellan had of Lee's positions took clear shape, galvanizing the Federal commander into a coordinated plan of action to attack the separate portions of Lee's army and, depending on Miles's resistance, to relieve the garrison at Harpers Ferry. McClellan therefore ordered the 1st and 6th U.S. Cavalry to ride for Jefferson as part of an effort to open communications with Harpers Ferry, and he directed Capt. William P. Sanders, commanding the 6th Cavalry to establish contact with Alfred Pleasonton so the two men could synchronize their movements in Middletown Valley.[24]

He then sat down to compose a lengthy set of orders for Maj. Gen. Franklin, whose Sixth Corps on the Army of the Potomac's left flank south of Frederick, provided the best option for attacking the pass over South Mountain closest to

---

23 McClellan suspected, for example, "I am beginning to think he (Lee) is making off to get out of the scrape by recrossing the river at Williamsport, in which case my only chance of bagging him will be to cross lower down and cut into his communications near Winchester." See George McClellan to Mary Ellen McClellan, 3:00 p.m., Sept. 12, 1862, in McClellan, *Own Story*, 570. The general also cabled Halleck at 11:00 p.m. on Sept. 13, "It may, therefore, in my judgment, be regarded as certain that this rebel army . . . intended to attempt penetrating Pennsylvania. The officers told their friends here that they were going to Harrisburg and Philadelphia." *OR* 19:1, 281.

24 *OR* 51:1, 107, 830.

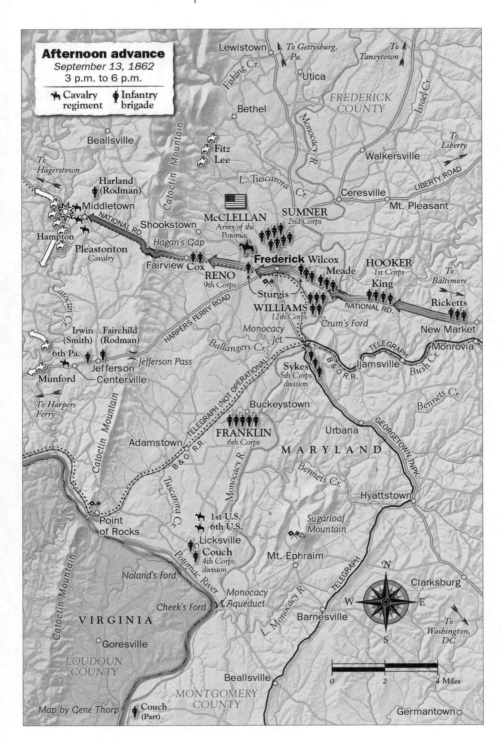

Afternoon advance
September 13, 1862
3 p.m. to 6 p.m.

🐎 Cavalry regiment   🔵 Infantry brigade

Map by Gene Thorp

Harpers Ferry at Crampton's Gap. These instructions, timestamped 6:20 p.m., outlined McClellan's response to reading Lee's dispatch, demonstrating that the general himself believed the information he gleaned was essential for planning the next phase of the army's operations. With Burnside's Ninth Corps already filling the road to Middletown, and the importance Lee placed on capturing Harpers Ferry now obvious, McClellan issued orders for the relief of Col. Miles's beleaguered garrison *before* he received confirmation of Special Orders No. 191's contents from Alfred Pleasonton. The general clearly felt he could no longer wait for a reply from his cavalry commander before acting, which is not something a timid general officer afflicted with a case of "the slows" would have done.

Telling Franklin "I have now full information as to movements and intentions of the enemy," McClellan added that Lee had divided his army into five parts. He also reasoned that the Federal garrison at Harpers Ferry remained intact because cannon fire from the southwest "shows that Miles still holds out." Little Mac then outlined his plan. Stating that "The whole of Burnside's command, including Hooker's corps, march this evening and early to-morrow morning, followed by the corps of Sumner and Banks (Williams) and Sykes's division," McClellan explained to Franklin that he intended to strike the Rebel army at Boonsborough and "carry that position." Lost in most analyses of the 6:20 p.m. orders is the fact that McClellan intended the attack on Boonsboro to be both his main thrust against Lee and chronologically the first engagement to take place on September 14. This is clear from the next series of instructions in the 6:20 p.m. orders. Informing Franklin that he had ordered Darius Couch's reduced division "to join you as rapidly as possible," McClellan stipulated that the Sixth Corps should not wait "for the whole of that division" to come up. Instead, Franklin was to "move at daybreak . . . by Jefferson and Burkittsville, upon the road to Rohrersville." Doing so would enable Franklin to seize Crampton's Gap over South Mountain and "cut off, destroy, or capture McLaws's command and relieve Colonel Miles." That is if the Rebels did not defend the pass at Crampton's Gap.

McClellan told Franklin he did not know if Confederate troops held positions near Burkittsville, writing, "If you find this pass (Crampton's) held by the enemy in large force, make all your dispositions for the attack, *and commence it about half an hour after you hear severe firing at the pass on the Hagerstown pike* [emphasis added], where the main body will attack." Continued McClellan, "My general idea is to cut the enemy in two and beat him in detail. I ask of you, at this important moment, all your intellect and the utmost activity that a general can exercise." Little Mac then concluded his 6:20 p.m. orders by telling the Sixth Corps' commander he was "fully authorized to change any of the details of this order as circumstances may change, provided the purpose is carried out, that purpose being to attack the enemy in detail and beat him."[25]

Franklin took full advantage of the leeway given to him on the next day, describing in his campaign report how "In compliance with the instructions of the commanding general, the corps advanced [at about 5:30–6:00 a.m.] on the morning of the 14th instant from a point 3 miles east of Jefferson, in the direction of the Blue Ridge."[26] Four to five hours afterward, at 10:30 a.m., Franklin then wrote to McClellan, "General. Finding a cross road at this point, I send a messenger. The head of my column is here well closed. I however have heard nothing from Couch and . . . have waited for him as long as I think proper," indicating that despite Little Mac's exhortation for him not to wait for Couch, Franklin did so anyway, ensuring his attack would jump off later in the day than McClellan expected.[27]

The 6:20 p.m. orders reveal that McClellan intended to thrust Franklin's nearly 13,000 man command through the "center" (assuming Jackson remained at Harpers Ferry and Longstreet at Boonsboro) of the Confederate army at Crampton's Gap after Burnside and the other commands had struck Longstreet and Hill's forces at Boonsboro.[28] Successfully completing this two-pronged offensive would pin a large portion of the Army of Northern Virginia at the north end of Pleasant Valley while the Sixth Corps inserted itself between that portion and the two Confederate divisions under McLaws hemming in Harpers Ferry at Sandy Hook. Once he had entered Pleasant Valley, and based on the evolving situation, Franklin could then pivot north to support Ambrose Burnside or turn south to confront Lafayette McLaws and Richard Anderson.[29]

As McClellan noted to Franklin, "If this pass (Crampton's Gap) is not occupied by the enemy in force, seize it as soon as practicable, and debouch upon

25 OR 19:1, 45–46. OR 51:1, Sec. 2, 825-826. Also see Reese, *High-Water Mark*, 31.

26 Franklin wrote to McClellan, "My command will commence its movement at 5:30 a.m." See William B. Franklin to George McClellan, Sept. 14, 1862, McClellan Papers, LOC Microfilm, Box C18, Reel 65. George Cook wrote that his regiment began its march at 6:00 a.m. See the Sept. 14 entry in the Diary of George H. Cook, January 1, 1862 – October 25, 1862, Principal Musician of the 27th Regt. NYSV, Pocket diary for 1862 (Salem, MA, 1862).

27 William B. Franklin to George McClellan, Sept. 14, 1862, McClellan Papers, LOC Microfilm, Box C18, Reel 65. The head of Franklin's column reached Burkittsville between noon and 1:00 p.m.

28 The two divisions in Franklin's Sixth Corps totaled about 12,800 men present for duty as of Sept. 10. See Appendix B.

29 Reese, *High-Water Mark*, 30 provides an excellent overview of what he calls "Franklin's three-way mandate of September 13."

Rohrersville, in order to cutoff the retreat of or destroy McLaws' command." Moving the Sixth Corps beyond South Mountain would place it squarely within the center of Lee's scattered army and trap McLaws between it and Miles's command, assuming the colonel still held Maryland Heights. Considered in total, the attack McClellan ordered Franklin to make amounted to an exceptionally aggressive move for a general commonly portrayed as meek and indecisive.

Concerning the oft-voiced reproach of McClellan for not ordering Franklin to march on Burkittsville overnight, this critique overlooks the fact that Little Mac designed what amounted to a corps-level *en echelon* attack intended to have the Sixth Corps to strike later than, and in support of, Burnside's assault. McClellan clearly sought to minimize the danger he knew Franklin would face by ordering him to attack Crampton's Gap *after* Burnside had already begun his assault on Boonsboro. The 6:20 p.m. orders show that McClellan wanted Franklin to break through at Crampton's Gap in order to open the way to Harpers Ferry. At the same time, McClellan did not wish to place Franklin's command in a more perilous position than it already would be in once the Sixth Corps moved into Pleasant Valley. The language in McClellan's 6:20 p.m. orders indicates that he considered the attack on Crampton's Gap to be a corollary to the main strike at Boonsboro. Accordingly, given the order of their importance in McClellan's plan, the general had Burnside's men march late into the night on September 13 to put him in place for a morning engagement on September 14 while Franklin's corps came up.

In other words, McClellan did not leave Miles to wither on the vine by delaying Franklin's advance. Pinning Longstreet and Hill at Boonsboro before Franklin made his move proved to be an essential element of McClellan's plan that critics of the general have ignored in favor of blaming him for Col. Miles's "shameful surrender," as the Harpers Ferry Military Commission put it.[30] McClellan did not confirm until the next day that Burnside's men would encounter D. H. Hill's troops atop South Mountain rather than on its western side. He did suspect it as a possibility, however, as evidenced in his September 13 warning for Pleasonton to approach Turner's Gap cautiously because "the pass through the Blue Ridge may be disputed by two columns." Nothing about this diminishes the reality that as a result of reading Lee's orders on September 13 McClellan ordered a two-pronged

30 OR 19:1, 799.

assault on Lee's army.[31] Whether these clashes erupted atop South Mountain or on its western slope made no difference.

Within thirty minutes of sending his orders to Franklin, McClellan also instructed Darius Couch to "call in all your command that you have left behind [along the Potomac], entrusting the guarding of the fords, etc., to the cavalry, and … march at once for Jefferson" to support General Franklin.[32] Then, at 8:45 p.m., McClellan ordered Sumner to "move punctually at 7 o'clock to-morrow morning," presumably in support of Burnside, per the 6:20 p.m. orders, but possibly also to reinforce the Sixth Corps should Franklin require it. As McClellan wrote to Franklin, "I think the force you have is, with good management, sufficient for the end in view. If you differ widely from me, and being on the spot you know better than I do the circumstances of the case, inform me at once, and I will do my best to re-enforce you."[33]

McClellan also took a moment at 8:45 p.m. to contact General-in-Chief Halleck and inform him of the situation. Writing, "We occupy Middletown and Jefferson," Little Mac addressed Halleck's ongoing concern about a possible Rebel attack on Washington from Virginia. "The whole force of the enemy [is] in front [of me]," he stated, "They are not retreating into Virginia." He then advised the War Department to "Look well to Chambersburg. Shall lose no time. Will soon have a decisive battle," indicating how despite reading Lee's orders McClellan still accepted the possibility of a Rebel strike into Pennsylvania.[34] At some point that

31 Copies of the attack orders to Burnside and Hooker have not survived, and may have never been issued beyond a verbal caution about the anticipated presence of Rebel troops at Boonsboro.

32 George McClellan to Darius Couch, 6:45 p.m., Sept. 13, 1862, McClellan Papers, LOC Microfilm, Box C18, Reel 65. Detaching regiments to guard the fords along the Potomac River from Washington all the way to Offutt's Cross Roads (present day Potomac, Maryland) left only a little more than half of Couch's division available for Franklin's use on Sept. 15.

33 OR 19:1, 45–46. For his orders to the Second Corps see George McClellan to Edwin Sumner, 8:45 p.m., Sept. 13, 1862, McClellan Papers, LOC Microfilm, Box C18, Reel 65.

34 George McClellan to Henry Halleck, 8:45 p.m., Sept. 13, 1862, McClellan Papers, LOC Microfilm, Box C18, Reel 65. Telegraph Corpsmen did not restore the line from Monocacy Junction to Frederick until late morning on Sept. 14 at the earliest. McClellan sent telegraph communications after 5:00 p.m. from the signal station in the cemetery southwest of Frederick by signal flag and torch to Sugarloaf Mountain, and from there by the same method to the Point of Rocks station, where the message was telegraphed through Monocacy Junction on to Washington. McClellan's sent time and date for this telegram in the *Official Records* is 11:00 a.m., Sept. 14, which is copied from the War Department's received copy. See George McClellan to Henry Halleck, 11:15 a.m., Sept. 14, 1862, NA, RG 107, Microcopy 473, Roll 79, No. 306. The

evening, a messenger also rode up to army headquarters with a response from Pleasonton verifying what McClellan had learned in the Lost Orders. "As near as I can judge the order of march of the enemy . . . has been followed as closely as circumstances would permit," revealed the cavalry commander, thus confirming the assumptions McClellan had relied on to develop his plans for the next day, which probably gave the general some relief.[35]

McClellan's 8:45 p.m. missive to Halleck radiates confidence, something Brig. Gen. John Gibbon attested to some years later. Having arrived at army headquarters near sundown, Gibbon remained there until well after dark waiting to speak with McClellan. "As it grew later and only one or two staff officers remained in the tent," recalled Gibbon, "General McClellan expressed himself freely in regard to his movements and taking from his pocket a folded paper, he said: 'Here is a paper with which if I cannot whip 'Bobbie Lee,' I will be willing to go home.' He spoke cheerfully and confidently and added, 'I will not show you the document now but there (turning down one of the folds) is the signature (showing 'R. H. Chiton Adjt. Gen.') and it gives the movement of every division of Lee's Army. Tomorrow we will pitch into his centre and if you people will only do two good, hard days' marching I will put Lee in a position he will find hard to get out of.'"[36]

Gibbon's statement further underscores the value McClellan placed on the intelligence he had gleaned from reading the Lost Orders. The general obviously thought seeing the document changed the game in his favor, although executing his plan would not be without complications, because resistance had already arrived in the form of a dispatch from Henry Halleck. In it the General-in-Chief signaled his strong disapproval of McClellan's order to remove Darius Couch's division from guarding the Potomac fords and march it to the main army. Despite having more than 84,000 troops present in and around the Washington defenses, the skittish

---

War Department's received copy is incorrect and does not match the original in McClellan's Papers which state the sent time as 8:45 p.m. on Sept. 13. McClellan's reference to Chambersburg reflects intelligence he had received from Gov. Curtin on Sept. 11 stating "Jackson is now in Hagerstown . . . Men all believed they were going to Pennsylvania. We shall need a large portion of your column in this valley to save us from utter destruction" and from Burnside on Sept. 12: "The soldiers all say they are going into Pennsylvania." See OR 19:2, 269 and 272. Halleck also expressed the opinion to McClellan at 10:30 a.m. on Sept. 13 "that the enemy will send a small column toward Pennsylvania, so as to draw your forces in that direction." OR 19:2, 280.

35 Alfred Pleasonton to Randolph Marcy, 6:15 p.m., Sept. 13, 1862, McClellan Papers, LOC Microfilm, Box A79, Reel 31.

36 John Gibbon, *Personal Recollections of the Civil War* (New York, NY & London, 1928), 73.

Halleck claimed he had no force to replace Couch's, and he warned McClellan not to uncover the capital, or to underestimate the danger that Lee intended to draw the Federal army north into Pennsylvania and then dart south to attack Washington from Virginia.[37]

McClellan responded forcefully to this dispatch in a message timestamped 11:00 p.m. Informing Halleck that "An order from General R. E. Lee . . . has accidentally come into my hands this evening (i.e., afternoon in nineteenth century parlance)—the authenticity of which is unquestionable," McClellan explained to the rattled General-in-Chief that it "discloses some of the plans of the enemy, and shows most conclusively that the main rebel army is now before us." General Pleasonton's front-line observations and the sound of heavy artillery firing from the southwest, wrote McClellan, confirmed that Lee had split his army into multiple columns to capture Harpers Ferry. "There is but little probability of the enemy being in much force south of the Potomac," McClellan argued.[38] "I do not, by any means, wish to be understood as undervaluing the importance of holding Washington . . . but upon the success of this army the fate of the nation depends. It was for this reason that I said everything else should be made subordinate to placing this army in proper condition to meet the large rebel force in our front."[39] This remarkable telegram shows how unlike earlier in the campaign when he had taken into account Halleck's concerns about the possibility of a Confederate attack

37 OR 19:2, 280–281. When Halleck wrote McClellan, General Nathaniel Banks had 84,253 troops present for duty in the Washington defenses. An additional 20,682 men stationed at Baltimore under the command of John Wool could be relied upon in an emergency. Over the next week, 7,953 more soldiers from the North would be added to Banks's command. See Abstract from tri-monthly return of the Defenses of Washington, Maj. Gen. N. P. Banks commanding, Sept. 20, 1862, Headquarters, Washington, D.C. and Abstract from tri-monthly return of the Middle Department (Eighth Army Corps), Maj. Gen. John E. Wool commanding, Sept. 20, 1862, Headquarters, Baltimore, Md. in OR 19:2, 337. The *Washington Evening Star* also reported the number of newly arriving troops.

38 Reports from the Sugarloaf Mountain signal station at 1:00 p.m. announced that "no enemy was visible or apparently near our left," reinforcing McClellan's belief that no large force of Confederates threatened his left flank. See OR 19:1, 120.

39 George McClellan to Henry Halleck, 11:00 p.m., Sept. 13, 1862, McClellan Papers, LOC Microfilm, Box A79, Reel 31. Nineteenth-century Americans commonly used the term "evening" to refer to the hours after noon. Here McClellan himself confirmed receipt of the Lost Orders on the afternoon of Sept. 13 and not before noon that day. Halleck's insistence on holding back tens of thousands of troops for the defense of Washington, which Lee's army no longer threatened, greatly frustrated McClellan. See, for example, McClellan's request to Halleck on Sept. 11, 1862: "Please send forward all the troops you can spare from Washington, particularly Porter's, Heintzelman's, Sigel's, and all the other old troops . . . General Banks reports 72,000 troops in and about Washington." OR 19:2, 253.

on Washington while he moved north, McClellan now doubled-down on his offensive strategy by arguing the value of pushing his army with the maximum force available to meet the enemy at South Mountain.

Orders McClellan sent out shortly afterward further confirmed his resolve. At 11:30 p.m.—in accordance with what he had earlier written to Franklin—he instructed Gen. Hooker to march his First Corps to Middletown at daylight. Then he directed Brig. Gen. George Sykes to move his Fifth Corps division, "punctually at 6 o'clock in the morning . . . in rear of Hooker and in advance of Sumner."[40] Fifteen minutes later, McClellan ordered Burnside to investigate rumors that a large body of Rebel cavalry had been spotted operating north of Frederick while at the same time he responded to an earlier message from Gov. Curtin by asking him to concentrate Pennsylvania state militia troops at Chambersburg to keep Lee boxed in, and to look out for Rebels near Gettysburg—an obvious reference to the cavalry after which he had sent Burnside prowling.[41]

It is only when all of this was said and done that Gen. McClellan finally sat down to compose his famous midnight "trophies" message to Abraham Lincoln.[42] Writing that he had "the whole rebel force" before him, McClellan assured the president "no time shall be lost" in pursuing it. Lee had, he continued, "made a

40 George McClellan to George Sykes, 11:30 p.m., Sept. 13, 1862, McClellan Papers, LOC Microfilm, Box C18, Reel 65.

41 George McClellan to Ambrose Burnside, 11:45 p.m., Sept. 13, 1862, and George McClellan to Gov. Andrew Curtin, 11:45 p.m., Sept. 13, 1862, McClellan Papers, LOC Microfilm, Box C18, Reel 65. McClellan had by this time sent Brig. Gen. John F. Reynolds to command these troops in Harrisburg and Fitz Lee's Rebel cavalry brigade operated north of Frederick as well.

42 McClellan's communication reached Washington at 2:35 a.m. on Sept. 14. See OR 19:2, 281. We know from Chief Signal Officer, Maj. Albert Myer, reporting on Oct. 6, that, "In the evening [on Sept. 13] a message was received from Washington, transmitted through the signal station at Point of Rocks, from the President of the United States to General McClellan. A reply was in the same manner returned." Since Operator Bickford at Monocacy Junction did not connect the wire from Washington to the Point of Rocks station until 5:00 p.m., we know the message was sent after that hour. We also know that the message was sent from Point of Rocks by flag or torch signals to the Sugarloaf Mountain signal station because it was the only location that had direct communication with Frederick City. The other flag route, via Middletown to Catoctin Mountain to Frederick, was not yet operational. See Report of Albert Myer, Oct. 6, 1862, OR 19:1, 120. Jim Rosebrock discovered the message referred to by Myer in the Signal Corps records at the National Archives. Dated Sept. 13 and addressed to General McClellan. It reads: "Sir; the telegraph line is open to Point of Rocks. The President is at the War Department Office and [is] anxious to hear from you." See NA, RG 111 "Records of the Office of the Chief Signal Officer, 1860-1982," 111.2.1 Correspondence, Messages Sent and Received, Jan. 1862-May 1863; Jan–Dec 1864, 3 Vols., Entry 13. The next entry is McClellan's "trophies" message. Our thanks to Jim Rosebrock via Scott Hartwig for the source.

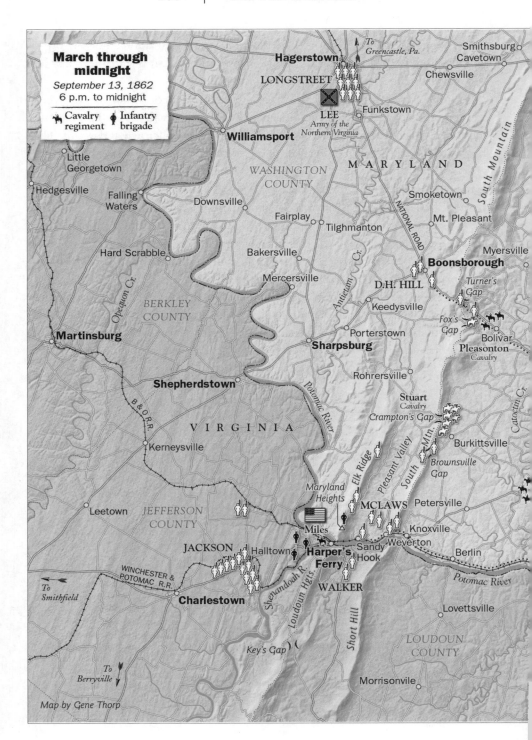

March through midnight

September 13, 1862
6 p.m. to midnight

Cavalry regiment   Infantry brigade

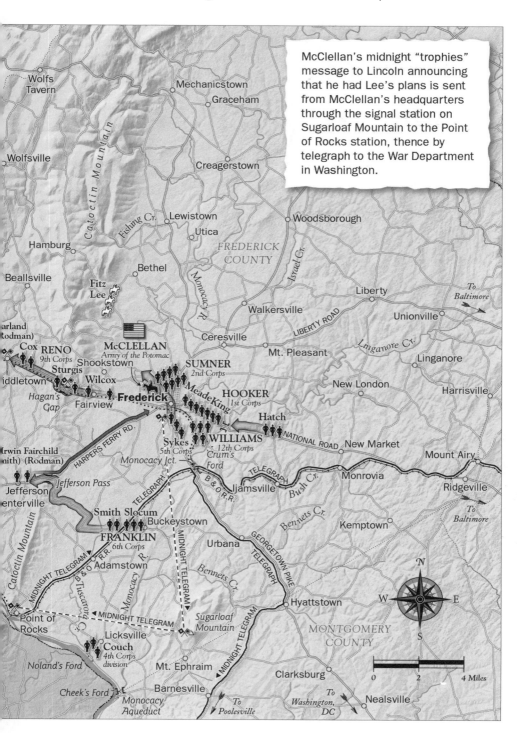

McClellan's midnight "trophies" message to Lincoln announcing that he had Lee's plans is sent from McClellan's headquarters through the signal station on Sugarloaf Mountain to the Point of Rocks station, thence by telegraph to the War Department in Washington.

Time Received *2.35 a.m.*   **United States Military Telegraph,**
/   War Department,
Washington, D.C. Sept 14 ___ *1862.*

Hd Qrs Fredirick Sept 13, 12 Midnight

The Presdt.

I have the whole Rebel force in front of me but am confident and no time shall be lost. I have a difficult task to perform but with Gods blessing will accomplish it. I think Lee has made a gross mistake & that he will be severely punished for it. The army is in motion as rapidly as possible. I hope for a great success if the plans of the Rebels remain unchanged. We have possession of Cotocktano. I have all the plans of the Rebels and will catch them in their own

18408

Time Received_____ United States Military Telegraph,
2 War Department,
Washington, D. C._____1862.

trap of my men are equal
to the emergency.
I now feel that
I can't count on them as of old.
All forces of Penna should
be placed to cooperate at
Chambersburg. My respects to
Mrs Lincoln. Received most enthusiastically by the ladies, Will send
you trophies. All well and
with Gods blessing will accomplish
it.

Geo B McClellan.

161

gross mistake [in dividing his army] and . . . he will be severely punished for it. The army is in motion as rapidly as possible. I hope for a great success if the plans of the rebels remain unchanged. We have possession of Catoctin Mountain (not captured by Pleasonton until 1:00 p.m.). I have all the plans of the rebels, and will catch them in their own trap if my men are equal to the emergency." Lastly, added McClellan, the "forces of Pennsylvania should be placed to co-operate at Chambersburg," a reference to the missive he dispatched to Curtin at 11:45 p.m., and the "look well to Chambersburg" caution sent to Halleck at 8:45 p.m. Closing with "Will send you trophies," McClellan added, "all well, and with God's blessing will accomplish it."[43]

Multiple points in the midnight message make it clear that George McClellan summed up the situation as it stood at the very end of the day on September 13, not as it had appeared at noon. He confirmed possession of Lee's orders, verified he had taken steps to exploit them, established that his army held Catoctin Mountain, referenced his 8:45 p.m. dispatch to Halleck concerning Chambersburg, and cited content in the message he sent to Gov. Curtin fifteen minutes earlier. McClellan had at that moment every reason to feel optimistic. With Burnside's command converging on Middletown, Franklin's Sixth Corps ordered to advance on Crampton's Gap in the morning, and Hooker's First Corps, Sykes's division, and, potentially, Sumner's wing of the Second Corps, as well as the Twelfth Corps prepared to support the attack where needed, he had put all of the pieces in place to effectively pounce on the fragmented pieces of Lee's army early the next day.

43 George McClellan to Abraham Lincoln, 12 Midnight, Sept. 13, 1862, (Telegram concerning military affairs), LOC, Manuscript Division, Lincoln Papers, Series 1. General Correspondence 1833-1916, Sept. 13, 1862, No. 18408. McClellan's original copy of this telegram has yet to be found, but the copy transmitted by the signal station on Sugarloaf Mountain to the telegraph station at Point of Rocks has been discovered in the Signal Corps records at the National Archives. See NA, RG 111, Entry 13.

September 14–15, 1862:
Where the Blame Rests for the
Fall of Harpers Ferry

Critics of George McClellan have raised numerous complaints over the years about the general's performance in Maryland. Thanks to the libel voiced by Henry Halleck during the inquiry of the Harpers Ferry Military Commission, and weaponized by William Swinton in 1864, they have repeatedly blasted McClellan for marching too slowly to have relieved Col. Miles's beleaguered garrison before it surrendered on September 15. Due to the honest mistake made by Jacob Cox several decades after the war that McClellan came into possession of Lee's orders at noon on September 13, a claim repeatedly emphasized by Stephen Sears and others a century later, they have also criticized the general for dawdling indecisively before moving to help Miles. According to those critics, Little Mac wasted eighteen hours that he could have used to advance his army. Then, even after his success at South Mountain, those same critics lambasted McClellan for not following up his victory rapidly enough on September 15.

This study has examined each of these subjects in turn, demonstrating the myth of Army of the Potomac's slow advance on Frederick, showing how the possession of Special Orders No. 191 by McClellan before noon is flat-out incorrect, and proving that McClellan responded aggressively to reading Lee's orders by ordering a two-pronged *en echelon* attack on the Rebel army within only four hours of receiving them, despite believing the Confederate force to be numerically stronger than his own. Concerning the surrender of Harpers Ferry, Henry Halleck pinned responsibility for saving the garrison on McClellan only on September 12. Before that date, Little Mac had counseled repeatedly that Miles's men should be removed. His warnings fell on deaf ears, however, due to either the stubbornness or incompetence of the General-in-Chief. But what about the brief two days that McClellan had the authority to command Col. Miles and his men? Could he realistically have contacted and rescued the Federal garrison during those 48 hours? McClellan himself certainly thought it was possible.

As early as September 11, the general had ordered his cavalry to make contact with Miles, even asking Alfred Pleasonton if he could "without too much risk, send a small party to communicate with Harper's Ferry by the south side of the Potomac?" Upon learning on September 12 that he could order Miles to evacuate his position if he managed to open communications with the Ferry, McClellan again immediately ordered his cavalry to open contact with Miles and, when it advanced into Middletown Valley on the following day, to fire artillery "at frequent intervals as a signal that relief was at hand."[1] Then, after reading Lee's orders shortly before 3:00 p.m. on September 13, he promptly devised a plan for attacking the South Mountain gaps, including Crampton's Gap near Burkittsville, with the intention of punching into Pleasant Valley to rescue Miles and his men. McClellan's minimum expectation of Miles was that he would hold Maryland Heights, the 1,400 foot ridge which towered over Harpers Ferry.

Reno's Ninth Corps spearheaded the advance that afternoon, marching west on the National Pike through Hagan's Gap, and filling the road until well after midnight. Further south, Franklin acknowledged at 10:00 p.m. that he had received McClellan's orders to break through to Miles after he had sent the balance of William F. Smith's Second Division over the Catoctin range to position them at Jefferson for an early start on the following day. When Little Mac finally retired in the early hours of September 14, he felt sure that even though he had heard nothing from Miles, he had done all in his power to alert the Harpers Ferry garrison to his advance, and set the wheels in motion for a powerful attack on the enemy that would ultimately lift the Rebel siege.

After only a two-hour break, the Army of the Potomac's advance from Frederick resumed at 3:00 a.m. on September 14, when Col. Harrison Fairchild's brigade, the last of Maj. Gen. Reno's eight Ninth Corps brigades to remain east of the Catoctin range, roused from a short slumber. Footsore from having marched all the way to Jefferson Pass and then back again on September 13, Fairchild's men had only a brief opportunity to rest before getting back onto the road. "It seemed as though they had scarcely rolled themselves in their blankets ere the order came to 'fall in,' which was obeyed with the greatest reluctance" recalled one member of the

---

1 *OR* 51:1, 818 and *OR* 19:1, 44.

brigade.[2] Fairchild's weary men led the Federal column out of Frederick on this day's march, and as they moved buglers blared and drummers beat reveille into the cool night air to wake the rest of the army. By sunrise, the men of Hooker's First Corps had begun flowing through the city on the National Road and then over Hagan's Gap while troops in the other corps waited their turn to follow.

Pleasonton's troopers scouted Fox's Gap at roughly the same time, investigating the place where the Old Sharpsburg Road crossed over South Mountain. Near the summit, the Federals encountered the 5th Virginia Cavalry under Col. Thomas Rosser, supported by a two-gun section from Capt. John Pelham's horse artillery, and a brigade of North Carolina troops under the command of Brig. Gen. Samuel Garland.[3] Pleasonton soon realized his troopers could not handle Rebel infantry, so he called on Jacob Cox to bring up his nearby Kanawha division. These two brigades of Buckeye troops hit Garland's men in the right flank and center, driving them back in only three hours and temporarily opening the Old Sharpsburg Road before reinforcements arrived that afternoon to stabilize the Rebel position.

Back in Frederick, Gen. McClellan had taken up pen and ink to write his wife before the fighting on South Mountain erupted at 9:00 a.m. Informing Mary Ellen "I have only time to say good-morning this bright, sunny Sunday, and then start to the front to try to relieve Harper's Ferry, which is sorely pressed by secesh," McClellan wrote, "It is probable that we shall have a serious engagement to-day, and perhaps a general battle; if we have one at all during this operation it ought to be to-day or to-morrow. I feel as reasonably confident of success as any one well can who trusts in a higher power and does not know what its decision will be."[4]

McClellan revealed in this letter that he fully expected a fight that day. Not only had he cautioned Alfred Pleasonton on the previous afternoon that "the pass through the Blue Ridge may be disputed by two columns," he also informed William Franklin of the orders he gave for Ambrose Burnside to "carry" (i.e., assault and take) the enemy position that he expected to find ahead of Boonsboro after reading Lee's orders. The mention of Boonsboro in Lee's orders did not imply that Little Mac thought Lee would cede the pass at Turner's Gap without a fight. As McClellan told Franklin, he expected the Sixth Corps to coordinate its attack on

---

2 Graham, *The Ninth Regiment*, 269.

3 OR 19:1, 817.

4 McClellan, *Own Story*, 571.

Crampton's Gap "after you hear severe firing at the pass on the Hagerstown pike, where the main body will attack."[5]

While he watched Hooker's long column flow westward, and listened for the sound of artillery to boom out beyond the Catoctin Range, McClellan still had no information about Col. Miles. A stroke of luck changed that when an intrepid officer from Harpers Ferry rode into the encampment with an aide after a difficult ride through enemy lines. This man, Capt. Charles Russell, bore important news. Miles still held out, he told McClellan, recalling the details of their journey. Russell had hand-picked nine men to accompany him and departed from Harpers Ferry after dark on September 13. Following a long, circuitous ride, said Russell, they "came to South Mountain," where they ran into an enemy picket line. "We got around them by taking a road through the woods," explained the captain, "and then we went directly over the center of South Mountain until I reached Middletown. I reported there to General Reno. He gave me a fresh horse, and directed me to report to General McClellan."[6]

Russell finally reached army headquarters at the Steiner Farm around 9:00 a.m. on September 14, or just about the time that the first cannon fire erupted at Fox's Gap. Reporting to Little Mac that Col. Miles "could hold out forty-eight hours," Russell clarified that the garrison "had subsistence for forty-eight hours" before informing McClellan "Maryland Heights had been evacuated." Incredulous that Miles had sacrificed the key position defending Harpers Ferry, McClellan asked Russell "if Colonel Miles held Loudoun Heights," on the far side of the Shenandoah River. He did not, replied the captain. Little Mac then stated, according to Russell, "that General Franklin was . . . on his way to relieve that garrison [and] he immediately sent off a messenger to General Franklin to urge him forward." Finally, McClellan inquired if Russell thought he "could get back to Colonel Miles," to which the captain responded, "I told him I did not think I could." McClellan then concluded the exchange by sending Russell to Franklin to personally offer the general assistance concerning local terrain and roads in case he needed it.[7]

---

5 Hartwig, *To Antietam Creek*, 304 argues contrary to the evidence "there were no plans . . . in the morning to seize the mountain gaps. The Federals planned nothing more than to reconnoiter the gaps on the 14th."

6 OR 19:1, 45, 720-721.

7 Ibid. The one piece of information Russell does not seem to have shared with McClellan is Col. Miles's admonishment for the captain to "try to reach somebody that had ever heard of the

Russell's testimony makes clear that as of 9:00 a.m. on September 14, Gen. McClellan "confidently expected that Colonel Miles would hold out until we had carried the mountain passes, and were in condition to send a detachment to his relief."[8] The key date for the general at this point became the morning of September 16 because this is when Miles had estimated his men would run out of food and be compelled to surrender. Little did McClellan know that he and Franklin had less than half that time to rescue the surrounded garrison. Miles would instead hoist the white flag within twenty-four hours, a full day sooner than he had promised to hold out.

In the meantime, the primary task for Little Mac remained defeating the enemy forces defending Turner's, Fox's, and Crampton's Gaps. Following his interview with Russell, McClellan attended to business at his headquarters. Hooker's column continued to make its way over Hagan's Gap, George Sykes's division of regular army troops filed onto the turnpike behind them, and Sumner's Second Corps and Williams's Twelfth Corps, the men of which had been awake since 3:00 a.m., tried unsuccessfully to work their way forward, too. One of Sumner's soldiers recalled his frustration at the initially fruitless march, complaining that, although his unit "left camp early" they did not make much headway "as we went some distance on the wrong road, and had to turn back almost to our starting point." Another wrote that the delay along the road, "was one of the worst I ever saw."[9]

Lee, too, had experienced a similar delay four days earlier when he had to squeeze his own army through the Hagan's Gap choke point, taking more than a day and a half to move more than 60,000 men from Frederick into Middletown

---

United States Army, or any general of the United States Army, or anybody that knew anything about the United States Army, and report the condition of Harper's Ferry . . . he told me that if I could get to any general of the United States Army, or to any telegraph station, or, if possible, get to General McClellan, whom he supposed was at Frederick—he thought he must be at Frederick." This statement indicates that Miles had received no word about the Army of the Potomac's advance since Sept. 11 when telegraphic communications with Washington went dead. The colonel therefore assumed that McClellan had reached Frederick, but he did not know it for certain. As for the question of Miles being able to hear the cannon fire on South Mountain on Sept. 14, Capt. Russell offered the opinion that he must have, "unless the cannonading there (at Harpers Ferry) was very great." OR 19:1, 723-724.

8 McClellan, *Report on the Organization and Campaigns of the Army of the Potomac*, 357.

9 Joseph R. C. Ward, *History of the One Hundred and Sixth Regiment Pennsylvania Volunteers, 2d Brigade, 2d Division, 2d Corps, 1861-1865* (Philadelphia, PA, 1906), 98–99. Aldrich, *The History of Battery A*, 120.

Valley.[10] Now, McClellan needed some 48,000 men to work their way through the gap to support Burnside. Fortunately, he had already sent Burnside and Pleasonton's combined 15,000 man force over the mountain on the late afternoon and night of September 13. A second rough and little used road crossed the Catoctin ridge at Shookstown several miles to the north, but this route veered away from the fight on South Mountain. Little Mac needed options to bypass the bottleneck. He therefore sent orders for Sumner to march his army wing, including the Second and Twelfth Corps, to Middletown via the Shookstown Pass. Once over the mountain, Sumner's men would need to cut across fields and woods to get back to the National Road. Taking this circuitous route ensured that they would miss the fight on September 14, although McClellan did not know this at the time. With these arrangements complete, the general finally took to the saddle between 10:00 and 10:30 a.m. According to Col. Strother, McClellan and his entourage "rode rapidly" to Burnside's headquarters at Middletown, a journey that took them approximately one hour despite the traffic filling the road.[11]

To the south, meanwhile, Henry Slocum's First Division of Franklin's Sixth Corps moved promptly at daylight, marching five miles over Catoctin Mountain to Jefferson, where it reunited with Smith's waiting Second Division.[12] Franklin then pushed his men another mile west, driving off Rebel pickets along Catoctin Creek, before halting his command at a rural crossroad three miles from Burkittsville to await a portion of Darius Couch's division. "The head of my column is here [and] well closed," he wrote to McClellan at 10:30 a.m. "I however have heard nothing from Couch & have seen nothing of him. I have waited for him as long as I think proper. I shall capture the pass as soon as I arrive at it, & will let you know what occurs as frequently as possible."[13]

Resuming his advance with Slocum in the fore, Franklin reached Burkittsville at noon about two hours after the morning's fight between Cox and Garland ended at Fox's Gap five miles to the north. Skirmishers from the Sixth Corps then traded

10 Thorp, "In Defense of McClellan at Antietam."

11 *OR* 51:1, Sec. 2, 831. McClellan sent a telegram location stamped Middletown at 11:45 a.m. See *OR* 51:1, Sec. 2, 833.

12 Slocum's official report estimated the distance at "about 3 miles east of Jefferson," but a review of contemporary roads combined with modern mapping shows the distance was greater than five miles. *OR* 19:1, 380. Also see Cook, *Diary*, Sept. 14, 1862: "Started 6 oc am for Scromptons [Crampton?] Gap."

13 William Franklin to George McClellan, 10:30 a.m., Sept. 14, 1862, McClellan Papers, LOC Microfilm, Box A79, Reel 31, No: 16164.

shots with Confederate troops at the base of Crampton's Gap, which, Franklin observed, was "occupied by the enemy in force." While positioning his command for its attack, Franklin sent McClellan another dispatch at 12:30 p.m. informing him, "I think from appearances that we may have a heavy fight to get the pass."[14]

Upon arriving at Burnside's headquarters just east of Middletown, McClellan likely found Franklin's 10:30 a.m. message waiting for him, replying to it in a 11:45 a.m. message with an update on the Ninth Corps' progress. Informing him that Miles had abandoned Maryland Heights, McClellan urged the Sixth Corps' commander in strong terms "to bear in mind the necessity of relieving Colonel Miles if possible."[15] Rescuing Harpers Ferry clearly continued to preoccupy Little Mac, even as the fight for South Mountain progressed. Colonel Strother, always an astute witness to the events, found the general "apprehensive in regard to Miles" during his visit to Burnside's headquarters. The general even called on the colonel to "find a man true and reliable to go to Harpers Ferry to carry a message to Miles."[16] Strother had no luck identifying a volunteer, but Allan Pinkerton, McClellan's civilian Chief of Secret Service eventually found three local men willing to take copies of the following message from McClellan to the besieged Col. Miles:

Colonel: The army is being rapidly concentrated here [at Middletown]. We are now attacking the pass on the Hagerstown road over the Blue Ridge. A column is about attacking the Burkettsville and Boonsboro' Pass. You may count on our making every effort to relieve you; you may rely upon my speedily accomplishing that object. Hold out to the last extremity. If it is possible, reoccupy the Maryland Heights with your whole force. If you can do that, I will certainly be able to relieve you. As the Catoctin Valley is in our possession you can safely cross the river at Berlin or its vicinity, so far as opposition on this side of the river is concerned. Hold out to the last.[17]

This missive makes clear both McClellan's concern for the safety of Miles's men and the fact that as of about 2 p.m. on September 14 he had still not heard any firing from the direction of Burkittsville. McClellan finally received Franklin's 12:30 p.m. message about that time. Responding to it immediately, he ordered the general to

14 William Franklin to George McClellan, 12:30 p.m., Sept. 14, 1862, McClellan Papers, LOC Microfilm, Box A79, Reel 31. Also see Sears, ed., *The Civil War Papers of George B. McClellan*, 460.

15 *OR* 51:1, Sec. 2, 833.

16 Eby, Jr., ed., *A Virginia Yankee*, 106.

17 *OR* 19:1, 45.

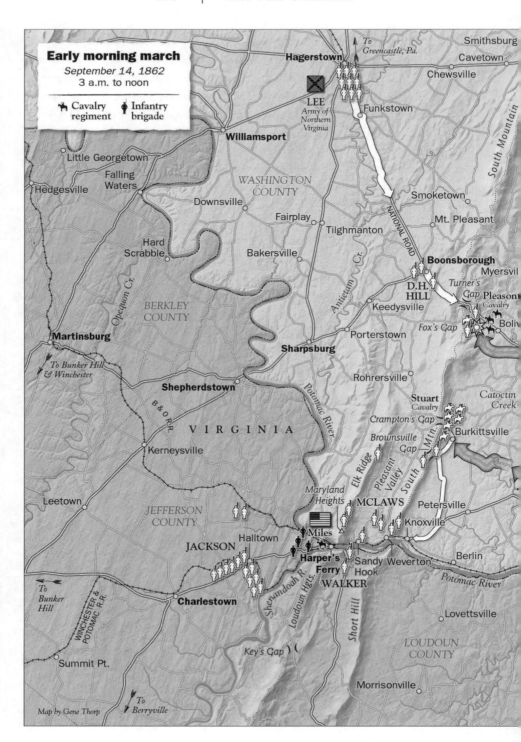

Early morning march
September 14, 1862
3 a.m. to noon

🐎 Cavalry regiment   ⚔ Infantry brigade

To Greencastle, Pa.

Smithsburg
Cavetown
Chewsville

Hagerstown

Funkstown

LEE
Army of Northern Virginia

Williamsport

Little Georgetown

Falling Waters

Hedgesville

WASHINGTON COUNTY

Downsville

Smoketown

Mt. Pleasant

South Mountain

Fairplay

Tilghmanton

NATIONAL ROAD

Hard Scrabble

Bakersville

Antietam Cr.

Boonsborough

Myersvil

D.H. HILL

Turner's Gap

Pleason
Cavalry

BERKLEY COUNTY

Keedysville

Fox's Gap

Boliv

Opequon Cr.

Martinsburg

Porterstown

To Bunker Hill & Winchester

Sharpsburg

Shepherdstown

Rohrersville

Stuart
Cavalry

Catoctin Creek

B. & O. R.R.

VIRGINIA

Potomac River

Crampton's Gap

Brownsville Gap

Burkittsville

Kerneysville

Elk Ridge

Pleasant Valley

South Min.

Leetown

JEFFERSON COUNTY

Maryland Heights

MCLAWS

Petersville

Halltown

Miles

Knoxville

JACKSON

Harper's Ferry

Sandy Hook

Weverton

Berlin

WALKER

Potomac River

To Bunker Hill

WINCHESTER & POTOMAC R.R.

Charlestown

Shenandoah R.

Loudoun Hgts.

Short Hill

Lovettsville

Summit Pt.

Key's Gap

LOUDOUN COUNTY

Map by Gene Thorp

To Berryville

Morrisonville

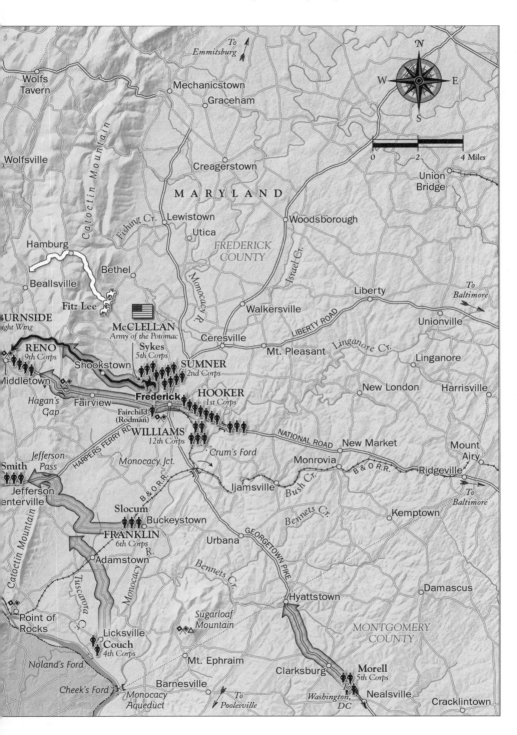

To Emmitsburg

Wolfs Tavern

Mechanicstown

Graceham

N
W E
S

Wolfsville

Creagerstown

Union Bridge

M A R Y L A N D

Catoctin Mountain

0 2 4 Miles

Hamburg

Fishing Cr.

Lewistown

Utica

FREDERICK COUNTY

Israel Cr.

Woodsborough

Liberty

To Baltimore

Bethel

Beallsville

Monocacy R.

Walkersville

Unionville

Fitz Lee

LIBERTY ROAD

BURNSIDE
Right Wing

McCLELLAN
Army of the Potomac

Sykes
5th Corps

Ceresville

Mt. Pleasant

Linganore Cr.

Linganore

RENO
9th Corps

Shookstown

SUMNER
2nd Corps

New London

Harrisville

Middletown

Hagan's Gap

Fairview

Frederick

HOOKER
1st Corps

Fairchild
(Rodman)

NATIONAL ROAD

New Market

Mount Airy

Jefferson Pass

HARPERS FERRY RD

WILLIAMS
12th Corps

Crum's Ford

Monrovia

B & O.R.R.

Ridgeville

Smith

Monocacy Jct.

Bush Cr.

To Baltimore

Jefferson
Centerville

B. & O.R.R.

Ijamsville

Catoctin Mountain

Slocum

Buckeystown

Bennets Cr.

Kemptown

FRANKLIN
6th Corps

Urbana

GEORGETOWN PIKE

R.R.

Monocacy

Adamstown

Bennets Cr.

Damascus

Tuscarora Cr.

Hyattstown

MONTGOMERY COUNTY

Point of Rocks

Licksville

Couch
4th Corps

Sugarloaf Mountain

Mt. Ephraim

Clarksburg

Morell
5th Corps

Noland's Ford

Cheek's Ford

Monocacy Aqueduct

Barnesville

To Poolesville

Washington, DC

Nealsville

Cracklintown

"Send back to hurry up Couch. Mass your troops and carry Burkittsville at any cost." Little Mac informed the Sixth Corps' commander that he anticipated "strong opposition at both passes," probably referring to Fox's and Turner's Gaps, and promised to "hold a reserve in readiness to support" the Sixth Corps if Franklin found the enemy in his front in great force. "Amuse them (the Rebels) as best you can, so as to retain them there," continued the general. "In that event I will probably throw the mass of the army on the pass in front of here. If I carry that, it will clear the way for you, and you must then *follow the enemy as rapidly as possible* [emphasis added]."[18] For the second time that day McClellan had urged the Sixth Corps' commander to press the Rebels with vigor and push through them into Pleasant Valley.

After sending his orders to Franklin, McClellan rode from Middletown to a ridge near the hamlet of Bolivar to observe the fighting. Riding up to Hooker's men as they moved into position that afternoon McClellan called out, "Boys, you have driven the enemy from those hills," referring to Cox's successful assault at Fox's Gap, "and now you must follow them up: yes, boys, follow them up."[19] A *New York Herald* newspaperman who witnessed the scene recounted how these words steeled the men for the task ahead. "From that moment the troops seemed to have been inspirited with new life," he wrote, perhaps a bit theatrically, "for they fought like tigers, and the result was a glorious victory."[20] McClellan then observed both Reno's renewed assault on Fox's Gap to his left and Hooker's attack on the heights overlooking Turner's Gap to the right. "During this contest we could hear heavy thugs of cannon and musketry from Franklin's attack at the Burkittsville pass," noted Col. Strother, who stood with the general on the ridge just east of South Mountain.[21]

The mention of gunfire by Strother indicated that McClellan could hear Franklin finally open his attack on Crampton's Gap at about 3:00 p.m. Advancing the three brigades of Slocum's First Division against the right and center of the

18 Ibid., 46. Regarding the location stamp of "Headquarters Army of the Potomac," the sources make clear that McClellan had already ridden with his staff to Middletown. For example, McClellan sent a message to Franklin from Middletown at 11:45 a.m. also headed "Headquarters Army of the Potomac." See OR 51:1, Sec. 2, 833. Gen. Fitz John Porter also reported to McClellan at Middletown and from that location telegraphed to Halleck at 12:30 p.m. "Am in sight of enemy, with General McClellan." OR 51:1, Sec. 2, 832.

19 *New York Herald*, Sept. 17, 1862.

20 Ibid.

21 Eby, Jr., ed., *A Virginia Yankee*, 107.

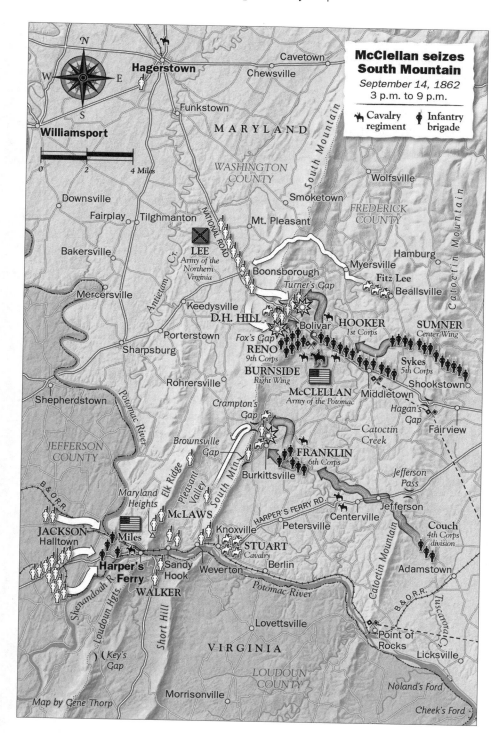

McClellan seizes South Mountain
September 14, 1862
3 p.m. to 9 p.m.

Cavalry regiment · Infantry brigade

Map by Gene Thorp

Confederate position along a stone wall at the base of the gap, the Federals struggled at first to dislodge the Rebel defenders. Soon, however, with the support of two brigades from Baldy Smith's division, the weight of their numbers told, forcing the Confederates to retreat up the east side of the mountain and then over the gap into Pleasant Valley. Slocum's elated men continued their pursuit until darkness finally ended the chase. By nightfall, recalled Franklin after the war, the men of Gen. Slocum's division held both the east and west sides of Crampton's Gap, occupying a position that Franklin later described as "astride of the mountain." Two brigades of Smith's division, the Second Brigade of Brig. Gen. William T. H. Brooks and Third Brigade of Col. William Irwin, held the ridge itself, and the First Brigade under Brig. Gen. Winfield Scott Hancock stationed at the base of the mountain near Burkittsville. As for Darius Couch, elements of his understrength division finally joined Franklin at about 10:00 p.m. following a sixteen mile march from Licksville.[22]

William Franklin and his men had much to celebrate after night fell on September 14. Since dawn, Slocum's division had marched more than fourteen miles, surmounted the Catoctin range, fought a stoutly posted Rebel force, and pursued the fleeing enemy over South Mountain. Yet more tough work lay ahead for Franklin to relieve the Harpers Ferry garrison. Seven miles and a narrow defile between the churning Potomac River and sheer cliffs of Maryland Heights still separated the Sixth Corps from Miles's besieged command. More importantly, Franklin now had to contend with Lafayette McLaws's and Richard H. Anderson's divisions in Pleasant Valley. Although Slocum's attack on Crampton's Gap had wrecked two Rebel brigades, McLaws still possessed eight additional infantry brigades, two cavalry brigades under Jeb Stuart, and ample artillery support to slow or repel any Federal advance. McLaws himself arrived on the west side of Crampton's Gap to assess the situation just as the sun went down on September 14. He rallied the remnants of his two broken brigades and brought up four of his eight remaining brigades to form a solid defensive line on the hills across the 1.5 mile wide Pleasant Valley. The only way Franklin could rescue Miles and his men would be to fight through these veteran Confederate troops.

Darkness had fallen two hours earlier by the time the struggle finally ceased on McClellan's end of the line. Burnside's troops had taken Fox's Gap and seized the heights above Turner's Gap, pushing back both of the Rebel defenders' flanks.

---

22 William B. Franklin, "Notes on Crampton's Gap and Antietam," in Johnson and Buel, eds., *Battles and Leaders*, 2:596.

Although Little Mac had good reason to be optimistic at this point, absolute victory still eluded him. "The question tonight was whether the enemy would retire during the night or reinforce and dispute the pass" wrote Col. Strother, reasoning, "He (Lee) evidently considers the point of great importance, and seems very reluctant to yield it."[23] Assuming the Confederates would hold their position on the following day, McClellan called up troops still working their way toward the front. The Second and Twelfth Corps had spent all of September 14 in a grueling trek over the Catoctins and across the countryside to Middletown. "It was a very hard march" confided a veteran captain with the 108th New York, a part of the Second Corps' Third Division, to his diary at the end of the day.[24]

The long blue column finally returned to the National Road around dusk as the fighting around Turner's and Fox's Gaps raged. Despite the onset of darkness, McClellan directed Sumner to move his army wing into supporting positions along the line of battle, resulting in the men of the two corps stumbling up the steep and rocky mountainside so they could be in position for a resumption of the assault at dawn. "We marched and halted, halted and marched, filed right, filed left, and climbed up the foot of the mountain" wrote Lt. John M. Gould of this exhausting work. "Then we jumped brooks, tumbled through cornfields, and finally halted after midnight, in a field well up in Turner's Gap, having marched, some said ten and some twenty miles. The men were completely played out, and straggled worse than ever they did under Pope."[25]

McClellan, in the meantime, retired a short distance to the rear to rest for the night. Then, sometime between midnight and 1:00 a.m. on September 15, he finally received word of Franklin's success at Crampton's Gap. Dictating a response to his aide-de-camp, Col. George Ruggles, McClellan directed Franklin to "occupy with your command the road from Rohrersville to Harper's Ferry, placing a sufficient force at Rohrersville to hold that position, in case it should be attacked by the enemy from Boonsboro." He then turned to the subject of Harpers Ferry, instructing Franklin to "open communication with Colonel Miles," if he could while "attacking and destroying such of the enemy as you may find in Pleasant Valley. Should you succeed in opening communication with Colonel Miles, direct

23 David. H. Strother, "Personal Recollections of the War. By a Virginian," in *Harper's New Monthly Magazine*, Vol. 36, No. 213 (New York, NY, 1868), 278-279 and Eby, Jr., ed., *A Virginia Yankee*, 107–108.

24 Washburn, *A Complete Military History and Record of the 108th Regiment N. Y. Vols*, 107.

25 Gould, *History of the First-Tenth-Twenty-Ninth Maine Regiment*, 226.

him to join you with his whole command, with all the guns and public property he can carry with him. The remainder of the guns will be spiked or destroyed; the rest of the public property will also be destroyed." Once Franklin had accomplished this, McClellan directed him to "proceed to Boonsboro—which place the commanding general intends to attack tomorrow—and join the main body of the army at that place. Should you find, however, that the enemy has retreated from Boonsboro towards Sharpsburg, you will endeavor to fall upon him and cut of his retreat."[26]

Based on movements undertaken by his command the next morning, it is definite that Franklin received McClellan's overnight instructions. Hancock's brigade and Couch's division marched out of Burkittsville for Crampton's Gap at dawn, while Smith's division shook out skirmishers for a cautious advance toward Harpers Ferry. The roar of heavy artillery fire rolled up the valley as Franklin himself passed through Crampton's Gap at 7:00 a.m. It is here that he first glimpsed McLaws's line of battle. "I had a good view of the enemy's force below," he recalled later, "which seemed to be well posted on hills stretching across the valley."[27] Per McClellan's overnight directive, the general had ordered two of Couch's three brigades three miles north to Rohrersville to guard against the possibility that Lee's force retreating from Boonsboro could attack him on the right flank that morning.

Following this, Franklin pushed Hancock's brigade down the valley to support Smith. Reverberations of cannon fire from Harpers Ferry continued to echo across the landscape as Franklin rode to the western foot of South Mountain. Joining the Second Division's commander to get a closer look at the Rebel line, Franklin and Smith concluded within a short time that "it would be suicidal to attack it." Then the artillery at Harpers Ferry fell silent, prompting Franklin to write McClellan at 8:50 a.m.: "The enemy is drawn up in line of battle about two miles to our front, one Brigade in sight. As soon as I am sure that Rohrersville is occupied I shall move forward to attack the enemy. This may be two hours from now. If Harper's Ferry has fallen, and the cessation of firing makes me fear that it has, it is my opinion that I should be strongly reenforced." Although he did not know it for sure, Franklin correctly suspected that Miles had surrendered. The capitulation took place after Federal officers signaled an intent to negotiate. General Julius White then went out

---

26 *OR* 19:1, 47.

27 Franklin, "Notes on Crampton's Gap and Antietam," 596.

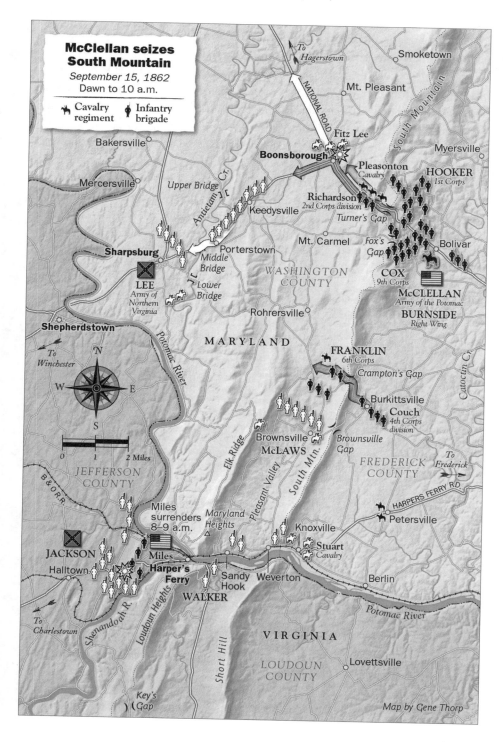

in place of the mortally wounded Miles and met with Jackson between the lines to unconditionally surrender the garrison at 8:00 a.m.[28]

Back at McClellan's headquarters, the general met with Burnside early on the morning of September 15. McClellan wanted the Rhode Islander to stay with him until definitive news came in about Franklin's attack, but as he later recounted, Burnside "begged me to let him go, saying that his corps had been some time in motion, and that if he delayed longer he would have difficulty in overtaking it; so I let him go."[29] McClellan then learned shortly after Burnside's departure that Franklin had seized Crampton's Gap and, better yet, that Lee had withdrawn his force from Fox's and Turner's Gaps. Immediately, Little Mac ordered a pursuit. He instructed Burnside to advance the four divisions of the Ninth Corps—now under the command of Jacob Cox due to the untimely death of Jesse Reno as night fell on September 14—along with Sykes's division, on the road direct to Sharpsburg.

---

28 William Franklin to George McClellan, 8:50 a.m., Sept. 15, 1862, McClellan Papers, LOC Microfilm, Box A79, Reel 31. Multiple sources in addition to Franklin's 8:50 a.m. dispatch provide a general timeframe for Miles's capitulation. The surrender appears to have taken place in stages with the combatants first declaring a ceasefire before the Federals formally capitulated. McClellan wrote Halleck on the morning of Sept. 16, for example, "I learn Miles surrendered 8 a.m. yesterday unconditionally." *OR* 19:2, 307-308. McClellan then repeated this in his post-campaign report: "Colonel Miles surrendered Harper's Ferry at 8 a.m. on the 15th." *OR* 19:1, 48. Captain Russell, the commander of the party that escaped Harpers Ferry overnight on Sept. 13 and later joined Franklin's command in Pleasant Valley, told the Harpers Ferry Military Commission in Oct. 1862, "General Franklin moved his force up through the gap, and formed a line of battle there about 9 o'clock . . . and while we were there in line of battle the firing at Harper's Ferry ceased." *OR* 19:1, 721. William Franklin offered somewhat confusing testimony after the campaign before the congressional Joint Committee on the Conduct of the War: "Early the next morning (Sept. 15) I heard by a messenger who had come from Harper's Ferry that the place had surrendered at nine o'clock the preceding day, I think. We found a dispatch on the field of battle, signed by McLaws, stating that Maryland Heights had been taken, and about eleven o'clock that morning a messenger arrived and informed us that the place had been surrendered. The firing stopped at half-past nine o'clock that morning, which gave us an intimation that the place had surrendered." *JCCW*, 626. Confederate sources suggest a similar period. Captain Henry King of Lafayette McLaws's staff recorded in his diary on Sept. 15, "Returned to H'd Qrs 10 A.M. Glorious! Report from Maryland Hts. that Harper's Ferry has surrendered!!" Helen Trimpi, ed., "Lafayette McLaws' Aide-de-Camp: The Maryland Campaign Diary of Captain Henry Lord Page King" in *Civil War Regiments: A Journal of the American Civil War*, Vol. 6, No. 2 (1998), 36. General McLaws himself recalled after the war, "About 10 A.M. it was telegraphed to me from Maryland Heights that the garrison or troops at Harper's Ferry had hoisted a white flag and had ceased firing." Lafayette McLaws, "The Maryland Campaign: An Address Delivered before the Confederate Veterans Association of Savannah, Ga.," (1896) in McLaws Papers, Collection Number 00472, Folder 30. Southern Historical Collection, The Wilson Library, University of North Carolina at Chapel Hill. Available online at https://finding-aids.lib.unc.edu/00472/.

29 McClellan, *Own Story*, 586.

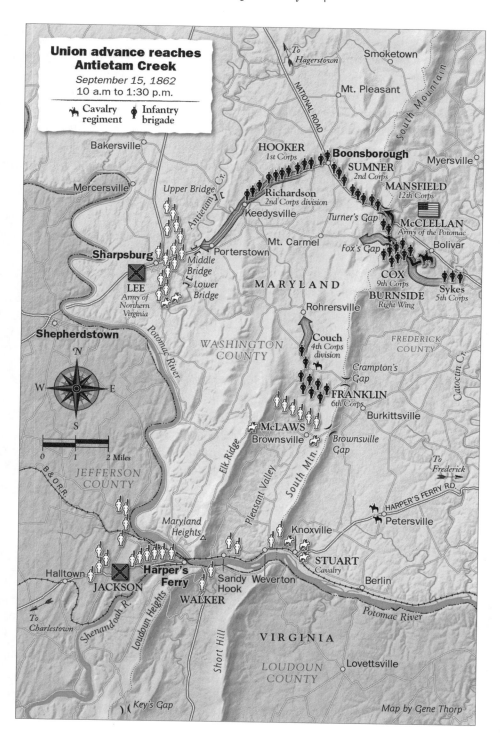

Union advance reaches Antietam Creek
September 15, 1862
10 a.m to 1:30 p.m.

🐎 Cavalry regiment   ⚑ Infantry brigade

To Hagerstown

Smoketown

South Mountain

Mt. Pleasant

Myersville

Bakersville

NATIONAL ROAD

HOOKER
1st Corps

Boonsborough

SUMNER
2nd Corps

MANSFIELD
12th Corps

Mercersville

Upper Bridge

Antietam Cr.

Richardson
2nd Corps division

Keedysville

Turner's Gap

McCLELLAN
Army of the Potomac

Mt. Carmel

Fox's Gap

Bolivar

Sharpsburg

Porterstown

Middle Bridge

Lower Bridge

MARYLAND

COX
9th Corps

Sykes
5th Corps

LEE
Army of Northern Virginia

BURNSIDE
Right Wing

Rohrersville

FREDERICK COUNTY

Shepherdstown

WASHINGTON COUNTY

Couch
4th Corps division

Potomac River

Catoctin Cr.

N
W   E
S

Crampton's Gap

FRANKLIN
6th Corps

Burkittsville

0   1   2 Miles

JEFFERSON COUNTY

McLAWS

Brownsville

Brownsville Gap

To Frederick

Elk Ridge

Pleasant Valley

South Mtn.

HARPER'S FERRY RD.

Maryland Heights

Knoxville

Petersville

B & O R.R.

STUART
Cavalry

Halltown

Harper's Ferry

Sandy Hook

Weverton

Berlin

JACKSON

WALKER

Loudoun Heights

To Charlestown

Shenandoah R.

Short Hill

Potomac River

VIRGINIA

LOUDOUN COUNTY

Lovettsville

Key's Gap

Map by Gene Thorp

Ordering Burnside to stay in contact with Hooker and Sumner on his right, and Franklin on his left, McClellan wanted the Rhode Islander to provide support to either until it could be confirmed that the Confederates did not intend to defend Boonsboro. If the Rebel retreat continued toward the Potomac River, Burnside was to advance via the Old Sharpsburg Road and cut off the enemy's route to safety on the Shepherdstown Pike. "General McClellan desires to impress upon you the necessity for the utmost vigor in your pursuit," read the orders, leaving Burnside no room for interpretation. Another order dictated by Little Mac then directed the First Division (Second Corps) of Maj. Gen. Israel Richardson at 9:30 a.m. to advance on Boonsboro, trailed closely by Hooker's First Corps, and afterward by the balance of Sumner's Second Corps and all of Williams's Twelfth Corps.[30]

Within a short time after issuing these orders, Little Mac learned that, instead of fighting for Boonsboro as expected, Lee had marched his battered force west toward Sharpsburg. McClellan instructed Sumner to "push on after the enemy as rapidly and far as possible, keeping your corps well in hand and doing them all the injury possible."[31] The general then sent an elated message to Henry Halleck confirming his army's victory. "I am happy to inform you that Franklin's success on the left was as complete as that on the center and right," he wrote, resulting "in his getting possession of the Burkittsville Gap, after a severe engagement." Colonel Strother conveyed the delight at headquarters to his diary on September 15, writing, "The morning news has assured us of further success. Franklin has forced the pass at Burkittsville and gangs of Rebel prisoners are occasionally seen passing toward Frederick."[32] Lastly, McClellan wrote Franklin to announce Lee's retreat, informing him that "much is left by the commanding general to your judgment, trusting that you will act promptly and vigorously and complete the success thus far gained."[33]

Rescuing Harpers Ferry still seemed within McClellan's grasp if Franklin could only get through to Col. Miles, but the news coming in soon hinted to the general that all was not as well as it had seemed. First, a telegram from Gov. Curtin

30 OR 51:1, Sec. 2, 834–837. McClellan temporarily attached Richardson's Second Corps division to Hooker's First Corps on the night of September 14. By the time Richardson received McClellan's 9:30 a.m. order, Hooker had already set his division and Pleasonton's cavalry in pursuit of the Confederates down the west side of South Mountain.

31 Ibid.

32 Strother, "Personal Recollections," 108.

33 OR 51:1, Sec. 2, 836.

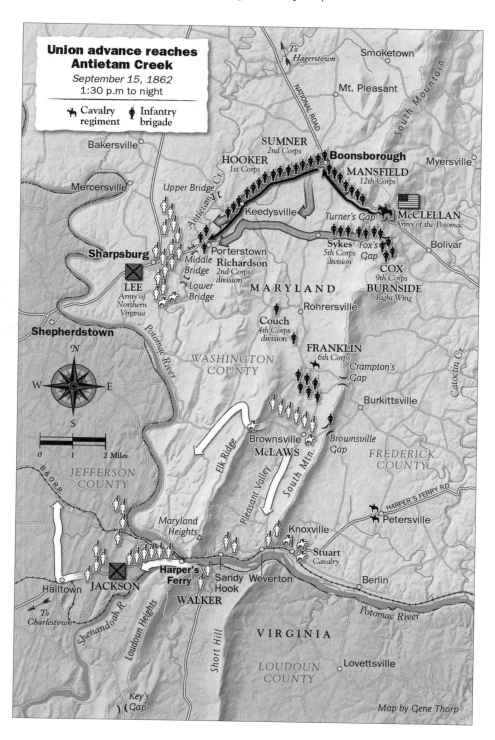

Map by Gene Thorp

announced the glorious news that 1,300 cavalry had escaped from Harpers Ferry overnight. Curtin relayed to McClellan that "fighting has been going on for two days at Harper's Ferry. The enemy occupy Maryland and Loudoun Heights, and were planting their cannon in front of Bolivar Heights all day yesterday." Ominously, though, Curtin then noted that Col. Benjamin Franklin Davis, the leader of the cavalry breakout, "says he thinks Colonel Miles will surrender this morning."[34] General Franklin's 8:50 a.m. dispatch arrived soon after this, reporting that the gunfire at Harpers Ferry had gone quiet and a large Confederate force blocked his path down Pleasant Valley. McClellan, then in Turner's Gap, responded to Franklin at 1:20 p.m. with the assurance the he would instruct Burnside and Sykes to "communicate with you at Rohrersville, and if necessary re-enforce you." Not knowing for certain if Miles had already surrendered, he implored Franklin "to drive in the enemy in your front, but be cautious in doing it until you have some idea of his force." McClellan further directed the Sixth Corps' commander to "closely, but warily" follow up their success so far and "attack whenever you see a fair chance of success."[35]

McClellan got on the road to Boonsboro soon after this, temporarily establishing his headquarters at that place until late in the afternoon when he rode to Keedysville to confer with Joseph Hooker. The First Corps' commander, along with other sources, reported in the afternoon that the Rebels had unexpectedly formed a new, formidable line of battle on the far side of Antietam Creek in front of Sharpsburg. Another dispatch from Franklin timestamped 11:00 a.m. soon followed, informing Little Mac, "The enemy is in large force in my front, in two lines of battle stretching across the valley, and a large column of artillery and infantry on the right of the valley looking toward Harper's Ferry." Franklin claimed that the Rebels, "outnumber me two to one," concluding "it will, of course, not answer to pursue the enemy under these circumstances." The Sixth Corps' commander assured McClellan he would "communicate with Burnside as soon as possible. In the mean time I shall wait here until I learn what is the prospect of re-enforcement. I have not the force to justify an attack on the force I see in front. I have had a very close view of it, and its position is very strong.[36]

Receiving this message must have come as a severe disappointment for George McClellan. Flush with victory and believing he had the enemy on the run, it now

34 *OR* 19:2, 305.

35 *OR* 51:1, Sec. 2, 836.

36 *OR* 19:1, 44.

became evident that Harpers Ferry had fallen. McClellan accordingly dictated a response to Franklin at 4:30 p.m., ordering him to "withdraw the two brigades left at Rohrersville and order them [to] join you, doing your best to hold your position without attacking unless you should see a very favorable opportunity." Then he revealed his thinking on the situation. "It is his (Gen. McClellan's) desire to concentrate everything this evening on the force at or near Sharpsburg, and he will be satisfied if you keep the enemy in your front without anything decisive until the Sharpsburg affair is settled, when he will at once move troops directly to your assistance, and also to endeavor to cut off the enemy in your front."[37]

Confirmation of Miles's surrender finally arrived late in the afternoon. After learning from Franklin that "The enemy (McLaws) has begun to retreat . . . Smith is in pursuit, with a brigade and battery, and will do good service," McClellan read the note's postscript. "I hear from General Smith that the enemy is drawing off through the valley too fast for him."[38] A second message from Franklin timestamped fifteen minutes later then verified what the general had suspected at 8:50 a.m.—that Miles had capitulated: "I send with the guard an aide-de-camp of General J. E. B. Stuart, who says that he was bearing a message from General Jackson to General Lee, at Keedysville; that the white flag was raised at Harper's Ferry this morning at 9.30, and that he was to take possession immediately."[39]

McClellan verified receiving this message at 9:00 p.m. By this time, however, it had also become clear that the belated substantiation of Harpers Ferry's fate had freed Jackson to march to Lee's relief. It remained uncertain if Lee would retreat across the Potomac on the following morning to meet Jackson, or if he would stand in Maryland and call Stonewall to him. All of this became clear after a heavy fog lifted late on the morning of September 16 when the presence of Confederate troops east of Sharpsburg indicated that Lee had gone nowhere, setting the stage for what McClellan would the next day call "the most terrible battle of the war" along Antietam Creek.[40]

37 OR 51:1, Sec. 2, 836.

38 OR 19:2, 296. Message timestamped 3:00 p.m.

39 Ibid.

40 OR 19:2, 312.

Evaluating McClellan's Performance
in Maryland Up to the Battle of Antietam

By the time George McClellan definitively learned of Dixon Miles's surrender on September 15, two days and six hours had passed since he first read Robert E. Lee's plans. And even though the orders had been written four days earlier, McClellan nevertheless gleaned enough information on September 13 to strike the separate columns of Lee's army quickly and with confidence. Reading Special Orders No. 191 may have provided an opportunity to free Miles from Stonewall Jackson's chokehold, but it is questionable if McClellan could have ever really exploited this small window given the handicaps that Henry Halleck placed in his path. McClellan also counted on Miles mounting a determined defense against Jackson in order to buy time for his command, but this is something the aging colonel did not do. Even without a single Confederate blocking his way, Gen. Franklin would have been hard pressed in the thirty-six hours he had available—twenty-one of which were at night—to march his corps twenty miles from Buckeystown, where he had first received McClellan's orders at about 8:00 p.m. on September 13, to Harpers Ferry before Miles surrendered at 8:00 a.m. on September 15. With the Harpers Ferry garrison in his hands, Jackson could move to wherever Lee needed him. By that time the intelligence contained in the Lost Orders had outlived its usefulness.

That his effort to save Harpers Ferry ended in failure must have come as a bitter disappointment for McClellan considering the victories his army had won on September 14. Regrettably, Col. Miles could not be saved, and not because of any failure on McClellan's part. As Maj. Gen. David Hunter, the President of the Harpers Ferry Military Commission, concluded one month later,

Colonel Miles was unfit to conduct so important a defense as that of Harper's Ferry. This Commission would not have dwelt upon this painful subject were it not for the fact that the officer who placed this incapable in command should share in the responsibility, and in the opinion of the Commission Major-General Wool is guilty to this extent of a grave disaster, and should be censured for his conduct. . . . The evidence thus introduced confirms the Commission in the opinion that Harper's Ferry . . . was prematurely surrendered. The garrison should have been satisfied that relief, however long delayed, would come at last, and that 1,000 men killed in Harper's Ferry would have made a small loss had the post been secured.[1]

Citing the testimony of General-in-Chief Halleck, and apparently ready to spread blame for the disaster, the Commission elected to condemn George McClellan as well for moving too slowly to relieve Miles. "Having received orders to repel the enemy invading the State of Maryland," wrote Hunter, McClellan "marched only 6 miles per day on an average when pursuing the invading enemy." To this Hunter added, "The General-in-Chief also testifies that, in his opinion. General McClellan could, and should, have relieved and protected Harper's Ferry, and in this opinion the Commission fully concur."[2]

Did McClellan deserve this censure on the part of the Commission as far as Harpers Ferry was concerned? The evidence presented in this study leads emphatically to the conclusion that he did not. It shows not only that the general marched his army at a faster pace than Halleck testified, it also demonstrates that McClellan designed an attack plan intended to lift the siege of Miles's command as rapidly as possible, and that he repeatedly urged William Franklin to press the enemy as hard as he could. Franklin's inability to break through to Harpers Ferry on September 15 did not result from any oversight on McClellan's part, or even on the part of Franklin himself. Miles simply did not resist for long enough to give Franklin a chance. Even as the Sixth Corps' commander busily moved men into place for an attack on the detached command of Lafayette McLaws, Miles gave out, raising the white flag of capitulation and effectively ending his chance of escaping from the Rebel trap.

McClellan could have succeeded in lifting the siege of Harpers Ferry if Dixon Miles had shown more backbone. As of the hour on September 15 when Miles surrendered, McClellan still believed, based on Miles's own assurance, that he had until September 16 to relieve the garrison. Colonel Miles did not know if the messengers he had sent on Saturday night made it through enemy lines, but he did

1 OR 19:1, 800.

2 Ibid.

hear the roar of battle at Crampton's Gap. To again cite Capt. Russell, in response to a question from Brig. Gen. Julius White concerning the possibility that the fighting at Crampton's Gap could be heard at Harpers Ferry, the captain stated unequivocally, "Yes, sir; unless the cannonading there (at the Ferry) was very great."[3] On September 14, it was not.

Consider on this subject the testimony of Lt. Henry Binney, Col. Miles's aide-de-camp, who told the Commission on October 7, "We heard heavy firing on Sunday [September 14] off in the direction of South Mountain . . . We heard firing on Saturday afternoon, and on Sunday pretty much all day; also on Monday afternoon, after the surrender."[4] The only conclusion one can draw from this is that Dixon Miles experienced a failure of courage at precisely the time when he needed it most. With the rumble of battle north of Harpers Ferry clear for all to hear on September 14, a sound that any military man could reasonably judge represented an effort by McClellan's army to lift the siege, Miles nevertheless elected on the following morning to surrender his post. Blaming George McClellan for this outcome is totally unreasonable when the responsibility for it rested squarely on the shoulders of Dixon Miles, John Wool, Henry Halleck and, of course, the determined and well-led Confederates under Stonewall Jackson.

The thoroughly documented chain of events surrounding McClellan's receipt of the Lost Orders recounted here demands a re-evaluation of the general's performance during the Maryland Campaign. The evidence shows not only that Little Mac did not dawdle upon reading Lee's orders, it also demonstrates that up to that point McClellan had handled his reconstituted army with consummate skill. Even before Lee's orders came to his attention on September 13, McClellan had directed Alfred Pleasonton's cavalry to break through the passes at Catoctin Mountain. He had shepherded the Second Corps through Frederick and begun pushing the Ninth Corps into Middletown Valley after Confederate defenses at Hagan's Gap collapsed at 1:00 p.m. McClellan had also concentrated the strung out First Corps around Frederick in readiness for a renewed advance the next day. Then, once he had Lee's orders in his hands, McClellan issued instructions related directly to the information they contained *before* Pleasonton confirmed the Rebel order of march. Little Mac ordered William Franklin to seize Crampton's Gap and he directed Darius Couch to hurry his division forward at the expense of defending the Potomac crossings.

3 Ibid., 724.

4 Ibid., 586.

When considered within the context of these events a more measured understanding of how the Lost Orders fit into the history of the Maryland Campaign comes into view. By the time they appeared at the Army of the Potomac's headquarters, McClellan had already developed a reasonably good idea that Lee's army occupied positions in Washington County, Maryland, and, from the sound of cannon fire to the southwest, around Harpers Ferry. Intelligence received over the preceding days from the War Department and from Gov. Curtin in Harrisburg also made it clear that Confederate troops had not crossed into Pennsylvania. If anything, columns of Rebel soldiers had been seen crossing back into Virginia at Williamsport, which is why as of September 12 McClellan toyed with the idea of marching directly on Harpers Ferry and cutting through Jefferson County to arrest Lee's theoretical retreat at Winchester.[5] What reading Lee's orders clarified to Little Mac were the movements of the Rebel army, the intentions of its commander, and the fact that the Rebel general had divided his force. McClellan knew there and then that he must strike Lee's force as swiftly as possible and he resolved to do so with Burnside's and Franklin's columns at South Mountain. More important still, he advanced his army and decided to attack Lee despite being hounded by Halleck about the fantastic possibility of a Rebel attack on Washington from Virginia.

The feckless General-in-Chief proved to be a thorn in McClellan's side throughout the campaign in Maryland, admonishing his field commander to stop moving too fast toward Frederick in case Lee slipped his army back south of the Potomac to attack Washington. Halleck's role in slowing McClellan's pursuit of Lee has not been sufficiently acknowledged. Even after McClellan confirmed the presence of Lee's entire army in Maryland and around Harpers Ferry, Halleck admonished McClellan on September 13 for "uncovering the capital," wiring him, "I am of the opinion that the enemy will send a small column toward Pennsylvania to draw your forces in that direction, then suddenly move on Washington with the forces south of the Potomac and those he may cross over."[6]

One day later, as McClellan's army engaged Lee's, Halleck cabled again to warn that "Scouts report a large force still on the Virginia side of the Potomac. If so, I

---

5 "I am beginning to think he [Lee] is making off to get out of the scrape by recrossing the river at Williamsport, in which case my only chance of bagging him will be to cross lower down and cut into his communications near Winchester." George McClellan to Mary Ellen McClellan, 3:00 p.m., Sept. 12, 1862, in McClellan, *Own Story*, 570.

6 OR 19:2, 280.

fear you are exposing your left and rear."[7] And on September 16, with the Army of Northern Virginia gathering at Sharpsburg, Halleck complained to Little Mac, "As you give me no information in regard to the position of your forces, except that at Sharpsburg, of course I cannot advise. I think, however, you will find that the whole force of the enemy in your front has crossed the river. I fear now more than ever that they will recross at Harper's Ferry or below, and turn your left, thus cutting you off from Washington. This has appeared to me to be a part of their plan, and hence my anxiety on the subject."[8] With leadership in Washington this fainthearted nipping at his heels it is remarkable that George McClellan managed to accomplish even what he did.

Little Mac's attack on September 14 did not destroy the Army of Northern Virginia. It did, however, put an end to any immediate plans that Lee might have had for further offensive action in Maryland. The Lost Orders contributed mightily to this outcome by quickening McClellan's resolve to punish Lee's overconfidence. Lee regained his balance at Sharpsburg, but on September 17 McClellan followed up his victory at South Mountain by inflicting so many casualties on the Army of Northern Virginia that he eventually forced Lee to withdraw.[9] This strategic victory shifted the war in the North's favor by allowing Lincoln to issue the preliminary Emancipation Proclamation on September 22. Elevating the abolition of slavery to an equivalent aim alongside restoration of the Union transformed the war into both a moral crusade and a national-political imperative. This outcome never would have materialized had George McClellan, a general with a supposed case of "the slows," as Lincoln once put it, not acted decisively throughout the Maryland Campaign, and with particular aggression in Frederick, Maryland, on September 13, 1862.

---

7 Henry Halleck to George McClellan, 1:00 p.m., Sept. 14, 1862, McClellan Papers, LOC Microfilm, Box A79, Reel 31. The intelligence from the scouts Halleck refers to had a timestamp of Sept. 13, but the date was crossed out and replaced with "14." From the context of the message, Halleck should have known the message was written on Sept. 13. See Operator Gaines to Henry Halleck, 10:10 a.m., Sept. 14, 1862, NA, RG 107, Microfilm Roll 18, No. 60, M473.

8 OR 19:2, 41.

9 For an in depth look at revised Confederate casualties during the Antietam Campaign, see Gene Thorp, "Defending McClellan", *The Washington Post* (Sept. 2012). Available at: https://www.washingtonpost.com/wp-srv/special/artsandliving/civilwar/mcclellan-graphic/.

Telegraphic Communications During the Army of the Potomac's March to South Mountain, September 6–13, 1862

One of the most enduring pieces of misinformation used to mar George McClellan's reputation over the years arose not out of spite or jealousy, but rather from an innocent telegraphic transmission error that remained unnoticed and unchallenged for more than 100 years. This error is of course the "12 M" notation made on McClellan's 12 midnight telegram sent to Abraham Lincoln from Frederick on September 13. Announcing that he held Lee's plans and would send the president "trophies," this message from McClellan arrived at the War Department only 2:35 hours after it had been sent. However, an army telegraphic operator on duty at the time incorrectly recorded the incoming message as being sent more than fourteen hours earlier at "12 M" or noon. As will be explained in detail below, the operator probably made this mistake when he decoded the sent timestamp. Jacob Dolson Cox then noticed the "12 M" time of the message printed in the voluminous *War of the Rebellion: A Compilation of the Official Records of the Union and Confederate Armies* and wrote about it in his 1900 military memoir. Ever since that moment historians and others used the erroneous information to spin grand tales of McClellan's incompetence, basing their narratives on the faulty assumption that timestamps derived from War Department telegrams are infallible. The fact is that some of the timestamps on telegram copies are simply wrong due to human error and those who refuse to accept this do so at the peril of their own professional reputation.

There is no better place for an historian to begin researching the American Civil War than the *Official Records* mentioned above. Besides holding thousands of after-action reports of battles and skirmishes, the *Official Records* contain correspondence between officials at the highest levels of the Union and

Confederate governments. Anyone using this vast collection of documents can read the most intimate and confidential conversations about strategy, intelligence, and orders between Civil War generals, politicians, the presidential cabinet, and even Abraham Lincoln himself. Most of the messages in the *Official Records* were sent by telegram, giving us a raw and unvarnished look at what decision makers understood about their situations at the time.

The telegrams printed in the *Official Records* typically provide the location where the message was written and the specific time it was sent. The telegraphic operator at the receiving end of the line usually marked the time when messages came in, allowing us to see how long it took for each telegram to be transmitted. Sometimes the length of time it took for a message to be received revealed the distance a sender was from a telegraph station as opposed to an indication of trouble with the wires themselves. When officers were in the field, telegram received times usually ran longer because couriers required additional time to deliver each message to the closest operating telegraph station before it could be transmitted. With explicit timestamps and locations, telegrams provide historians an excellent means to establish time benchmarks to assemble and understand the order of any chain of events.

This said, great care must be taken when using telegraph timestamps found in the *Official Records* because they are not always accurate. The only way to certify a timestamp is to review it on the *original* written message and compare it to the later printed version. Copies of many of these original messages can be found on microfilm at the Library of Congress or the National Archives. For some collections, like the McClellan Papers, researchers can now view the microfilm online. If the microfilm is too difficult to read, a researcher can ask to view the original documents in person under the care of an archivist, as we have sometimes needed to do. Unfortunately, great numbers of original messages cannot be found. Many have been permanently lost over time.[1] Some were undoubtedly destroyed during the war, while others probably still exist, but to this day remain in private hands.

---

1 A fire in the 1880s destroyed many of McClellan's personal papers. See Unknown Writer to Ezra Carman, May 27, 1897, NYPL, Carman Correspondence, Box 2, Folder 4. McClellan himself also wrote on Nov. 8, 1881, "The labor of years in the preparation of my memoirs having been destroyed by fire, it remains to recommence the tedious work and replace the loss as best I may." See McClellan, *Own Story*, 27. Our thanks to Tom Clemens for the Carman source.

In 1864, as the Civil War raged on, the War Department began the herculean task of compiling the official reports and correspondence of the U.S. armies, a process that would eventually take sixty-three years to complete.[2] Compilers of the *Official Records* faced a daunting task. More often than not, the officers or officials who sent the telegraphic messages retained their original copies. Locating and collecting all these original telegrams presented a major challenge because it required the compilers to find the thousands of officers and officials who sent the telegrams—many of whom were dead—and once located, to then ask each for permission to access their personal papers. The War Department needed a simpler solution. Compilers therefore decided to use the received telegraphic copies they had on file. This turned out to be no easy task either, as the high-stress environment in the War Department's telegraph room during the war years had left little time for telegrams to be properly filed away. David H. Bates, the manager of that office, recorded the hectic scene: "The operators were fully occupied in the work of transmitting and receiving these messages over the wires, and the cipher operators in translating the more important ones into and out of cipher. There was no time to spare for the task of filing them away in an orderly, careful manner."[3] From this loose collection of War Department telegram receipts, Maj. Albert E. H. Johnson, Secretary of War Edwin Stanton's private secretary, carefully organized and filed the thousands of messages he was able to locate so they could eventually be copied and published in the *Official Records*.[4]

Historians, including the authors of this book, rely heavily on the War Department copies of the original telegrams found in the *Official Records* because they are easily accessible, and, being reduced to print, are easier to read than the handwritten originals. The drawback is that many of these copies cannot be trusted. An example of this issue can be found in the following telegram from George McClellan to Henry Halleck at midnight on September 11, 1862. McClellan's original telegram is clearly timestamped "12 Midnight," whereas the timestamp on the copy of the same telegram in the *Official Records* incorrectly reads "Noon."

To learn how this mistake happened it is first necessary to understand something about telegraphic operations during the Antietam Campaign and how

---

2 For additional background on the compilation of the *Official Records* see https://www.essentialcivilwarcurriculum.com/official-records-of-the-union-and-confederate-armies.

3 David H. Bates, *Lincoln in the Telegraph Office, Recollections of the United States Military Telegraph Corps During the Civil War* (New York, NY, 1907), 47–48.

4 Ibid., 48.

ORIGINAL telegram sent from McClellan's headquarters

The original message is from "Middleburg" with a timestamp of "12 Midnight".

The reproduced message has a location of "Middlebrook" with a timestamp of "12 Noon".

Source: George McClellan to Henry Halleck, 12 Midnight , Sept. 11, 1862, Library of Congress, Manuscript Division, George Brinton McClellan Papers: Letterbooks and Telegram Books, 1852-1862; Aug. 30–Oct. 21, 1862, Box C16, Reel 65.

COPY of McClellan's telegram printed in the *Official Records*

HEADQUARTERS ARMY OF THE POTOMAC,
Middlebrook, Md., *September* 11, 1862—12 noon.
(Received 3.45 a. m., September 12.)

Major-General HALLECK :

I was informed by Mr. Garrett, president of the Baltimore and Ohio Railroad, previous to leaving Washington, that he could transport 28,000 infantry in one day in the cars under his control. In view of this, and the importance of having General Porter's command join me soon, I would suggest that it be sent by rail to Frederick. By this means it

George McClellan to Henry Halleck, Sept. 11, 1862, *OR* 19:2, 252

the process of sending and receiving telegrams worked. Quick communication from Washington to the outside world was vital for Lincoln and his military commanders. In the fall of 1862, only two telegraph lines connected the capital city to the rest of the Union. Both of these lines ran north out of the district. The first followed the country's oldest telegraph line northeast to Baltimore, and beyond, along the Baltimore and Ohio Railroad. As long as this line remained open, Lincoln could communicate with the rest of the northern states.

The U.S. Army built the second telegraph line in late 1861 to keep Union commanders apprised of Confederate activity along the Potomac River. This line ran out of Washington—likely along Seventh Street—to Leesboro, Maryland. From there, the line turned west to Rockville, where it left the pike and continued along the rough road through Darnestown to Poolesville. Spurs off of this route went to Great Falls and Edwards' Ferry. From Poolesville, the line followed roads north to Hyattstown where the telegraph line returned to the Georgetown Pike and followed it northwest through Urbana and over the Monocacy River to the railroad

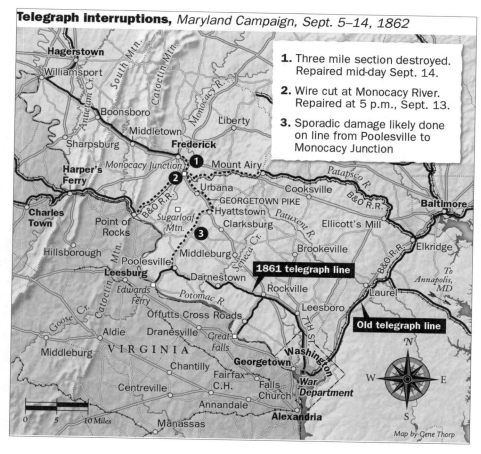

Telegraph interruptions, *Maryland Campaign, Sept. 5–14, 1862*

1. Three mile section destroyed. Repaired mid-day Sept. 14.

2. Wire cut at Monocacy River. Repaired at 5 p.m., Sept. 13.

3. Sporadic damage likely done on line from Poolesville to Monocacy Junction

Map by Gene Thorp

tracks at Monocacy Junction.[5] At this point, the telegraph line split in three directions. One line followed the B&O Railroad due east to Baltimore. Another line followed the B&O Railroad southwest to Point of Rocks, Harpers Ferry, and west into western Virginia and Ohio. The third hugged the short B&O Railroad spur north into Frederick City, then followed the National Pike to Williamsport, Hagerstown, and beyond. When Lee's army entered Maryland in 1862 it temporarily disrupted this carefully laid network.

On the night of September 4, Confederate forces began crossing the Potomac into Maryland, and over the next week they occupied Frederick and the surrounding area. They cut the main telegraph line over the Monocacy River and

5 William R. Plum, *The Military Telegraph During the Civil War in the United States* (Chicago, IL, 1882), 82–84 and 230.

completely destroyed the three mile long spur into the city. Near the Monocacy they made a small break in the line and skillfully concealed it to give the impression the line was still intact on that section. Sporadic damage may also have been done on the line from Poolesville to Monocacy Junction as J. E. B. Stuart's cavalry worked their way north from the Potomac River to Urbana. This appears to be the extent of damage to the telegraph line between Washington and Frederick during the occupation.

On September 7, the day after the Confederates first set foot in Frederick, George McClellan left the capitol to set up his headquarters on the newly developing front. He wrote to his wife at 2:30 p.m., "I shall go to Rockville tonight and start out after the rebels tomorrow."[6] Rockville lay along the macadamized (paved) Georgetown to Frederick Pike, the most direct route from Washington to Lee. Conveniently located where the telegraph line to Frederick crossed the pike, Rockville provided a central location where McClellan could be in close proximity to all three of his advancing army wings while at the same time he retained direct contact with the War Department by telegraph.

During his four day stay there, McClellan sent and received a flurry of telegrams. A review of those sent from Rockville on September 11 show that messages traveling over fully functional wires took between 20 and 75 minutes to be received by the War Department. Singling out two of these telegrams provides an example of a typical timestamp error made later in the day. The first message is from McClellan to Halleck with a location stamp of "Rockville" and a timestamp of "12 M" (noon) requesting the General-in-Chief to "Please order Peck's division, upon its arrival, to proceed at once to Rockville, where it will find orders for its further movements."[7] Halleck responded to this request an hour later, wiring McClellan, "Peck's division will not be here for some days. Weber's troops will be sent forward as soon as they can get transportation. Why not order forward Porter's corps, or Sigel's? If the main force of the enemy is in your front, more troops can be spared from here."[8]

The second message is also to Halleck from McClellan. Stamped "Rockville" and "3:45 p.m.," it asked for the general to "Please send forward all the troops you can spare from Washington, particularly Porter's, Heintzelman's, Sigel's and all the other old troops . . . General Banks reports 72,000 troops in and about

6 McClellan, *Own Story*, 569.

7 OR 19:2, 253. The War Department received this message 20 minutes later at 12:20 p.m.

8 Ibid.

Telegram transmission times from McClellan's headquarters in the field to the War Department, Sept. 11, 1862

Headquarters location	Time sent	Time received	Transmission time	Telegram number*
Rockville	9:45 a.m.	10:15 a.m.	30 minutes	No. 290
Rockville	10:45 a.m.	12 p.m.	1:15 hours	No. 291
Rockville	12 p.m.	12:20 p.m.	20 minutes	No. 292
Rockville	3:45 p.m.	4:25 p.m.	40 minutes	No. 293
Middleburg	11 p.m.	4 a.m., Sept. 12	5 hours	No. 297
Middleburg	11:15 p.m.†	3:55 a.m., Sept. 12	4:40 hours	No. 296
Middleburg	11:30 p.m.	3:45 a.m., Sept. 12	4:15 hours	No. 294
Middleburg	12 a.m.	3:45 a.m., Sept. 12	3:45 hours	No. 295

*All telegram sent and received times are from the National Archives and Records Administration, Record Group 107, Records of the Office of the Secretary of War, Microfilm Publication M473, Roll 50.

†No sent time is listed on this telegram. The content of the telegram strongly implies it was sent shortly after 11 p.m. The 11:15 p.m. time is the author's estimated sent time.

Washington. I will move my headquarters immediately."[9] Shortly after sending this telegram, McClellan got on the road. Col. Strother wrote in his diary of that day, "we moved about four o'clock across the fields to the Frederick road" and McClellan's staff followed the turnpike for nine miles to "a little meadow near the Seneca" at a place shown on period maps as Middlebrook or Middleburg.[10] Now at his new headquarters, McClellan resumed sending messages at 7:00 p.m. He wired at least ten of these telegrams before midnight, with six going to his field commanders and four to Washington. All ten messages bore the location heading "Middleburg."

McClellan's headquarters sat at the center of a 17 mile long stretch of the Georgetown Turnpike where no telegraphic wire had been strung. According to their timestamps, the four telegrams he sent from Middleburg to the War Department took between 3.5 and 5 hours to be received, underscoring that it took couriers three hours to carry each message back to Rockville, then the same 20 minutes to 2 hours to get them through the wires to the War Department. Before midnight, McClellan received a much-anticipated response from President Lincoln, who had approved sending reinforcements, informing the general that Porter "is ordered to-night to join you as quickly as possible." A second message from Halleck arrived after this confirming that, "General Fitz John Porter's corps

9 Ibid.

10 Eby, Jr., ed., *A Virginia Yankee*, 104.

Original telegram sent telegram from McClellan's headquarters,
September 11, 1862, 12 Midnight

has been ordered to move to-morrow to Brookville, via Leesborough, to report to you for duty in the field."[11] These two telegrams answered McClellan's noon and 3:45 p.m. telegrams sent earlier in the day. At 11:30 p.m., McClellan replied to Halleck, "I am much obliged to you for sending me Porter's corps, and should like the remainder of Keyes' corps (Peck's division) as soon as possible. I shall follow up the rebels as rapidly as possible."[12] Thirty minutes later, at midnight, McClellan again wrote to Halleck, this time with a suggestion for getting Porter's Fifth Corps to the front more quickly. Stating he "was informed by Mr. Garrett, president of the Baltimore and Ohio Railroad, previous to leaving Washington, that he could transport 28,000 infantry in one day in the cars under his control," McClellan continued, "In view of this, and the importance of having General Porter's command join me soon, I would suggest that it be sent by rail to Frederick. By this means it would reach me two days earlier than by making the overland march, and would be fresh on its arrival. Porter's trains might come by land."[13]

Both the "12 Midnight" timestamp on this last telegram and the "Middleburg" location stamp are accurate, and, judging by the content of this last message, it is clear that the midnight message concluded the sequence of telegrams between McClellan, Halleck, and Lincoln on September 11. What makes this last document so interesting is that both Halleck's received copy of the telegram and the War Department copy have a timestamp of "12 M," which means meridian, or noon. The noon timestamp makes no sense, however, since McClellan had already sent a different telegram to Halleck at noon that day. No one would send two separate telegrams to the same person at that same time. Furthermore, at noon McClellan had not yet left for Middleburg, so how did this "12 M" mistake happen?

When McClellan handed the midnight message over to one of his three telegraphic operators, either A. H. Caldwell, Jesse H. Bunnell or J. H. Emerick, the man put it into cipher and transmitted it from headquarters.[14] Putting a message into cipher involved four primary steps:

1.) Rearranging the words of the message according to a common key held by operators at both ends of the line.

11 OR 19:2, 254–255.

12 Ibid., 254.

13 Ibid., 255.

14 Plum, *The Military Telegraph*, 232.

When telegrams were put into cipher the timestamps were changed to code words. In Cipher Key Number Nine shown below, 12 a.m. would be converted to the word Gertrude, while 12 p.m. would be written as Mary.

CIPHER NUMBER NINE COMPLETE.

A. M.   **TIME**

Ann 1.30, Agnes 2.30, Anna 3.30, Amelia 4.30, Alice 5.30, Betsy 6.30, Barney 7.30, Barbara 8.30, Cora 9.30, Clara 10.30, Catherine 11.30, Clotilda 1, Delia 2, Deborah 3, Dorothy 4, Emma 5, Eugenia 6, Emily 7, Elizabeth 8, Fanny 9, Florence 10, Frances 11, Gertrude 12.

P. M.

Harriet 1, Hannah 2, Helen 3, Henrietta 4, Imogen 5, Jennie 6, Julia 7, Katy 8, Lucy 9, Laura 10, Libby 11, Mary 12, Martha 1:30, Minnie 2:30, Nancy 3:30, Nelly 4:30, Rosalie 5:30, Rosetta 6:30, Rebecca 7:30, Reliance 8:30, Sarah 9:30, Susan 10:30, Topsy 11:30, Viola 12:30.

MESSAGE OR DIVISION OF THREE LINES—COMMENCEMENT WORDS:

| Army, Anson, Action, | Five columns. | Astor, Advance, Artillery, | Six columns. | Anderson, Ambush, Agree, | Four columns. |

Six Column Route: Up the fourth column, down the third, up the second, down the first, up the fifth, down the sixth.

Four Column Route: Down the first, down the fourth, down the second, up the third.

Five Column Route: Up the second, up the third, up the fourth, down the first, down the fifth.

MESSAGE OR DIVISION OF FOUR LINES—COMMENCEMENT WORDS:

| Battle, Boston, Blair, | Six columns. | Banks, Board, Battery, | Four columns. | Brigade, Beverly, Bates, | Five columns. |

Six Column Route: Up the fifth column, down the fourth, up the sixth, down the third, up the second, down the first.

Four Column Route: Up the second, down the first, up the third, down the fourth.

Five Column Route: Up the third, up the fifth, up the first, up the fourth, up the second.

Source: William R. Plum, The Military Telegraph During the Civil War in the United States (Chicago, IL, 1882), 370.

2.) Adding random nonsensical words to the message.

3.) Replacing sensitive names with code words. For instance, using cipher key number nine, "Lincoln" became the code word "Adam" and "McClellan" became the code word "Axis"[15]

4.) Replacing times, including the timestamp, with code words. Again, referencing cipher key number nine, "noon" became the code word "Mary" and "Midnight" became the code word "Gertrude."

Once McClellan's message had been transcribed in cipher it no longer read "12 Midnight." Instead, the word "Gertrude" stood in for the timestamp received at the War Department.

A little more than 3.5 hours after McClellan finished his midnight message (three hours for the courier to deliver the message to the Rockville station and thirty minutes for the message to be transmitted), one of the four operators at the War Department in Washington received and translated the message from cipher. This would have been done by either Albert B. Chandler, Charles A. Tinker, David H. Bates, or Frank Stewart.[16] One of these four operators used his matching cipher key and a seven-column worksheet to put the words back in the correct order, discard the nonsensical words, and convert the code words back into their original names and times. With McClellan's September 11, "12 Midnight" telegram, however, an operator made a critical mistake translating the ciphered timestamp. Either one of McClellan's three operators in Middleburg had used the wrong code for the timestamp from the cipher key, the cipher keys for the time-related code words did not match between the two locations, or, most likely, one of the War Department operators made a simple mistake translating the coded timestamp back into the original time. Cipher keys changed frequently throughout the war and it is possible during this confusing time when multiple armies were being fused into one that the cipher key used by the War Department was slightly different than that being used in the field by the Army of the Potomac, so perhaps the operator thought "Gertrude" meant noon instead of midnight. Whatever the reason, the mistake on this telegram remained unnoticed for more than 150 years.

---

15 For a complete version of Cipher Key Nine, see Ibid., 370–377.

16 The *Brooklyn Daily Eagle*, Jul. 22, 1894. "Their day began at 8 o'clock, but often lasted until 2 or 3 o'clock the following morning" This is generally the timeframe in which McClellan sent his telegrams.

Original sent telegram from McClellan's headquarters
Correct timestamp is "12 Midnight"

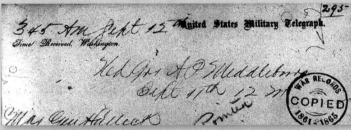

Source: George McClellan to Henry Halleck, 12 Midnight , Sept. 11, 1862, Library of Congress, Manuscript Division, George Brinton McClellan Papers: Letterbooks and Telegram Books, 1852-1862; Aug. 30–Oct. 21, 1862, Box C16, Reel 65.

Halleck's received copy of McClellan's telegram
Timestamp has changed from "12 Midnight" to a garbled "12 M"

George McClellan to Henry Halleck, National Archives and Records Administration, Halleck Papers, Record Group 94, Entry 159N, Vol. 17, No. 1445

War Department's copy of McClellan's telegram
Timestamp had changed from "12 Midnight" to "12 M"

George McClellan to Henry Halleck, Sept. 11, 1862, National Archives and Records Administration, Record Group 107, Records of the Office of the Secretary of War, Microfilm Publication M473, Roll 50, No. 295

Copy of McClellan's telegram printed in the Official Records
Timestamp has changed from "12 Midnight" to "12 Noon"

> HEADQUARTERS ARMY OF THE POTOMAC,
> *Middlebrook, Md., September* 11, 1862—12 noon.
> (Received 3.45 a. m., September 12.)
>
> Major-General HALLECK:
>
> I was informed by Mr. Garrett, president of the Baltimore and Ohio Railroad, previous to leaving Washington, that he could transport 28,000 infantry in one day in the cars under his control. In view of this, and the importance of having General Porter's command join me soon, I would suggest that it be sent by rail to Frederick. By this means it would reach me two days earlier than by making the overland march, and would be fresh on its arrival. Porter's trains might come by land.
>
> GEO. B. McCLELLAN,
> *Major-General.*

George McClellan to Henry Halleck, Sept. 11, 1862, *OR* 19:2, 252

When prioritizing the message for Gen. Halleck, the War Department operator rewrote the telegram with the incorrect sent time from the worksheet on to a new piece of paper with War Department letterhead. This telegram can be found in the Halleck Papers at the National Archives.[17] The operator then made a file copy and at least one carbon copy of the file copy.[18] After the war, when the compilers of the *Official Records* did not have access to either McClellan's original copy or Halleck's received copy because both were still in the possession of their owners, they used the next best thing, the War Department's carbon copy of Halleck's file copy. When the compilers finished copying the telegram they placed a "War Records" stamp in the upper right corner of the document which can clearly be seen today. However, they did not copy the information verbatim, they changed the timestamp of "12 M" to "Noon." Every copy of the *Official Records* printed since then—both in paper and digital format—contains this timestamp error.

Ttimestamp mistakes like this were not unique. Exactly the same mistaken "12 Midnight" to "12 M" error happened again only two days later with McClellan's "trophies" telegram. We know that Operator Bickford at Monocacy Junction reconnected the wire from Washington to the Point of Rocks station at 5:00 p.m., and that afterward McClellan received a message directly from Lincoln through a telegraphic operator that read, "Sir; the telegraph line is open to Point of Rocks. The President is at the War Department Office and anxious to hear from you." The same source shows that Lincoln's message reached McClellan "from Point of Rocks via Sugar Loaf Mountain."[19] Chief Signal Officer, Maj. Albert Myer, further confirmed in his report on October 6, 1862, stating, "In the evening [of September 13] a message was received from Washington, transmitted through the signal station at Point of Rocks, from the President of the United States to General McClellan. A reply was in the same manner returned."[20]

As the analysis in Chapter 4 of this study makes clear, the content of McClellan's midnight telegram provides clues about when it was sent. It states, for example, that he had possession of the Catoctin Mountain range, when at noon he

---

17 NA, RG 94, Entry 159N, Vol. 7, No. 1445.

18 NA, RG 107, Microcopy 473, Roll 50, No. 295.

19 NA, RG 111 "Records of the Office of the Chief Signal Officer, 1860-1982," 111.2.1 Correspondence, Messages Sent and Received, Jan. 1862–May 1863; Jan–Dec 1864, 3 Vols., Entry 13. The next entry is McClellan's "trophies" message. Our thanks to Jim Rosebrock via Scott Hartwig for the source.

20 OR 19:1, 120.

Original sent telegram from McClellan's headquarters
McClellan's original telegram has never been located.

Lincoln's received copy of McClellan's telegram
The timestamp is "12 Midnight".

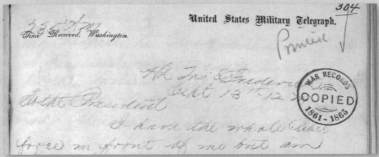

Source: George McClellan to Abraham Lincoln, 12 Midnight , Sept. 13, 1862, No. 18408, The Abraham Lincoln Papers at the Library of Congress, Series 1. General Correspondence. 1833-1916. Series 1. General Correspondence. 1833-1916.

The War Department's received copy of McClellan's telegram
The timestamp had changed from "12 Midnight" to "12 M".

National Archives, Series: Generals' Papers and Books, compiled 1830 - 1884 HMS Entry Number(s): PI17 159A PI17 159AA, Record Group 94: Records of the Adjutant General's Office, 1762 - 1984

Copy of McClellan's Sept. 13 telegram printed in the Official Records
The timestamp reflects the War Department carbon copy, not Lincoln's accurate recevied copy.

> HEADQUARTERS, *Frederick, September* 13, 1862—12 m.
> (Received 2.35 a. m., September 14.)
> To the PRESIDENT:
>   I have the whole rebel force in front of me, but am confident, and no time shall be lost. I have a difficult task to perform, but with God's blessing will accomplish it. I think Lee has made a gross mistake, and that he will be severely punished for it. The army is in motion as rapidly as possible. I hope for a great success if the plans of the rebels remain unchanged. We have possession of Catoctin. I have all the plans of the rebels, and will catch them in their own trap if my men

George McClellan to Abraham Lincoln, Sept. 13, 1862, *OR* 19:2, 281 did not. For six hours Pleasonton had been fighting for the gap and his last message to McClellan before noon indicated the difficulty he was having in driving the Confederates from their position. McClellan also repeated the appeal he had made fifteen minutes earlier to Gov. Curtin, and three hours earlier to Halleck, to concentrate Pennsylvania's militia forces at Chambersburg. Beyond the telegram's contents and timestamp, at least eight primary sources, many of which are recounted in Chapter 3, show that the Twelfth Corps did not halt until about noon, meaning Lee's lost orders could not have been found until after that time.

McClellan sent his return telegram "from Gen. McClellan's Hd. Qrs. at Frederick, Md by Signal from Point of Rocks via, Sugar Loaf Mountain" and the War Department received it 2:35 hours later on September 14.[21] Judging by the telegraphic operator's handwriting, the same person who had misinterpreted the timestamp coding of McClellan's midnight letter to Halleck two nights earlier, again incorrectly interpreted the same code word for midnight as noon.

At the top of a 7 column worksheet used to decode the received telegram, the operator wrote the timestamp in error as "12 M." From that worksheet a clean copy was made for Lincoln, also with the wrong timestamp of "12 M."After sending off Lincoln's copy, the operator took out two pieces of paper with the War Department heading and placed a piece of carbon paper between them. He then re-copied the telegram from the worksheet, still with the incorrect timestamp, sending the top copy to Secretary of State Seward and retaining the bottom copy for the War Department's records.[22] Yet unlike the September 11 midnight telegram to Halleck, it appears someone corrected the timestamp on the stcopy sent to President Lincoln.[23] Who had the authority to make such a change on the president's personal copy? In a *Washington Post* online debate in 2012, Stephen W. Sears, the loudest modern advocate of the noon "trophies" telegram theory, conjectured that "some unknowing civilian clerk organizing the Lincoln Papers" who was "ignorant of military telegraph usage" made the change. Before giving serious consideration to a view which fails to consider that the clerk, or whomever, altered the document at the time, the history of Lincoln's personal papers needs to be closely reviewed.

21 NA, RG 111, Vol. 1, Entry 13.

22 NA, RG 94, Vol. 7, Entry 304–305.

23 George McClellan to Abraham Lincoln, Sept. 13, 1862, Lincoln Papers, LOC, Ser. 1: 18408 and George McClellan to Abraham Lincoln, Sept. 13, 1862, NA, RG 107, No. 295.

Judging by the handwriting samples below, both McClellan's midnight September 11 telegram to Henry Halleck and his midnight September 13 telegram to Abraham Lincoln appear to have been received and recorded by the same telegraph operator at the War Department. In the numbered examples below note how the operator writes the same characters identically in each telegram receipt.

Halleck's received copy of McClellan's September 11, 1862 midnight telegram

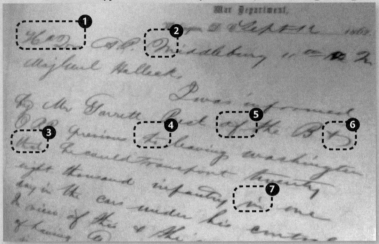

George McClellan to Henry Halleck, National Archives and Records Administration, Halleck Papers, Record Group 94, Entry 159N, Vol. 17, No. 1445

Lincoln's received copy of McClellan's September 13, 1862 midnight telegram

George McClellan to Abraham Lincoln, 12 Midnight, Sept. 13, 1862, The Abraham Lincoln Papers at the Library of Congress, Series 1. General Correspondence. 1833-1916. Series 1. General Correspondence. 1833-1916.

Lincoln's copy of the "trophies" telegram, along with thousands of his other papers, remained in Lincoln's possession until his assassination on April 15, 1865. Within two weeks, all of his papers had been sequestered.[24] Deeply concerned that some of Lincoln's papers "would be damaging to men now living," Lincoln's oldest son Robert asked trusted friend, Associate Judge David Davis, on April 27 to administer his father's estate. Within two weeks, Judge Davis had Lincoln's trusted personal secretaries, John Nicolay and John Hay, pack up the papers and secure them in a vault at the National Bank in Bloomington, Illinois. From a letter Robert wrote a few weeks later it is clear that "the papers relating to the Administration" were "in such a confused state" that they could not then "be got at." The papers then remained in the vault until 1874, when they were sent to Nicolay in Washington for use in producing Lincoln's authorized biography. The papers were still in the custody of Nicolay upon his death in 1901, after which, under Hay's supervision, they were moved to the Department of State.[25]

When Hay died four years later, Robert Lincoln retrieved the papers and held them under lock and key in Chicago until his retirement, after which they traveled with him between Washington, DC, in the winter, and Manchester, Vermont, in the summer. In 1919, Robert secretly moved the papers to the Library of Congress under the condition that their presence there not be disclosed. Then, a few years later, he formally conveyed them to the library by a deed of gift with the stipulation that they should be kept from "official or public inspection or private view" until 21 years after his death. Robert Lincoln died on July 26, 1926, and exactly 21 years later, in 1947, officials at the library opened the papers to the public. During his life, and for years after his death, Robert Lincoln did not let anyone except his father's two most trusted aides review the papers.[26] Taking this into consideration, it would seem impossible that Robert or Lincoln's former secretaries would ever allow someone of the character described by Mr. Sears to access Lincoln's unorganized papers, much less be given the sanction to write directly on them. The far simpler explanation is that immediately upon receiving McClellan's "trophies" telegram, Lincoln added "idnight" to the "12 M" himself. Only a few hours earlier, Lincoln had been at the War Department office anxious to hear from McClellan. When McClellan's response eventually came in at 2:35 a.m., Lincoln knew that the reply

24 About the Lincoln Papers collection (https://memory.loc.gov/ammem/alhtml/alabout.html)

25 Ibid.

26 Ibid.

timestamped "12 M" was wrong because he had not requested an update from McClellan until hours after that time in the evening. He then added "idnight" himself to correct the timestamp for his own use.

These examples of two telegraphic transcription errors in only two days emphasize the need for historians to be critical of the sent timestamps shown on telegrams if they come from anywhere other than the original source, especially when the contents of a message seem out of context. Although innocently created, the incorrect "12 M" timestamp has been used by authors ever since Jacob Cox to misinform generations about McClellan's performance during the Maryland Campaign. Rather than question when the "trophies" telegram might have been sent based on an analysis of its content and surrounding events, too many authors have chosen instead to twist their narratives into a timeline that relies on the message being sent at noon. In the process they have ignored, dismissed, renounced, or misquoted the vast array of readily available primary accounts that show otherwise. Thankfully, a new era of Civil War scholarship is evolving which provides a more balanced appraisal of George McClellan based on the fact that he sent his "trophies" telegram at midnight on September 13 and not at noon.

Army of the Potomac Strength
on September 10, 1862

Chart appears on the facing page

Army of the Potomac strength, September 10, 1862

On Sept. 10 Gen. McClellan had an estimated 86,000 men under his immediate control for operations against the Confederate army at Frederick, Maryland. No contemporay reports exist that reveal the size of McClellan's army from the time he was put in command of Washington's defenses on Sept. 2, 1862, until the Army of the Potomac's consolidated report of Sept. 20, 1862.

McClellan's estimated strength for Sept. 10 is reached by adding all Union casualties received during the Antietam Campaign to the consolidated report of Sept. 20, 1862, then subtracting those units which would not have reached McClellan by Sept. 10.

		Aggregate present for duty, Sept. 20[1]	Casualties Sept. 3–20[2]	Total after casualties returned	Troops not with AoP Sept. 10	Army of the Potomac Sept. 10
McClellan	HQ	1,393		1,393		1,393
Meade	1st Corps	12,237	+3,552	15,789		15,789
Sumner	2nd Corps	13,604	+5,209	18,813	-2,300[3]	16,513
Couch	4th Corps Div.	7,219	+9	7,228	-953[4]	6,275
Porter	5th Corps	19,477	+476	19,953	-14,433[5]	5,520
Franklin	6th Corps	11,862	+971	12,833		12,833
Reno	9th Corps	10,734	+3,151	13,885	-1,963[6]	11,922
Williams	12th Corps	8,383	+1,743	10,126		10,126
Pleasonton	Cavalry Div.	4,543	+109	4,652		4,652
Allen	Frederick	1,110		1,110		1,110
Kenly	Williamsport	2,269			-2,269[7]	0
Scott	Boonsborough	318		318		318
TOTAL		**90,880**	**+15,220**	**106,100**	**-19,649**	**86,451**

[1] *Statement showing the number of men composing the Army of the Potomac on the 20th day of September, 1862.* O.R. Ser. 1, Vol. 19, Pt. 2, Ser. 28, p. 336

[2] Casualties from Sept. 29, 1862 report, *Statement of Casualties in the Army of the Potomac September 3-20, 1862, inclusive,* at O.R. Ser. 1, Vol. 19, Pt. 1, Ser. 27, p. 36

[3] Weber's brigade arrived in Washington, D.C. on Sept. 9, 1862 and did not reach McClellan until the evening of Sept. 16, 1862. They had an estiated 2,300 men. Seville, William P., History of the First Regiment, Delaware Volunteers, (Wilmington: The Historical Society of Delaware, 1884), p. 47, O.R. Ser. 1, Vol. 18, Ser. 26, p. 389

[4] 139th Pennsylvania Infantry had 953 men and did not join McClellan until Sept. 17. Strength: O.R. Ser. 3, Vol. 3, Ser. 124, p. 759, Arrival time: Bates, Samuel P., History of Pennsylvania Volunteers, 1861–5; Vol. IV, (Harrisburg: B. Singerly, State Printer, 1870), p. 378.

[5] Only Sykes' division was with McClellan on Sept. 10, 1862. A report of Sept. 6, shows he had 3,820 troops at that time. Morell's division did not reach McClellan until the evening of Sept. 16, 1862. A report of Sept. 6, shows Morell had 5,256 troops at that time not including Piatt's brigade. Before the division marched to join McClellan on Sept. 12, 1862, Piatt's brigade was detached, and the 118th Pennsylvania (1,016 men), 20th Maine, (961 men), and 2nd District of Columbia, (more than 600 men), were added. Sykes and Morell's division strength, O.R. Ser. 1, Vol. 19, Pt. 2, Ser. 28, p. 195, 118th Pennsylvania strength; O.R. Ser. 3, Vol. 3, Ser. 124, p. 759, 20th Maine strength; O.R. Ser. 3, Vol. 3, Ser. 124, p. 771. 2nd District of Columbia strength; Washington Evening Star, Aug. 27, 1862.

[6] 16th Connecticut Infantry, 999 men. Strength: O.R. Ser. 3, Vol. 3, Ser. 124, p. 203, The regiment reached McClellan on Sept. 16, Blakeslee, B. F., History of the Sixteenth Connecticut Volunteers, (Hartford: The Case, Lockwood & Brainard Co., Printers, 1875), p. 11, 9th New Hampshire Infantry, 964 men, O.R. Ser. 3, Vol. 3, Ser. 124, p. 779, The regiment reached McClellan on Sept. 13, Lord, Edward O., Ed. History of the Ninth Regiment New Hampshire Volunteers in The War of The Rebellion (Concord, N.H.: Republican Press Association, 1895), p. 56

[7] Kenly's brigade did not leave Baltimore until Sept. 18, 1862. O.R. Ser. 1, Vol. 19, Pt. 2, Ser. 28, p. 312.

Appendix C

Special Orders No. 191
Hd. Qrs. Army of Northern Va., Sept. 9, 1862

I. The citizens of Fredericktown being unwilling, while overrun by members of this army, to open their stores, in order to give them confidence, and to secure to officers and men purchasing supplies for benefit of this command, all officers and men of this army are strictly prohibited from visiting Fredericktown except on business, in which case they will bear evidence of this in writing from division commanders. The provost-marshal in Fredericktown will see that his guard rigidly enforces this order.

II. Major Taylor will proceed to Leesburg Va., and arrange for transportation of the sick and those unable to walk to Winchester, securing the transportation of the country for this purpose. The route between this and Culpepper Court-House east of the mountains will no longer be travelled. Those on the way to this army already across the river will move up promptly; all others will proceed to Winchester collectively and under command of officers, at which point, being the general depot of this army, its movements will be known and instructions given by the commanding officer regulating further movements.

III. The army will resume its march to-morrow, taking the Hagerstown road. General Jackson's command will form the advance and, after passing Middletown, with such portions as he may select, take the route toward Sharpsburg, cross the Potomac at the most convenient point, and by Friday morning take possession of the Baltimore and Ohio Railroad, capture such of the enemy as may be at Martinsburg, and intercept such as may attempt to escape from Harper's Ferry.

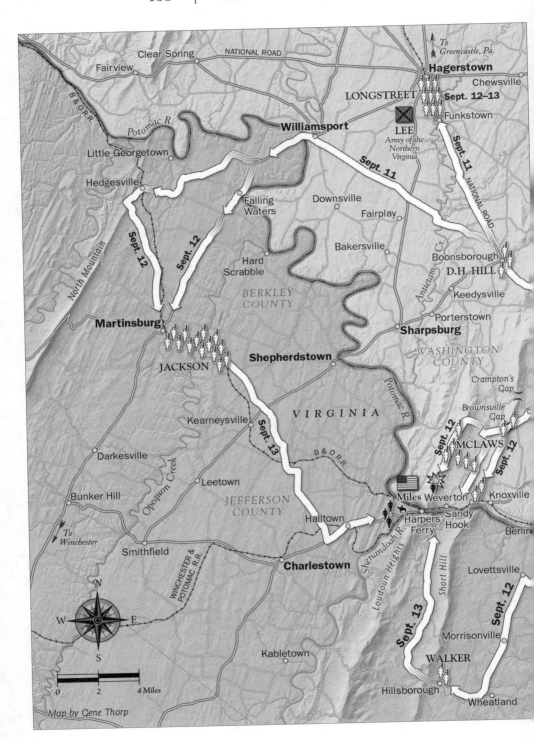

Map by Gene Thorp

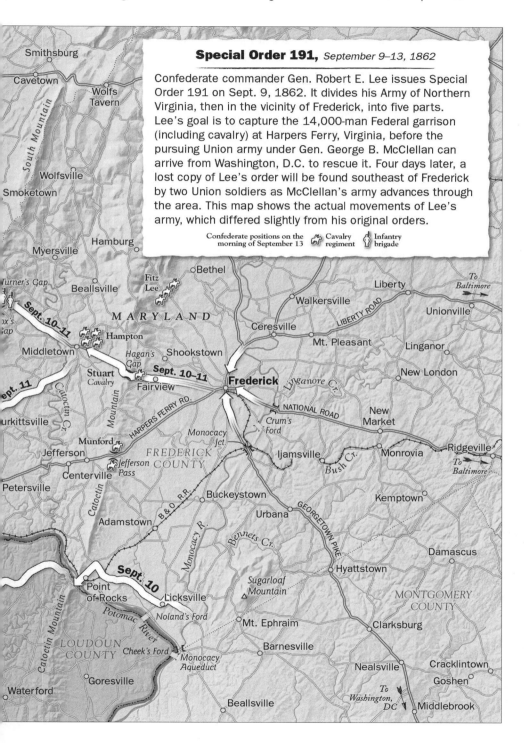

Special Order 191, *September 9–13, 1862*

Confederate commander Gen. Robert E. Lee issues Special Order 191 on Sept. 9, 1862. It divides his Army of Northern Virginia, then in the vicinity of Frederick, into five parts. Lee's goal is to capture the 14,000-man Federal garrison (including cavalry) at Harpers Ferry, Virginia, before the pursuing Union army under Gen. George B. McClellan can arrive from Washington, D.C. to rescue it. Four days later, a lost copy of Lee's order will be found southeast of Frederick by two Union soldiers as McClellan's army advances through the area. This map shows the actual movements of Lee's army, which differed slightly from his original orders.

Confederate positions on the morning of September 13   Cavalry regiment   Infantry brigade

IV. General Longstreet's command will pursue the main road as far as Boonsborough, where it will halt, with reserve, supply and baggage trains of the army.

V. General McLaws, with his own division and that of R.H. Anderson, will follow General Longstreet. On reaching Middletown will take the route to Harper's Ferry, and by Friday morning possess himself of the Maryland Heights and endeavor to capture the enemy at Harper's Ferry and vicinity.

VI. General Walker, with his division, after accomplishing the object in which he is now engaged, will cross the Potomac at Cheek's Ford, ascend its right bank to Lovettsville, take possession of Loudon Heights, if practicable by Friday morning, Key's Ford on his left, and the road between the end of the mountain and the Potomac on his right. He will, as far as practicable, co-operate with Generals McLaws and Jackson, and intercept the enemy.

VII. General D. H. Hill's division will form the rear guard of the army, pursuing the road taken by the main body. The reserve artillery, ordinance, and supply trains &c., will precede General Hill.

VIII. General Stuart will detach a squadron of cavalry to accompany the commands of Generals Longstreet, Jackson, and McLaws, and with the main body of the cavalry, will cover the route of the army, bringing up all stragglers that may have been left behind.

IX. The commands of Generals Jackson, McLaws, and Walker, after accomplishing the objects for which they have been detached, will join the main body of the army at Boonsborough or Hagerstown.

X. Each regiment in the march will habitually carry its axes in the regimental wagons, for use of the men at their encampments to procure wood & c.

By command of General R. E. Lee:
R. H. Chilton
Assistant Adjutant-General

Bibliography

Unpublished Primary Sources

Pittman, Samuel E. "Civil War Papers of Samuel E. Pittman, Lt. Col., 1861-1925." Chapin Library, Williams College, Williamstown, MA.

Schaeffer, Ann R. L. "Records of the Past: Ann R. L. Schaeffer Civil War Diary, September 4–23, 1862." Transcribed by Kira Vaughan. Frederick, MD.

Taber, Joseph S. C. "The Civil War Diary of Private Jos. C. Taber, dating from July 15, 1861 to August 16, 1863." Transcribed by Frank and Denise Marrone. Frederick, MD.

Vautier, John D. "Civil War Daily Diary." Transcribed by Phyllis Weaver Bickley. Philadelphia, PA.

Newspapers and Periodicals

Baltimore American
Brooklyn Daily Eagle
Harper's Weekly
National Tribune
New York Herald
New York Times
Old Fort News
Washington Evening Star

Published Primary Sources

Aldrich, Thomas M. *The History of Battery A, First Regiment Rhode Island Light Artillery, In the War to Preserve the Union, 1861–1865.* Providence, RI: Snow & Farnham, 1904.

Allen, George H. *Forty-Six Months with the Fourth R.I. Volunteers in the War of 1861 to 1865.* Providence, RI: J. A. & R. A. Reid, Printers, 1887.

Bates, David H. *Lincoln in the Telegraph Office, Recollections of the United States Military Telegraph Corps During the Civil War.* New York, NY: The Century Company, 1907.

Benedict, George G. *Vermont in the Civil War, A History of the part Taken by the Vermont Soldiers and Sailors in the War for the Union, 1861–5*, Vol. 1. Burlington, VT: The Free Press Association, 1886.

Bosbyshell, Oliver C. *The 48th in the War, Being a Narrative of the Campaigns of the 48th Regiment Infantry, Pennsylvania Veteran Volunteers, During the War of the Rebellion*. Philadelphia, PA: Avil Printing Co., 1895.

Brown, Edmund R. *The Twenty-Seventh Indiana Volunteer Infantry in the War of the Rebellion 1861 to 1865*. Monticello, IN: No Publisher, 1899.

Burnham, Uberto A. "76th NY." *The National Tribune*. Washington, DC (1928).

Castleman, Alfred L. *The Army of the Potomac: Behind the Scenes*. Milwaukee, WI: Strickland & Co., 1863.

Child, William. *A History of The Fifth Regiment New Hampshire Volunteers of the American Civil War, 1861–1865*. Bristol, NH: R.W. Musgrove, 1893.

Colgrove, Silas. "The Finding of Lee's Lost Order." Robert Underwood Johnson and Clarence Clough Buel, eds. *Battles and Leaders of the Civil War*, Vol. 2. New York, NY: The Century Company, 1887.

Cook, Benjamin E. *History of the Twelfth Massachusetts Volunteers* (Webster Regiment). Boston, MA: Regiment Association, 1882.

Cook, George H. *Diary, January 1, 1862 – October 25, 1862. Principal Musician of the 27th Regt. NYSV, Pocket Diary for 1862*. Salem, MA: D. B. Brooks & Bros., Blank Book Manufacturers and Publisher, 1862.

Cox, Jacob D. *Military Reminiscences of the Civil War, Volume I: April 1861-November 1863*. New York, NY: Charles Scribner's Sons, 1900.

Croffut, William A. and Morris, John M. *The Military and Civil History of Connecticut During The War of 1861–65*. New York, NY: Ledyard Bill, 1868.

Davis, Jr. Charles E. *Three Years in the Army: The Story of the Thirteenth Massachusetts Volunteers from July 16, 1861, to August 1, 1864*. Boston, MA: Estes and Lauriat, 1894.

Denison, Frederic. *Sabres and Spurs, The First Regiment Rhode Island Cavalry, In the Civil War, 1861–1865*. Central Falls, RI: The First Rhode Island Cavalry Veteran Association, 1876.

Dwight, Eliza Amelia. *Life and Letters of Wilder Dwight, Lieut.-Col. Second Mass. Inf. Vols.* Boston, MA: Ticknor and Fields, 1868.

Eby, Jr., Cecil D, ed. *A Virginia Yankee in the Civil War: The Diaries of David Hunter Strother*. Chapel Hill, NC: University of North Carolina Press, 1961.

Ellis, Thomas T. *Leaves from the Diary of an Army Surgeon; or, Incidents of Field Camp, and Hospital Life*. New York, NY: Bradburn, 1863.

Fenner, Earl. *The History of Battery B, First Regiment Rhode Island Light Artillery, In the War to Preserve the Union, 1861-1865*. Providence, RI: Snow & Farnham Printers, 1894.

Ford, Andrew E. *The Story of the Fifteenth Regiment Massachusetts Volunteer Infantry in the Civil War, 1861-1864*. Clinton, MA: Press of W. J. Coulter, Courant Office, 1898.

Gibbon, John. *Personal Recollections of the Civil War.* New York, NY: G.P. Putnam's Sons, 1928.

Gordon, Edward C. "Memorandum of a Conversation with General R. E. Lee, February 15, 1868." Gary W. Gallagher, ed. *Lee the Soldier.* Lincoln, NE: University of Nebraska Press, 1996.

Gould, John M. *History of the First-Tenth-Twenty-Ninth Maine Regiment.* Portland, ME: S. Berry, 1871.

Graham, Matthew J. *The Ninth Regiment New York Volunteers, Being A History of the Regiment and Veteran Association, From 1860 to 1900.* New York, NY: E. P. Coby & Co., Printers, 1900.

Hall, Isaac. *History of the Ninety-Seventh Regiment New York Volunteers ("Conkling Rifles") in the War for the Union.* Utica, NY: L. C. Childs & Son, 1890.

Hughes, William E., ed. *The Civil War Papers of Lt. Colonel Newton T. Colby,* New York Infantry. Jefferson, NC: McFarland, 2003.

Johnson, Charles F. *The Long Roll: One of the Hawkins Zouaves, 1861–1863.* East Aurora, NY: The Roycrofters, 1911.

Judd, David W. *The Story of the Thirty-Third N. Y. S. Vols. or Two Years Campaigning in Virginia and Maryland.* Rochester, NY: Benton & Andrews, 1864.

Lane, David A. *A Soldier's Diary: The Story of a Volunteer, 1862–1865.* Jackson, MI: No Publisher, 1905.

Lord, Edward O. *History of the Ninth Regiment New Hampshire Volunteers In The War of the Rebellion.* Concord, NH: Republican Press Association, 1895.

McClellan, George B. *Report on the Organization and Campaigns of the Army of the Potomac.* New York, NY: Sheldon & Company, 1864.

_____. *McClellan's Own Story: The War for the Union.* New York, NY: Charles L. Webster & Company, 1887.

_____. "From the Peninsula to Antietam: Posthumous Notes by George B. McClellan." Robert Underwood Johnson and Clarence Clough Buel, eds. *Battles and Leaders of the Civil War,* Vol. 2. New York, NY: The Century Company, 1887.

McClenthen, Charles S. *A Sketch of the Campaign in Virginia and Maryland of Towers Brigade of Ricketts Division From Cedar Mountain to Antietam by a Soldier of the 26th N. Y. V.* Syracuse, NY: Masters & Lee, 1863.

Mills, J. Harrison. *Chronicles of the Twenty-First Regiment New York State Volunteers.* Buffalo, NY: 21st Regiment Veteran's Association, 1887.

Page, Charles D. *History of the Fourteenth Regiment, Connecticut Vol. Infantry.* Meriden, CT: The Horton Printing Co., 1906.

Pease, Theodore C., ed. *The Diary of Orville Hickman Browning: Vol. I, 1850-1864.* Springfield, IL: The Trustees of the Illinois State Historical Library, 1925.

Quaife, Milo M., ed. *From the Cannon's Mouth: The Civil War Letters of General Alpheus S. Williams.* Lincoln, NE: University of Nebraska Press, 1995.

Robertson, Robert S. "Diary of the War." *Old Fort News*, Vol. XXVIII, No. 1 (January-March 1963).

Seward, Frederick W. *Seward at Washington as Senator and Secretary of State: A Memoir of His Life, With Selections from His Letters, 1861-1872*, Vol. 2. New York, NY: Derby and Miller, 1891.

Spangler, Edward W. *My Little War Experience*. York, PA: New York Daily Publishing Co., 1904.

Steiner, Lewis H. *Report of Lewis H. Steiner, Inspector of the Sanitary Commission Containing a Diary Kept During the Rebel Occupation of Frederick, MD, and an Account of the Operations of the U.S. Sanitary Commission During the Campaign in Maryland, September 1862*. New York, NY: Anson D. F. Randolph, 1862.

Strother, David H. "Personal Recollections of the War. By a Virginian." *Harper's New Monthly Magazine*, Vol. 36, No. 213 (New York, NY: Harper & Brothers, 1868).

Terrill, J. Newton Terrill. *Campaign of the Fourteenth Regiment New Jersey Volunteers*. New Brunswick, NJ: Daily Home News Press, 1884.

Thorpe, Sheldon B. *The History of the Fifteenth Connecticut Volunteers in the War for the Defense of the Union*. New Haven, CT: The Price, Lee & Adkins, Co., 1893.

Todd, William. *The Seventy-Ninth Highlanders New York Volunteers in the War of Rebellion, 1861–1865*. Albany, NY: Brandow, Barton & Co., 1886.

U. S. House of Representatives. *Report of the Joint Committee on the Conduct of the War in Three Parts*. Washington, DC: Government Printing Office, 1863.

U. S. War Department. *The War of the Rebellion: A Compilation of the Official Records of the Union and Confederate Armies*. 128 Vols. Washington, DC: Government Printing Office, 1880-1901.

Walcott, Charles F. *History of the Twenty-First Regiment Massachusetts Volunteers in the War for the Preservation of the Union, 1861-1865*. Boston, MA: Houghton Mifflin, 1882.

Wallace, William W., et al. *History of the One-Hundred and Twenty-Fifth Regiment Pennsylvania Volunteers, 1862-1863*. Philadelphia, PA: J.B. Lippincott, 1906.

War Talks in Kansas, A Series of Papers Read before the Kansas Commandery of the Military Order of the Loyal Legion of the United States. Kansas City, MO: Franklin Hudson Publishing Company, 1906.

Ward, Joseph R. C. *History of the One Hundred and Sixth Regiment Pennsylvania Volunteers, 2d Brigade, 2d Division, 2d Corps, 1861-1865*. Philadelphia, PA: F. McManus, Jr. & Co., 1906.

Washburn, George H. *A Complete Military History and Record of the 108th Regiment N. Y. Vols., From 1862 to 1894*. Rochester, NY: E. R. Andrews, 1894.

Westbrook, Robert S. *History of the 49th Pennsylvania Volunteers*. Altoona, PA: Altoona Times, 1898.

Weymouth, Albert B., ed. *A Memorial Sketch of Lieut. Edgar M. Newcomb of the Nineteenth Mass. Vols*. Malden, MA: Alvin G. Brown, Steam Book and Job Printer, 1883.

Secondary Works

Bloss, R. Richard. *Bloss Genealogy, Edmund and Mary Bloss and Their Descendants in North America.* Beaumont, TX: No Publisher, 1959.

Burlingame, Michael. "Nicolay and Hay: Court Historians." *Journal of the Abraham Lincoln Association*, Vol. 19, No. 1 (Winter 1998).

Campbell, James H. *McClellan: A Vindication of the Military Career of General George B. McClellan, A Lawyer's Brief.* New York, NY: The Neale Publishing Company, 1916.

Carman, Ezra A. *The Maryland Campaign of September 1862, Vol. 1: South Mountain.* Thomas G. Clemens, ed. El Dorado, CA: Savas Beatie, 2010.

Catton, Bruce. *The Army of the Potomac: Mr. Lincoln's Army.* New York, NY: Doubleday & Company, 1951.

D'Aoust, Maurice. "Little Mac Did Not Dawdle." *Civil War Times* (October 2012).

D'Orleans, Louis Philippe. *History of the Civil War in America*, Vol II. Trans. Louis F. Tasistro. Philadelphia, PA: Porter & Coates, 1876.

Dew, Charles B. "How Samuel E. Pittman Validated Lee's 'Lost Orders' Prior to Antietam: A Historical Note." *Journal of Southern History*, Vol. 70, No. 4 (November 2004).

Draper, John W. *History of the American Civil War*, Vol. II. New York, NY: Harper and Brothers, Publishers, 1868.

Gallagher, Gary W., ed., *Lee the Soldier.* Lincoln, NE: University of Nebraska Press, 1996.

Gavin, William G., ed. *Infantryman Pettit, The Civil War Letters of Corporal Frederick Pettit, Late of Company C, 100th Pennsylvania Veteran Volunteer Infantry Regiment, "The Roundheads", 1862–1864.* Shippensburg, PA: White Mane Publishing, 1990.

Grimsley, Mark. "The Impact of the Lost Order: Rethinking the Significance of the Discovery of Special Orders No. 191." *Civil War Monitor*, Vol. 9, No. 2 (Summer 2019).

Harsh, Joseph L. *Taken at the Flood: Robert E. Lee and Confederate Strategy in the Maryland Campaign of 1862.* Kent, OH and London: Kent State University Press, 1999.

Hartwig, D. Scott. *To Antietam Creek: The Maryland Campaign of September 1862.* Baltimore, MD: The Johns Hopkins University Press, 2012.

_____. "Who Would Not Be a Soldier: The Volunteers of '62 in the Maryland Campaign." Gary W. Gallagher, ed. *The Antietam Campaign.* Chapel Hill, NC: University of North Carolina, 1999.

Heysinger, Isaac W. *Antietam and the Maryland and Virginia Campaigns of 1862.* New York, NY: The Neale Publishing Company, 1912.

McPherson, James M. *Crossroads of Freedom: Antietam, The Battle that Changed the Course of the Civil War.* New York, NY: Oxford University Press, 2002.

Macartney, Clarence E. *Little Mac: The Life of General George B. McClellan.* Philadelphia, PA: Dorrance and Company, 1940.

Menuet, Robert W. "Corporal Barton W. Mitchell and the Lost Orders." *America's Civil War* (Sep. 2007).

Michie, Peter S. *General McClellan*. New York, NY: Appleton and Company, 1901.

Murfin, James V. *The Gleam of Bayonets: The Battle of Antietam and the Maryland Campaign of September 1862*. New York, NY: Bonanza Books, 1965.

Nicolay, John G. and Hay, John. *Abraham Lincoln: A History*, Vol. 6. New York, NY: The Century Company, 1890.

Palfrey, Francis W. *The Antietam and Fredericksburg*. New York, NY: Charles Scribner's Sons, 1882.

Plum, William R. *The Military Telegraph During the Civil War in the United States*. Chicago, IL: Jansen, McClurg & Company, Publishers, 1882.

Rafuse, Ethan S. *McClellan's War: The Failure of Moderation in the Struggle for the Union*. Bloomington, IN: Indiana University Press, 2005.

Reese, Timothy J. *High-Water Mark: The 1862 Maryland Campaign in Strategic Perspective*. Baltimore, MD: Butternut and Blue, 2004.

Ropes, John C. *The Story of the Civil War: A Concise Account of the War in the United States of America between 1861 and 1865, Part I – To the Opening Campaigns of 1862*. New York, NY: G. P. Putnam's Sons, 1895.

Rossino, Alexander B. *Their Maryland: The Army of Northern Virginia from the Potomac Crossing to Sharpsburg in September 1862*. El Dorado, CA: Savas Beatie, 2021.

Schmiel, Eugene D. *Citizen-General: Jacob Dolson Cox and the Civil War Era*. Athens, OH: Ohio University Press, 2014.

Sears, Stephen W., ed. *The Civil War Papers of George B. McClellan: Selected Correspondence, 1860-1865*. New York, NY: Da Capo Press, 1989.

Sears, Stephen W. *Landscape Turned Red: The Battle of Antietam*. Boston, MA: Mariner Books, 1983.

_____. George B. McClellan: *The Young Napoleon*. New York, NY: Da Capo Press, 1988.

_____. "The Twisted Tale of the Lost Order." *North and South Magazine*, Vol. 5, No. 7 (October 2002).

_____. "Last Words on the Lost Orders." *Controversies & Commanders: Dispatches from the Army of the Potomac*. Boston, MA: Houghton Mifflin, 1999.

_____. "The Curious Case of the Lost Order." *Civil War Monitor*, Vol. 6, No. 4 (Winter 2016).

Sherlock, Scott M. "The Lost Order and the Press." *Civil War Regiments: A Journal of the American Civil War*, Vol. 6, No. 2 (1998).

Starr, Louis M. *Bohemian Brigade: Civil War Newsmen In Action*. New York, NY: Alfred A. Knopf, 1954.

Stotelmyer, Steven R. *Too Useful to Sacrifice: Reconsidering George B. McClellan's Generalship in the Maryland Campaign from South Mountain to Antietam*. El Dorado, CA: Savas Beatie, 2019.

Swinton, William. *McClellan's Military Career Reviewed and Exposed: The Military Policy of the Administration Set Forth and Vindicated.* Washington, DC: Union Congressional Committee, 1864.

_____. *Campaigns of the Army of the Potomac: A Critical History of Operations in Virginia, Maryland, and Pennsylvania from the Commencement to the Close of the War, 1861-1865.* New York, NY: C. B. Richardson, 1866.

Tap, Bruce. *Over Lincoln's Shoulder: The Committee On the Conduct of the War.* Lawrence, KS: University Press of Kansas, 1998.

Thorp, Gene M. "In Defense of McClellan at Antietam: A Contrarian View." *The Washington Post* (Sep. 2012).

Wood, Walter B. and Edmonds, Sir James E. *A History of the Civil War in the United States, 1861-5.* New York, NY: G. P. Putnam's Sons, 1905.

Index

The following is an excerpt from
Six Days in September by Alexander B. Rossino,
a novel of Lee's Army in Maryland, 1862
(Savas Beatie, 2017)

336 pages, maps, cloth, dust jacket. $19.95
Six Days in September is available in print, digital, and
audio editions. Order directly from the publisher and
get a signed author bookplate
at no extra charge: www.savasbeatie.com

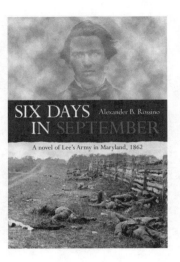

Chapter 5

Sunday, September 14, 1862 (Sunrise to Midnight)

Encampment of the Sixth Alabama Volunteer Infantry Regiment,
Robert Rodes' Brigade, D. H. Hill's Division,
Army of Northern Virginia

Boonsborough, Maryland

Three figures strode through a grassy field in the first light of day. The tallest, an officer, walked out in front, his black leather boots shiny with morning dew. Two youths trailed him dressed in jackets of homespun cloth. One of the boys toted a battered brass bugle, the other a drum dangling from his shoulder by a worn leather strap.

Stopping on a low crest in the middle of the field, the bugler pushed wispy strands of blonde hair from his eyes. The drummer, his round face dotted with freckles, positioned a pair of sticks in his hands.

"You boys ready?" inquired the officer.

They nodded and the officer told them to proceed. The bugler wet his lips, drew a deep breath, and blew into his horn for all he was worth, accompanied by the staccato rattling of the drum. The piercing notes shattered the morning silence, drawing curses and groans from the sleeping men scattered across the field.

Gilbert Farney's eyes snapped open as the blaring bugle separated him once again from the loving embrace of his wife. Her face hung suspended in his mind before fading back into the dream world from which it had come.

"I'm gonna murder that goddamned bugler!" Farney growled as he sat up.

Looking down at his bed mate, Farney clasped a hand on the skinny man's shoulder and shook him.

"Wheat, get up."

"Don't bother me. I ain't ready yet," Billy grumbled, yanking his thin blanket up to his chin.

Farney smacked his lips and rose to his feet, stretching in tandem with the hundreds of other men shaking themselves awake. He pulled on his coonskin cap and shivered, for it had grown cool the past few nights. His bladder aching, Farney hurried to relieve himself. Then he stepped into the trees to search for firewood. Other men also gathered wood so he sought an area not already picked clean. Making his way deeper into the underbrush, Farney took a bite of the stolen ham he kept tucked away in his jacket. A second bite completed his impromptu breakfast and he stuffed it back inside.

The sky had grown lighter by the time Farney returned. Striding to his comrades, he dropped the kindling next to the fire pit where Pat Cannon worked at stoking the smoldering coals into life. Flecks of orange flared brightly as he blew at the gray ashes and a wispy column of smoke rose into the air.

Farney looked over at Billy, who dug busily in his knapsack. "It's about time you got up," he said.

"You're just full of it this morning," Billy grumbled as he pulled out a small pouch of coffee and reached for a battered tin cup.

"You got enough for all of us?" Farney asked.

"No, sir, this here's the last of it," the slim young man replied with a quick shake of his head.

Farney frowned. The lack of food caused enough hardship. Now they had no coffee either. He stared at the gray rooftops of nearby Boonsborough. They were much closer to the town this morning after General Hill had ordered the division's brigades to change position the previous afternoon. Some of the boys had gone to the top of the mountain to join Colquitt's Georgians. Farney considered himself and his friends lucky. Climbing a mountain late in the day did not fit his idea of fun.

After setting up the new encampment, they received orders to cook three days rations. "Three days rations?" he had scoffed. "We ain't got one day's rations between the three of us." . . .

Farney's column followed the road across the gap and down the eastern side before veering onto a narrow dirt track that led sharply up the ridge. The hill fell away to their right as they climbed, its fields dotted with clumps of lichen-encrusted rock.

Suddenly, the whoosh of incoming shells filled the air, rocking the hillside above the men with heavy explosions.

WHUMP!

A shell exploded close to the ground, throwing dirt onto them.

"Ahead at the double-quick!" came the order.

The column surged forward, the men huffing and panting as they labored up the steep hillside. Farney ducked when another shell burst nearby and hoped that no one had been hit. Near the crest of the ridge, the column turned onto a grassy knoll that cascaded down to a shelf on which sat a battery of guns. Marching to the rear of the battery, the men were told to halt behind a low fieldstone wall. Farney dropped his Enfield to the ground and bent over, gasping for breath.

"Holy … mother … of God," Billy gulped. "That … was close!"

The order came for them to deploy in line of battle, and regiment after regiment swung into ranks two men deep. Then they were told to rest. Farney plopped onto the ground and gazed at the patchwork landscape below. Well to their right, the mountainside sloped precariously into a gorge before rising to a distant spur that slanted down to the east. Heavy fighting roared along the top of the spur, sending thick clouds of powder smoke into the sky. The macadamized road they had marched on from Boonsborough zigzagged through the center of the gorge before rolling off to the eastern horizon. Masses of men in dark blue moved into assault positions at the base of the mountain.

Cannon whistled at the sight of the vast enemy army, exclaiming, "Lord have mercy! We're gonna need more ammunition."

A rider appeared on the road behind them. Steering his horse toward General Rodes, the man reined in and drew a note from his jacket. Rodes read the paper and ordered his bugler to sound assembly.

"Colonel Gordon!" Rodes shouted above the guns firing in front of them. "General Hill has ordered me to extend our line to the crest of that spur!" Rodes pointed north to a partially forested ridge more than one thousand yards away that sloped down to the east. "Your regiment is to cross the upper rim of the gorge and take position on our far left. The Sixth will anchor our flank, John, and you must hold. At all hazards, you must hold!" Rodes emphatically ordered.

"Yes, general, I understand," saluted Gordon, and wheeling his horse about, he cried for the Sixth Alabama to fall in. The hair-raising scream of an incoming projectile filled the air as the companies filed into place.

WHUMP!

The shell landed close by, showering dirt and throwing hot slivers of iron in every direction. A second round fell just beyond them and, a few seconds later, a third.

"We've gotta get out of here!" Farney yelled to his friends.

"Gil?" Billy said in a shaky voice.

"Yeah, Wheat?"

"I-I couldn't help it," said Billy, his cheeks flushing red.

Farney looked on as a wet stain spread down the front of Billy's pants. "Aw, Wheat, that ain't nothing," chuckled Farney. "I near shit myself the first time under cannon fire. Plenty brave boys here done the same. No man's going to think less of you." He clapped a hand on Billy's shoulder and ducked as yet another explosion rocked the hillside.

"Sixth Regiment, left face, forward ... march!"

"It's about damned time!" Cannon cussed. "I can't take sitting here for bluebelly target practice."

The column moved back to the pitted road and made its way toward the far side of the gorge. Winding their way over the broken ground, the Roughs struggled through the underbrush to encounter a wagon track cutting north across the spur. Gordon filed the regiment down the lane and halted at its far end.

"Right face!"

The men shifted to face the tree line before them as Gordon rode past to examine their position. Beyond the trees on their left, nothing but empty meadows rolled downhill. God help us if the Yankees suddenly appear from that direction, thought Farney as he realized the extent of their isolation. . . .

The bugler sounded the call and the regiment climbed out of the lane. The roar of musket fire in the gorge muffled as they entered the trees and the crunch of men's feet on dry leaves drowned out most of the guns. The men fell silent and tension hung thick in the air. After forty paces they received the order to halt. The

Six Days in September Excerpt

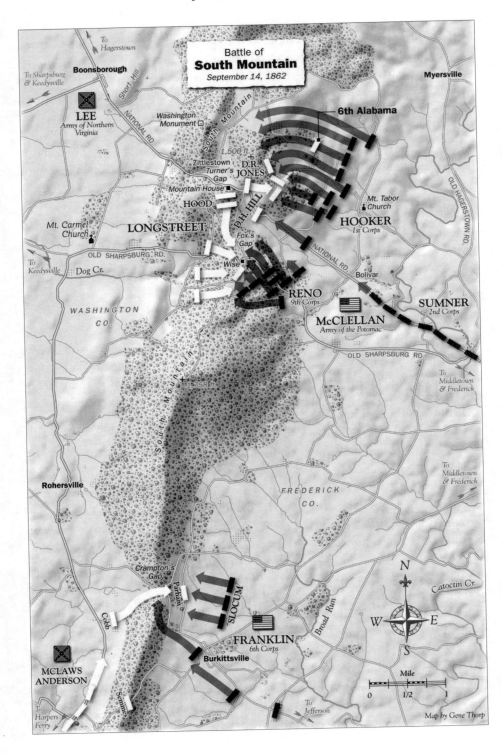

Battle of
South Mountain
September 14, 1862

To Hagerstown

Boonsborough

To Sharpsburg
& Keedysville

Short Hill

Myersville

LEE
*Army of Northern
Virginia*

NATIONAL RD.

Washington
Monument

South Mountain

6th Alabama

1,500 ft.

Zittlestown
Turner's
Gap

**D.R.
JONES**

Mountain House

OLD HAGERSTOWN RD.

HOOD

D.H. HILL

Mt. Tabor
Church

LONGSTREET

Fox's
Gap

HOOKER
1st Corps

Mt. Carmel
Church

Wise

OLD SHARPSBURG RD.

Dog Cr.

RENO
9th Corps

Bolivar

NATIONAL RD.

To
Keedysville

McCLELLAN
Army of the Potomac

SUMNER
2nd Corps

**WASHINGTON
CO.**

OLD SHARPSBURG RD.

To
Middletown
& Frederick

South Mountain

1,758 ft.

To
Middletown
& Frederick

Rohersville

**FREDERICK
CO.**

Crampton's
Gap

Parham

SLOCUM

Broad Run

Catoctin Cr.

N

Cobb

FRANKLIN
6th Corps

W   E

S

**McLAWS
ANDERSON**

Burkittsville

Semmes

To
Jefferson

Mile

0   1/2   1

To
Harpers
Ferry

Map by Gene Thorp

forest ahead of them gave way to pasture split lengthwise by a low stone wall. In the center of the field Gordon's skirmishers exchanged shots with the enemy.

Farney squinted at the tight double-lines of Federal troops downslope. "Wheat, what's that pinned to their caps?"

Billy peered through the leaves. "It looks like fur. . . deer tails."

Balls from the enemy's muskets zipped through the branches overhead, sending leaves fluttering down past Farney's face.

Captain Burton approached from the right. "Fix bayonets!"

Farney clicked his into place on the end of his musket. The minutes ticked by. He nervously licked his dry, cracked lips. Then, without warning, the firing from the Federal line stopped. Stillness descended over the field and Farney could hear his heart beating in his chest. He tightened the grip on his Enfield, his sweating palms creaking against the wooden stock. A bugle sounded and, with a lusty cheer, the Federal line began advancing toward them up the slope. Sweat trickled down the back of Farney's neck and he glanced at Billy. The sandy-haired man chewed his lip, his knuckles white around the rifle held tightly in his hands.

Burton stepped into a spot to Farney's right. "Steady, boys," he said.

With the sun in their eyes, the Federals drew closer, pushing Gordon's skirmishers back into the trees. A man Farney did not know settled in beside him. Craning his neck to see down the line, Farney spotted the colonel. Now on foot, Gordon wrenched his sword from its scabbard.

"Forward, boys, and give them hell!" he roared.

A high-pitched yell erupted as Farney and his comrades bolted from the trees. The Federal line wavered with surprise at the sudden attack and men turned to run. Farney put a ball between the shoulders of a fleeing man and slowed his pace to reload as the force of their charge petered out. Ramming the round home in his rifled-musket, he saw that only the first enemy line had cracked. Behind them, a second line stood firm, spreading ranks to allow their comrades to pass through. When the last man had cleared the way, the bluecoats lowered their weapons.

"FIRE!"

The enemy line erupted in a wall of flame and smoke.

Minié balls zipped past Farney's head as the fellow to his left sank silently to the ground. Captain Burton shouted for Company D to dress on the colors and load. Farney jogged into place next to Billy. He seated a percussion cap and pulled back the hammer of his Enfield.

"AIM!"

Farney took a bead on the belt buckle of a man in the center of the enemy line.

"FIRE!"

End of Excerpt

About the Authors

Alexander B. Rossino

Alexander B. Rossino, PhD, resides in Washington County, Maryland. An award-winning independent historian, who earned his degree from Syracuse University and worked at the U.S. Holocaust Memorial Museum in Washington, D.C. from 1994 to 2003. He is the author of *Their Maryland: The Army of Northern Virginia from the Potomac Crossing to Sharpsburg in September 1862* (Savas Beatie, 2021), and has published several articles on the Maryland Campaign. He has also written a two-part series of historically accurate Civil War novels published by Savas Beatie, *Six Days in September: A Novel of Lee's Army in Maryland, 1862* (2017) and *The Guns of September: A Novel of McClellan's Army in Maryland, 1862* (2022).

Gene M. Thorp

Gene M. Thorp is an award-winning cartographer, an author, historian, and businessman. He is a lifetime researcher of the American Civil War with a focus on historical data and geography in the eastern theatre. Gene spent 15 years as a cartographer and graphics editor at *The Washington Post*. In addition to his responsibilities covering daily news, he helped guide the newspaper's five-year coverage of the Civil War sesquicentennial. Gene currently works at the U.S. Department of State, Bureau of Intelligence and Research, where he helps advance U.S. diplomacy. As a freelance cartographer, his deeply researched and visually appealing maps can be found in an abundance of books on the *New York Times* bestseller list and throughout major museums and parks across America.